GIFFORD PINCHOT

GIFFORD PINCHOT

SELECTED WRITINGS

EDITED BY

CHAR MILLER

The Pennsylvania State University Press
University Park, Pennsylvania

Library of Congress Cataloging-in-Publication Data

Names: Pinchot, Gifford, 1865–1946, author. | Miller, Char, 1951– , editor.
Title: Gifford Pinchot : selected writings / edited by Char Miller.
Description: University Park, Pennsylvania : The Pennsylvania State University
Press, [2017] | Includes bibliographical references and index.
Summary: "Collection of essays by Gifford Pinchot (1865–1946), founding chief
of the U.S. Forest Service and twice governor of Pennsylvania. The social,
political, and scientific insights in these essays anticipate many contemporary
environmental-policy dilemmas and the growing demand for
environmental justice"—Provided by publisher.
Identifiers: LCCN 2016058255| ISBN 9780271078410 (cloth : alk. paper) |
ISBN 9780271078427 (pbk. : alk. paper)
Subjects: LCSH: Forests and forestry. | Pennsylvania—Politics and
government—1865–1950. | LCGFT: Essays.
Classification: LCC SD123 .P56 2017 | DDC 634.909748—dc23
LC record available at https://lccn.loc.gov/2016058255

For Al Sample

CONTENTS

PART 4: WATER, ENERGY, AND POWER   177

PART 5: NATURAL ENGAGEMENTS   217

Introduction

Gifford Pinchot had a keen sense of his place in history. With reason: he was one of the central forces behind the emergence of the conservation movement in the United States. As the founding chief of the U.S. Forest Service and a key political ally of President Theodore Roosevelt, as well as a relentless publicist for the cause, Pinchot helped make conservation a household term. Yet as illustrious as his forestry career was, his political impact was of equal significance. Historians of Pennsylvania consider Pinchot's two terms as governor of the Commonwealth to be among the most important in the state's modern history. During his first term in the Roaring Twenties, this no-nonsense crusader instituted critical administrative and budgetary reforms, and, during his second, battered as the industrialized state was by the worst of the Great Depression, Pinchot created jobs and generated hope in communities that had little of either.

So when it came time to write his autobiography, Pinchot had a lot to talk about. Fittingly enough, he opened his memoir, *Breaking New Ground*, with a blunt declaration about why his version of events should be understood as *the* version. "It is the story of an eyewitness, an account of events in which I had a part, written to tell not only what happened but also why and how it happened." This insider perspective, Pinchot allowed, was essential to understanding the past, for "personal experience beats documentary history all hollow." Although he conceded that documents were crucial to historical analysis, he made it clear to his readers that his "respect for history written from documents alone, after the men who lived it and made it have passed away, is distinctly qualified." In so saying, he rejected the "common statement that actions or events cannot be properly appraised until after generations have passed," arguing against its illogical implication—"that actions and events cannot be understood until there is nobody left alive who knows the inside causes which produced them, or the true conditions which gave them their meaning." His autobiography was not a "formal history, decorated and delayed by references to authorities. As to nearly every statement it contains, you will have to take it on my say-so."[1]

What Pinchot would say about this selected collection of his writings is anyone's guess—he has been dead since 1946, and that makes these texts the kind of dread (and dead) documentation he believed could mislead

1. Gifford Pinchot, *Breaking New Ground*, 4th ed. (Washington, D.C.: Island Press, 1998), xviii–xx.

subsequent readers unaware of their origins or their author's original intentions. "I have been in on, or have known about the making of too many documents," he asserted, "not to know how often they tell but part of the real story, or even distort it altogether."[2] Duly noted: Caveat lector!

That sensible caution notwithstanding, there is good reason to reengage with Pinchot's essays, speeches, and articles, the literary leavings of his lengthy, and at times controversial, career as a public servant, political activist, and social critic. For more than fifty years, he wrote penetratingly about the enduring need for Americans (and all people) to manage their natural resources with greater care. The deliberate stewardship of timber, minerals, grass, and water, he believed, would ensure national prosperity, a matter of considerable concern to the newly powerful nation-state of the late nineteenth and early twentieth centuries. But Pinchot was more than an able technocrat devoted to the careful production of wood fiber to fuel a booming economy. Who benefitted from that growth, and who did not, were also matters of great concern to Pinchot; for forestry to fulfill its promise it must enhance the life chances of all Americans. So, too, with politics. Elected officials, Pinchot argued, must be committed to the commonweal, especially to those without access to the levers of power, to the marginalized and disenfranchised. Indeed, the social, political, and scientific insights that emerge in this collection of Pinchot's writings—on war and the rights of women and minorities; education, prohibition, and hydropower; the art of fishing and the craft of politics—testify to the range of his interests and to his enduring progressive commitments. A complex figure, he also anticipated many of the dilemmas confronting those in the twenty-first century who are deliberating over environmental policy in an era of climate change; the cultural tensions implicit in American nature writing that focuses on the wild amid a rapidly urbanizing society; and the growing demands for environmental justice by those whose rural landscapes and city neighborhoods are disproportionately polluted. Even as Pinchot was resolutely a man of his time, he speaks to our own.

This claim of Pinchot's continued relevance comes with a conundrum: how did someone born into a family of wealth and standing, who never lacked for anything material during his eighty years of life, become such a powerful advocate for sustained—or, as his legion of conservative critics argued, radical—social change? The answer depends in part on the very privilege that enveloped him at his birth on August 11, 1865. Pinchot's parents, Mary Eno (1838–1914) and James Pinchot (1831–1908), had themselves grown up in comfort. The Enos, particularly Mary's father, Amos

2. Ibid., xviii.

Eno, had amassed a fortune speculating in New York City's pre–Civil War land boom. On a smaller scale, the Pinchot family, who were French émigrés, owned significant acreage in Milford, Pennsylvania, that they logged and farmed, and through their general store they structured much of that community's economic activity. When James left Milford in 1855 to pursue his entrepreneurial dreams in New York City, he struck gold by catering to the rising middle and upper classes' desires for imported wallpaper and other domestic furnishings. His marriage to Mary Eno brought a sizeable dowry, to be sure, but also a life partner strongly convinced that the pursuit of mammon was less important than doing right in the world. To that end, she convinced her husband that he should retire in his mid-forties to serve as an example to their children—Gifford, Antoinette (1868–1934), and Amos (1873–1944)—for how to engage with the world. Rank had its duties and privileges.

The question was how to fulfill those duties, how to use those privileges. To judge from the three Pinchot siblings' adult activism, their parents trained them well. In line with her older brother's public career, Antoinette, who married a titled English diplomat, threw herself into progressive social movements in her adopted country; during World War I, she turned her home into a hospital and served as a nurse. Amos, trained as a lawyer, was a more mercurial presence in the civic arena. One of the founders of the American Civil Liberties Union, he wrote blistering critiques of entrenched power during the Progressive Era and then in the Great Depression swung hard right, lambasting Franklin Roosevelt's New Deal. With other disaffected intellectuals, he established America First, an organization opposing the nation's entrance into World War II. Whatever their political leanings, Mary and James Pinchot's children were forces with which to be reckoned.

One of them, at least in their mother's eyes, gleamed brighter. "My children have grown more than I," Mary Pinchot wrote in her diary in 1909—Gifford "more than one could have imagined." She reiterated this preferential point a year later to a reporter from the *Detroit News:* "I record as the paramount blessing of my life the fact that I am Gifford Pinchot's mother and in a way one who helped to form his ideals, [and] who has always ardently sympathized with all that he hoped to do."[3]

What young Pinchot hoped to do was become a forester, a career option his parents encouraged him to pursue. They appreciated that his love of the great outdoors was a clue to his outgoing personality and his

---

3. Mary Eno Pinchot, Diary, Box 43, Pinchot Papers, Library of Congress, December 31, 1909; *Detroit News*, January 30, 1910.

professional possibilities. There was only one problem: the forestry profession did not yet exist in the United States of the 1880s. Here the family saw opportunity: might not Gifford become its progenitor? Theirs was no idle speculation, as is evident in the fact that within fifteen years of the family's initial conversation about this glittering prospect, Gifford had made it happen. But the steps Gifford had to take to fulfill this seemingly far-fetched goal were as many as they were improvised. He would attend Yale, a member of the class of 1889, but knew going in that it offered no classes in anything approximating forestry, so he sampled the curriculum as best he could, earning the requisite gentleman's Cs (except in French, his paternal family's native tongue). His linguistic proficiency led to his receiving the college's French prize as a senior, a fluency that would determine where he would study forestry; and, in another bit of foreshadowing, he also snagged the Townsend Prize for public debate. The latter earned him an invitation to speak at the 1889 Alumni Banquet following his graduation ceremonies. Well prepared to talk on "some subject long since forgotten," on a whim Pinchot jettisoned his original speech and delivered an extemporaneous pitch for the importance of forestry to the country and himself, "my first public declaration that I had chosen it for my life-work."[4]

Since there was no going back, he went forward, to Europe, where forestry was being formalized as a profession and certified through an emerging set of schools devoted to its study. Embedded in monarchical nation-states, European forestry quickly flourished in this paternalistic environment, James Scott argues, largely because this fledgling science made nature legible and manipulable. It turned scruffy natural forests into geometrically structured plantations, standing timber into board feet, and the seemingly valueless into a taxable commodity. All of this also gave the state new powers—a matter of considerable importance later, when Pinchot worked with Theodore Roosevelt to designate 150 million acres as National Forests and expand the regulatory authority of the national forest system. Not that Pinchot understood these implications when he disembarked in Southampton and traveled to London in hopes of purchasing some relevant books and treatises; he described himself at the juncture as "still being lost in the fog."[5]

The fog cleared slowly, mostly as a result of a series of fortuitous encounters: a high-ranking official in the Indian Civil Service secured

4. Char Miller, *Gifford Pinchot and the Making of Modern Environmentalism* (Washington, D.C.: Island Press, 2001), 71–72; Pinchot, *Breaking New Ground*, 6.
5. James C. Scott, *Seeing like a State: How Certain Schemes to Improve the Human Condition Have Failed* (New Haven: Yale University Press, 1999); Pinchot, *Breaking New Ground*, 6.

letters of introduction for Pinchot to two eminent German foresters, Sir William Schlich, head of the British forest school, and Sir Dietrich Brandis, formerly the inspector general of forests for the British government in India. These two men encouraged the young American to attend the École forestière in Nancy, France, putting his French to good use. Once properly schooled, Schlich counseled, Pinchot should then return to the States and advocate for the establishment of a system of national forests and an agency to manage them. Pinchot would prove an able student.

Yet even as he learned the scientific nomenclature of forestry and embraced its technical approach to timber management, Pinchot recognized this discipline's essential interdisciplinarity. Foresters had to know more about a tree than its capacity to produce wood fiber. They also must be expert in soils, light, and temperature, geology and geography, economics and politics: about forests as living, breathing entities and the human context in which such well-wooded lands were admired, utilized, and regulated. That meant that forestry was at once site specific—trees grew in particular ways within specific ecosystems—and global in its reach and ramifications. The illustrious careers of his German mentors, who brought European ideas of forest management to the Indian subcontinent on behalf of their British employers, made clear that these concepts, with modifications, were transportable to the United States and, by extension, to the empire it would secure following the Spanish-American War of 1898. It was not by happenstance that in 1902, Pinchot, then head of the Bureau of Forestry—precursor to the Forest Service—would travel to the Philippines to advise U.S. colonial administrators about how to introduce forestry to a tropical rainforest ecosystem, or that he would send agency staff to do the same for Puerto Rico. "Putting empire and environment in the same frame," notes Ian Tyrrell, "enables us to better understand the consolidation of national power under Roosevelt." No member of Theodore Roosevelt's administration contributed more to the "process of creating a stronger American state," home and abroad, than the forester Pinchot.[6]

Although these expansive ambitions lay in the future, Pinchot was no less ambitious for the more immediate opportunities to promote forest work and himself, a twinned subject that occupied his attention as he sailed back to New York in late 1890. A born promoter, Pinchot had been sending regular dispatches about aspects of European forestry to *Garden and Forest*, the leading conservationist journal in the United States at that time, transferring the knowledge he was gleaning to its readers, many of

6. Char Miller, *America's Great National Forests, Wildernesses, and Grasslands* (New York: Rizzoli, 2016); Ian Tyrrell, *Crisis of the Wasteful Nation: Empire and Conservation in Theodore Roosevelt's America* (Chicago: University of Chicago Press, 2015), 18.

whom would become early adopters of Pinchot's cause. These articles won him some renown, though they did little to appease his maternal grandfather; Amos Eno, who wanted his talented grandson to join his money-making operations, was "still soured on forestry," Pinchot noted in his diary. But other family members and friends rallied to his side, so much so that he began to resent the attention. "No talks on forestry," he noted after one social event, "which was a relief, for people seem to think I have distinguished myself. Which is nonsense."[7]

There was nothing nonsensical about his articulation of the principles he thought essential to establishing forestry in the United States. Most crucial, and thus most far-reaching, was the need for an interventionist nation-state: a strong federal government administering national forests was necessary for forestry to flourish in a society too long given to destructive, wasteful lumbering. He laid out what he believed was the best means of controlling the "gigantic and lamentable massacre of trees" in a speech to the American Economic Association, whose annual meeting was held within days of his December 1890 return to New York. Strikingly, his talk's thesis statement doubled as the call to action that would define his activism for the next two decades. "A definite, far-seeing plan is necessary for the rational management of any forest," he declared, but to create such plans and ensure their long-term viability required consistent oversight: "forest property is safest under the supervision of some imperishable guardian; or, in other words, of the State."[8]

Establishing this supervisory state took some doing, work that was not Pinchot's alone; its creation was one of the hallmarks of the Progressive Era and the reformist energies that animated it. Pinchot was in close touch with many of these like-minded women and men, including Jane Addams, Louis Brandeis, Theodore Roosevelt, John Muir, Charles Beard, Florence Kelley, Stephen S. Wise, and a host of others pressing for a more

7. Diary, January 7 and 11, 1891, in *The Conservation Diaries of Gifford Pinchot*, ed. Harold K. Steen (Durham, N.C.: Forest History Society, 2001), 11.

8. Pinchot's adoption of European models, however modified to fit American conditions, was in line with the actions of other contemporary reformers who visited the Old World to locate ideas they could bring back to the New, a transatlantic exchange that is the subject of Daniel T. Rodgers's *Atlantic Crossings: Social Politics in a Progressive Age* (Cambridge: Belknap Press, 2000); Gifford Pinchot, "Government Forestry Abroad," in this volume. His conviction that the nation-state was best situated to manage natural resources on public lands (a position that he would later extend to private woodlands), routinely tested and refined while he served as chief of the Forest Service and as governor of Pennsylvania, offers a counter to Donald Worster's argument that Pinchot and his progressive peers did "not consider deeply the possibility that their beloved state might be ill equipped to serve as developer rather than protector. . . . With so much power in their hands and yet so little self-examination, government conservationists were likely to be more, not less, wasteful than businessmen, pursuing grand designs that could not meet the test of practicality, let alone the test of a higher ethic." See Donald Worster, *Shrinking the Earth: The Rise and Decline of America's Abundance* (New York: Oxford University Press, 2016), 119–20.

conscientious government and beneficent society. His particular contribution to their shared crusade—forestry—only appeared to be disconnected from the social questions that shaped the others' actions. For him, forest management could not be divorced from the human context in which it was to be established; it was as political as the demand for unionization and women's rights or the need for enhanced public health, consumer protection, and child welfare. That for a time Pinchot had an office in the United Charities Building in New York City, which then served as the epicenter of "middle-class social politics," underscores the self-conscious links he forged with contemporary change agents.[9]

These connections, when combined with Pinchot's public relations acumen, propelled him and forestry forward. It helped, too, that the public at large, and scientists and activists in particular, had become deeply concerned by the mangled nature of American forests. Although the early settler-colonists who invaded North America immediately began swinging axes, wielding firebrands, and letting livestock loose to clear away the woods to convert the land to agriculture, their collective impact was largely concentrated along waterways; it took nearly two hundred years to clear-cut New England. The felling of trees accelerated with the nineteenth-century advent of the industrial revolution and its enormous appetite for wood. New, more powerful and efficient saws and mills, in combination with the intensifying demand for timber for housing, wharves, highways, canals, railroads, and mine shafts, among a thousand other needs, led loggers to follow the rapidly shifting lumberman's frontier—from Maine to the Great Lakes and then to the South. Millions of board feet were cut down and sent to market, often rafted to port along snowmelt-driven rivers that every spring became logjammed. Henry David Thoreau reported that in 1837 an estimated 250 mills were operating along the Penobscot and its tributaries above Bangor, Maine, annually turning out 200 million board feet. "To this is to be added the lumber of the Kennebec, Androscoggin, Saco, Passamaquoddy and other streams. No wonder we hear so often of vessels becalmed off our coast being surrounded a week at a time by floating lumber from the Maine woods."[10]

A half century later, after Pinchot's return from France, the neophyte forester was stunned by the celerity with which his compatriots were slicing through forests thick and deep. The iron horse was especially insatiable. By 1890, one billion board feet had gone into the creation of railroad ties alone. Pinchot and his generation bore witness to what he described

9. Rodgers, *Atlantic Crossings*, 27–28.
10. Henry David Thoreau, *The Portable Thoreau* (New York: Penguin Books, 1977), 78.

as "the most rapid and extensive forest destruction ever known." All resources were threatened: "The nation was obsessed, when I got home, by a fury of development. The American Colossus was fiercely intent on appropriating and exploiting the riches of the richest of all continents—grasping with both hands, reaping what he had not sown, wasting what he thought would last forever." As the exploiters pushed "farther and farther into the wilderness," the losses mounted—losses that were environmental and ethical. "The man who could get his hands on the biggest slice of natural resources," Pinchot lamented, "was the best citizen. Wealth and virtue were supposed to trot in double harness."[11]

Given his critique, there is no little irony that George W. Vanderbilt, grandson of Cornelius Vanderbilt, the steamboat and railroad magnate, offered Pinchot his first significant opportunity to put forestry—and its conservation measures designed to slow down the colossus—into practice. The site was palatial: Vanderbilt's 250-room house, Biltmore, near Asheville, North Carolina, a manse reputed to have been the largest in the United States. One of Pinchot's jobs was to develop a forest-management plan to bring the burned-over, grazed down woods back to life. A second was to recommend another 100,000 acres for Vanderbilt to purchase. Yet his professional enthusiasm for these initiatives did not blind him to what Biltmore also represented: "Its setting was superb, the view from it breathtaking, and if it was a feudal castle it would have been beyond criticism, and perhaps beyond praise. But in the United States of the nineteenth century and among the one-room cabins of the Appalachian mountaineers, it did not belong. The contrast was a devastating commentary on the injustice of concentrated wealth. Even in the early nineties I had sense enough to see that."[12]

That sensibility did not stop him from seizing this chance to make his mark. Ever the publicist, Pinchot produced a small, heavily illustrated book identifying the experiment's profitability as a promotional tool. His media-savvy approach to his work continued during subsequent years as a consulting forester to other owners of large wooded acreage: each project generated another article testifying to forestry's prospects and possibilities, a branding that made forestry a matter of public record and debate and that gave Pinchot a wider audience. Few of his attentive peers were surprised when in 1898 he was tapped to become the fourth head of the Division (later, Bureau) of Forestry in the Department of Agriculture. It looked like a dead-end job: the agency had a tiny budget,

11. Pinchot, *Breaking New Ground*, 23.
12. Ibid., 48.

few personnel, and did not manage a single acre of forest, as the nation's forest reserves were then under the control of the Department of the Interior. But Pinchot had a plan. He was convinced that he could flip these disadvantages into advantages.

The speed with which he instituted his ideas is remarkable. Within seven years of entering government service, he had launched a professional organization, the Society of American Foresters (1900). Many of the group's earliest members would come from the first wave of students graduating from the Yale Forest School (1900), the nation's first graduate program in forestry. (Pinchot and his parents had donated the school's foundational gift.) During their first summer at the school, students would get hands-on lessons in forest management at the Milford Experimental Forest, woodlands that were contiguous to the Pinchot estate in northeastern Pennsylvania and were leased to Yale College by the family. In subsequent summers, the students would intern with the Bureau, gaining invaluable experience in forests across the country. And as Pinchot convinced Congress to expand his agency's budget and increase the salaries he could offer, who better to hire but the sons of Yale? The demand for them would only escalate in 1905, following President Roosevelt's signing of legislation that transferred 86 million forested public lands from Interior to Agriculture and created the Forest Service to steward them—with Pinchot as its first chief. The forty-year-old Pinchot had had plenty of allies in the White House and on the Hill, but these culminating outcomes were largely his handiwork.

The new chief's job description and mission statement, conveyed in a letter that Agriculture Secretary James Wilson sent him on day one, bear Pinchot's fingerprints, too. He wrote it for his boss to sign! Although the full text is reproduced in this volume, one of its key phrases has remained a guiding principle for the Forest Service for more than a century: "where conflicting interests must be reconciled" on the national forests, "the question will always be decided from the standpoint of the greatest good for the greatest number in the long run." The last four words tempers the utilitarian bent of the concept of the greatest good. Sustainable management across time was to be—and has largely remained—the agency's objective. That kind of enduring influence might have softened Amos Eno's initial dismissal of his grandson's choice of profession.

Eno, a whiz-bang land speculator in New York City, might have recognized himself in Pinchot's expansive ambitions for the new agency's reach and impact, as well as in his creative leadership of the fledgling organization. To effectively manage the millions of acres now under the Forest Service's purview, Pinchot needed to secure larger budgets and a

stream of additional personnel. He routinely walked the corridors of
power on Capitol Hill, negotiating for more funding, building up alliances
across the aisle in support of the agency's actions, and using his clout in
the White House—he was a close friend and confidant of President Roosevelt—to gain additional resources. Recognizing that he was to be the
public face (and voice) of the Forest Service, Pinchot hired a group of
individuals at all levels who had the expertise he lacked. Three in particular are of note. For day-to-day management, he tapped Overton Price to
oversee the agency's internal workings, an arrangement that Pinchot later
credited with much of the organization's success. Because developing a
robust science of forest management would be critical to those working
on the ground, he turned that initiative over to Raphael Zon; research
stations and experimental forests, and the data that they generated, were
essential then (and are still today) for managerial decision-making. Albert
Potter was also emblematic of Pinchot's astute hiring practices. The new
chief knew little about rangelands management but knew enough to see
that grazing was, as he once put it, the "bloody angle." If the agency could
not figure out how to work with and manage those using its grasslands,
which constituted roughly 50 percent of the national forests, it would die
aborning. Pinchot had met Potter on an inspection trip in 1900; Potter
had worked for the livestock industry in Arizona at the time. He made
such an impression on the forester that within a year Pinchot had hired
Potter to develop the new Branch of Grazing. Giving such key personnel
their lead was a cornerstone of Pinchot's managerial strategy as chief
forester and, later, as governor.[13]

What this strategic approach also achieved was to free Pinchot to do
what he did best, keeping the organization on message and mission, gal-
vanizing public opinion through countless speeches and articles, and daily
championing the Roosevelt administration's conservation commitments.
A key component of this work was rebutting what we now call the first
Sagebrush Rebellions (whose troubling legacy extends to the January 2016
armed takeover of the Malheur National Wildlife Refuge). The rebellions
initially erupted because western resource interests—mining, livestock,
and logging operators, along with a sizeable segment of voters and their
political representatives—denied the right of the federal government to
designate national forests or to manage and regulate the use of these lands.
The rhetoric could become white-hot, and Pinchot came in for his share
of heated pushback—a *Rocky Mountain News* Republican anti-Pinchot

---

13. Pinchot, *Breaking New Ground*, 177–81; Harold K. Steen, *The U.S. Forest Service: A History*
(Durham, N.C.: Forest History Society and Pinchot Institute for Conservation, 2004), 75–96.

cartoon was titled "Czar Pinchot and His Cossack Rangers Administering the Forest Reserves." Yet the chief forester did not shy away from this charged debate. In 1907, he was invited to attend the Denver Public Lands Convention and was loudly heckled when he stepped up to the dais. Unfazed, Pinchot assured his skeptical audience that their economic future looked better with careful resource management than with the rapid exploitation of minerals, grasslands, and timber, as was then under way. Conservation protected land and water and stymied the growth of monopolies, and that meant prosperity for the West. At the close, the jeers reportedly had turned to cheers.[14]

That moment, like many others, also revealed the role that Pinchot played within the Roosevelt administration. He was its lightning rod, absorbing its critics' anger so that the chief executive could appear—and be—above the fray. Pinchot's commitment to the president extended across his lifetime, for he routinely identified himself as a Roosevelt Progressive whenever he hit the hustings, deference movingly reflected in Pinchot's 1919 remembrance of TR's definitive impact on his political ideals.[15]

This close identification made it difficult for Pinchot to imagine the Forest Service without Roosevelt's supportive presence. In retrospect, the twenty-sixth president's decision in 1908 not to run for reelection might have been the best time for Pinchot to step aside, too. As it was, although he initially hoped that President William Howard Taft, who as governor general of the Philippines had worked with Pinchot on his forestry initiatives in the archipelago, would uphold the Rooseveltian conservationist standard, he grew steadily disenchanted. Most concerning was that Taft, a lawyer by profession, was not as enthusiastic about his predecessor's willingness to use his executive authority without consultation with the Congress. Taft was much more cautious and consultative, traits that Pinchot pushed against. (Taft, for his part, recognized that Pinchot and Roosevelt "sympathized much more than [Pinchot] and I can, for they both have more of a Socialist tendency.")[16]

These tensions came to a head in 1909. Already worried that the newly inaugurated president seemed willing to go along with those powerful resource-extraction industries that the Forest Service was supposed to

---

14. Pinchot's speech is printed in "Resolutions of Land Convention," *Idaho Statesman*, June 21, 1907, and in this volume; Miller, *Gifford Pinchot*, 163–67; Char Miller, *Public Lands, Public Debates: A Century of Controversy* (Corvallis: Oregon State University Press, 2012).

15. Gifford Pinchot, "Roosevelt's Part in Forestry," in this volume.

16. Henry F. Pringle, *The Life and Times of William Howard Taft* (New York: Farrar and Rinehart, 1939), 492.

regulate, additional evidence seemed manifest in news that the secretary of the interior, Richard A. Ballinger, planned to lease Alaskan coalfields located within the Chugach National Forest to the well-heeled, New York–based Guggenheim syndicate. The story is complicated, but Pinchot came to believe that the administration's decision was corrupt. He first challenged it quietly within the executive branch, then let the president know in advance that he intended to go public with his concerns. What became known as the Ballinger-Pinchot controversy exploded across the front pages of every major newspaper in the country, damaging the Taft administration and leading the president to fire Pinchot for insubordination. The imbroglio continued as congressional investigations deepened and extended the controversy, one consequence of which was that Theodore Roosevelt would decide to return to the political arena, challenging Taft for the Republican presidential nomination in 1912. Losing that bid, he then mounted a third-party bid for the White House via the Bull Moose ticket, with Pinchot as a key advisor, donor, and speechwriter. With the GOP badly split, the Democratic candidate, Woodrow Wilson, prevailed that November, an outcome that disappointed Pinchot but which he did not regret. The forester had been bitten by the political bug.[17]

Between 1914 and 1938, a relentless Pinchot seemed forever in campaign mode, repeatedly running for the House and Senate at the national level and for governor at the state level; periodically, too, he had allies float the possibility of a White House bid. He only won twice, serving as governor first between 1923 and 1927, and again from 1931 to 1935, but he had a decided impact on the state: balancing budgets in good times and bad; staunchly advocating for all citizens' civil rights; building roads and other infrastructure to reduce unemployment; promoting rural economies and schools in an urban-dominated state; and vigorously enforcing Prohibition. (So, not perfect.)

That he tooted his own horn is to be expected: that's a given in the political rough-and-tumble. More notable is that he as assiduously beat the drum for his wife's aspirations. Cornelia Bryce Pinchot, an indispensable advisor whenever her husband sought office, was on the receiving end of his support during her own three campaigns for Congress. She never won, but like her husband, she understood that the fight was worth such setbacks. "My feminism tells me," she wrote in the *Nation* in the 1920s, "that a woman can bear children, charm her lovers, boss a business, swim

17. James L. Penick, *Progressive Politics and Conservation: The Ballinger-Pinchot Affair* (Chicago: University of Chicago Press, 1968).

the Channel, stand at Armageddon and battle for the Lord—all in the day's work!" An early sign of her steadfast convictions, and Gifford's, emerged in their decision, within hours of their marriage in August 1914, to put their honeymoon on hold so that they could crisscross Pennsylvania, earnestly pressing the flesh during Gifford's first, if unsuccessful, run for office. Before Franklin and Eleanor, before Bill and Hillary (and before Hillary and Bill), there were Gifford and Cornelia.[18]

The couple's intensely public life had private consequences. Their only child, Gifford Bryce Pinchot, was never easy in the glare of attention that followed his parents (and which they avidly courted). Whether his father was in or out of office, the family's home base, Grey Towers, offered little respite; Gifford Bryce's parents invited scores of guests to visit, with meals often taking on the aura of a debating society. The same was true if it was just family around the table, as Gifford Bryce recalled of the "arguments between the liberal Giffords and the more conservative Amoses." A threat to kidnap Gifford Bryce during his father's first term as Pennsylvania's chief executive—a threat taken very seriously, given the tragic outcome of the much-publicized Lindbergh baby's abduction—led his parents to send him back to Milford (which he loved) under round-the-clock guard (which he did not). Even a multi-month cruise in 1929 across the South Pacific had its political undertones. The power couple had their departure from Philadelphia, down the Delaware River, filmed, with the moving images distributed across the state; they kept in close contact with Pennsylvania's public affairs by radio, telegraph, and correspondence; and much to their son's disappointment, they cut short their itinerary when they got wind that the Depression was disrupting Pennsylvania's political order, potentially opening the way for another run for the Governor's Mansion. It is no wonder that Gifford Bryce vowed never to take up his parents' (pre) occupation. Instead, he became a biologist and medical researcher, and when not in the lab or classroom, this gifted sailor could be found at sea.[19]

However blind Gifford may have been to the degree to which being "Gifford Pinchot" shaped his relations with his family, he saw quite clearly another aspect of his years in the civic arena: he lost a lot of elections. His lack of success at the polls was not a liability, exactly. Learning that his sister Antoinette's son, Harcourt Johnstone, a perennial candidate for the British House of Commons, had been defeated in the 1927 elections, he

18. Cornelia Bryce Pinchot, "In Search of Adventure," in *These Modern Women: Autobiographical Essays from the Twenties*, ed. Elaine Showalter (New York: Feminist Press, 1979), 126.

19. Char Miller, *Seeking the Greatest Good: The Conservation Legacy of Gifford Pinchot* (Pittsburgh: University of Pittsburgh Press, 2013), 25–34.

cheered his nephew on and urged him not to be downcast: "I have been licked so many times in so many different ways," Gifford noted, "that I have sort of become immune to it." For all its travails, politics was an elixir.[20]

It also offered an unparalleled opportunity to do good, for public service was service. That was why Pinchot wanted the Forest Service to be so named, a signal to the American people that these public lands were public, owned by all citizens, and that those who managed them were there to serve the land and the people who depended on its manifold resources. This ethos also was integrated into his political discourse. Why enter politics if not to serve the larger community? Pinchot's faith in the reciprocal relationship between the government and the governed gained its first expression when he was but twenty-four. In 1889, asked to speak at Milford's centennial celebration of the U.S. Constitution, he assured his fellow citizens that together they were "trustees of a coming world." To fulfill that high office, and the mutual responsibilities that come with it, required the (then all-male) electorate to realize, "every man of us, not only that we have a share in the commonwealth, but that the common-wealth has a share in us."[21]

Pinchot upheld this conviction that the citizenry and their represen-tatives had a shared responsibility, even in the most fiercely contested of political brawls—and he was embroiled in, and sparked, any number of them. Note the language Pinchot deployed in 1926 when rebutting those members of his own Republican party who tried to get rid of the direct primary system, which granted voters the power to select the final candi-dates to run in the general election. Invoking the nation's revolutionary past—"One hundred and fifty years ago our ancestors laid down their lives for the principle that taxation without representation was tyranny and could not be tolerated by a free people. They won that fight and with it the right to vote and choose their own representatives"—he argued that that principle was "under attack. A handful of politicians have set on foot a movement designed to rob the people of this country of their fundamen-tal right to govern themselves. If the politicians have their way, they and not the people will really govern." A savvy Pinchot was not surprised that this attempt came shortly after women began to exercise their right to vote; its purpose, he argued, was to disenfranchise them. A free people

20. Gifford Pinchot to Harcourt Johnstone, quoted in Miller, *Gifford Pinchot*, 200.

21. "An Address of Gifford Pinchot, Esq., Delivered at the Celebration on Center Square, August 28, 1889, to Commemorate the Second Centennial of the Republic," *Milford Dispatch*, September 9, 1889.

required free choice, and, logically enough, candidate Pinchot hoped they would exercise that choice in his favor.[22]

To persuade them of the power of his ideas, whether as forester or politician, required more than political acumen. It also demanded a voice. Early on, Pinchot found it through his command of words. An award-winning debater in college, he loved to speak in public and could be blunt or conciliatory depending on the occasion. He was also a vigorous stylist, engaging his readers directly and without flourish. There is an economy to his writing; short, tight sentences were his preferred form. Even *Breaking New Ground* (1946), which weighs in at 510 pages, is a quick read (well, most of it is). By the time he began to write this tome, Pinchot had had a lot of practice, dating back to his first professional publication in *Garden and Forest*, which appeared more than five decades before his final book hit the bookstores. Practice made perfect.

Yet his commitment to writing can be further backdated: from the moment he could form letters, James and Mary Pinchot insisted that Gifford keep a diary, and whenever he was separated from them for even a short period of time, he was to send home detailed notes about his day and his doings. When the anticipated missive failed to arrive, or was late—a not infrequent occurrence during Gifford's youth—the senior Pinchots scolded their firstborn, worried that his inexactness was a sign of personal laxity. They were no less concerned as he matured. While the twenty-five-year-old studied forestry in Europe, he was expected to send a steady stream of letters describing his courses, teachers, fellow students, and most of all his plans for the future. The trio's transatlantic exchanges are revelatory, for in them the family collectively mapped out the next ten years of Gifford's career. That said, should their son have been tardy in replying promptly to every request for information embedded in the letters he received in a week's time from one or another of his parents, he could expect a passive-aggressive query wondering whether he had taken ill, or a stern remonstrance to fulfill his filial duties as a correspondent.[23]

These parental corrections were not the only ones Pinchot received during his time at the French forestry school. His German mentor, Dietrich Brandis, had his ambitious American charge write a weekly report about what he had learned in his classes and out in the field. Instructed to use only the left-hand side of a page for his notes, Pinchot was to leave blank the right-hand side so that Brandis could critique Pinchot's recitations of

22. Gifford Pinchot, speech, *New York World*, August 30, 1889, in editor's possession; Gifford Pinchot, "Politicians or the People?," in this volume.
23. Miller, *Gifford Pinchot*, 59–69, 81–93.

his lessons. In English, French, and German, the message was consistent. Words matter.

Pinchot was not shy about emphasizing that same point to those who worked for him in the Bureau of Forestry and later the Forest Service. Every forest ranger and supervisor had to submit quarterly and annual reports to the office in Washington, D.C., and although they might have chafed at the red tape–like nature of this paperwork, they learned soon enough that the chief took their accounts seriously. More than a few found themselves on the wrong end of his thick blue pencil. Pinchot slashed through their prose, demanding greater clarity of expression and a cleaner narration before requiring the chastened to revise and resubmit. As Pennsylvania's governor, he followed the same practice; efficiency in prose, like a speedy response, was the hallmark of a good memo, letter, or report.[24]

He was as tough when he put pen to paper. The drafts of Pinchot's speeches and articles located in his voluminous papers in the Library of Congress reveal the same attention to word choice, texture, and tone that he demanded of his subordinates. The talks he delivered demonstrate as well his sharp ear for how words might sound to those gathered in an auditorium or around a radio: the blue pen underlined words or phrases he was to stress, editing that structured his cadence.

This willingness to revise himself was a key to the successful and collaborative revision of Pinchot's *The Training of a Forester*. Originally published in 1914, it was reissued twice in the succeeding decades, but in 1937, when its publisher proposed yet another uncorrected edition, Pinchot balked, thinking the book too out-of-date. No longer in close touch with the latest research in forestry, he hired Massachusetts State College forester Robert P. Holdsworth to help make the book more relevant to its intended readers—contemporary students and those interested in the field more generally. Over that summer, as Holdsworth reworked each chapter, Pinchot followed behind him, blue pencil to hand, cutting, rewriting, and rearranging, a process that carried on through three full drafts of the manuscript.[25]

As smooth as that process was, Pinchot had a hard time replicating it in his faltering efforts to write what would become *Breaking New Ground*. There were too many moments when he despaired of completing his magnum opus. This was not for the lack of help—he had more than enough colleagues willing to pitch in, including some of his former Forest Service staffers, such as Raphael Zon, as well as Holdsworth again. He did not

24. Steen, *Forest Service*, 75–76.
25. Miller, *Gifford Pinchot*, 335–36.

suffer from a small data bank with which to craft his life story, either. Thanks to his parents' insistent (and incessant) demands that he stay in close touch with them, and as a result of their pack-rat tendencies to save everything Gifford wrote, he had access to every diary, post card, and letter he had written since childhood. This remarkable archive made it possible for *Breaking New Ground* to be quite faithful to these many texts that had preserved his (almost) every thought or reflection.[26]

What bedeviled Pinchot was how to frame this wealth of information into a cogent argument and coherent narrative. By the late 1930s, he had an array of sections written but could not figure out how to link them into a satisfying whole. Like a barometer measuring changes in atmospheric pressure, Pinchot's diary registers his every high and low while seeking a way out of this literary impasse. Finally, in February 1937, he asked Charles Beard for the secret to his "enormous production of books." The distinguished historian, author of such landmark texts as *An Economic Interpretation of the U.S. Constitution* (1913) and, with his wife, Mary, of *The Rise of American Civilization* (1927), laid out his surefire strategy: before he began to write any of his bestselling volumes, Beard told Pinchot, he first constructed a highly detailed outline that consisted of a series of subject subdivisions, one after the other. Once this was completed, "all you have to do is to put in the verbs and the book is done." For the record, Beard's prose reads as flat as his regimented methodology; Pinchot's is a good deal more vibrant. But for the blocked writer, Beard's approach seemed ideal—though it still took Pinchot the better part of a decade to finish his autobiography. At his death in October 1946, the book was at the printer.[27]

Once in print, *Breaking New Ground* confirmed his lifelong desire to make history. He also wanted to curate—if not control—its contours; through that book, in which he righted (some) old wrongs, he gained a modicum of management over his message and its meanings. By contrast, the selected collection of Pinchot's writings in this volume deliberately does not include any excerpts from his memoir. Rather, it reproduces Pinchot's words captured at those moments in which they were spoken and/or written. The texts included here are as purposeful as his autobiography, but they are not as polished, with an eye to how history would receive and interpret them. Pinchot wrote these speeches, articles, and essays for his contemporary listeners and readers, not necessarily for those

26. Pinchot also requested and received a trove of reminiscences that the first generation of forest rangers had sent to him. Bibi Gaston, whose great-grandfather was Amos Pinchot, has published a selection of these remarkable narratives in *Gifford Pinchot and the First Foresters* (New Milford, Conn.: Baked Apple Club Productions, 2016).

27. Steen, ed., *Conservation Diaries*, 208–11.

of us to come, and this gives them an immediacy precisely because they were crafted at and for a particular time, place, and audience. They therefore offer us an unparalleled view of his active engagements as he lived them, thought about them, and captured them on the page. His past can become part of our present, history brought back to life.

PART ONE

FORESTS, FORESTRY, AND FORESTERS

Four key moments in the history of the forestry profession in the United States hit notable marks in 2015: Gifford Pinchot would have been 150 years old, the Yale School of Forestry and Environmental Studies (née The Yale Forest School) and the Society of American Foresters (SAF) celebrated their 115th birthdays, and the U.S. Forest Service reached its 110th. Pinchot was not responsible for the first event, but he was present at the creation of the other three. In fact, he was their father—and midwife.

These latter births were part of a plan. In the early 1890s, as Pinchot turned his considerable energy into becoming the first scientifically trained American forester, he was already conceiving the steps needed to create the forestry profession. Its adherents would need graduate training, which the Yale Forest School, with funding from the Pinchot family, would provide. That program's graduates would need a professional organization to help certify their careers; enter the SAF. And these recent graduates would need to apply their scientific insights on the ground; many of them became the new agency's workforce. Call this a closed ecological system.

Yet for all this system's commitment to the scientific analysis of environmental factors shaping forested landscapes, progenitor Pinchot knew that forestry was also a social project born with an ineluctable moral code.

Pinchot had a well-developed sense of an all-encompassing duty to the commonweal, as evident in an 1889 speech he delivered at a local celebration of the U.S. Constitution's centenary, arguing that the state and nation-state had a right to "our service, our thought, and action." One year later, while studying forestry in Europe, he began to make good on that promise. As compelling as the scientific basis of his chosen profession was, Pinchot was more attracted to the political environments in which it was situated. That attraction was manifest in his first professional paper, "Governmental Forestry Abroad" (1891), an in-depth survey of the significance of global forestry. It contains two telling takeaways. The first was that while forestry science was consistent across cultures, its application was not; that is why republican Switzerland was a much better model for the United States than monarchical Prussia, Pinchot would declare. The second was that government action was essential because forestry's goal must be to protect and utilize forest resources across time, and that could only be achieved with a government that would be willing to guard these resources in perpetuity.

Foresters, in short, must be virtuous citizens and upright public servants. Theirs was a moral calling. He made that case in speeches and newspaper articles in the run-up to the establishment of the national forest system—and its later expansion. The application of forestry in overseas colonies like the Philippines was similarly essential and reflective of a people's character, just as the inability or unwillingness to adopt or maintain these land-management principles boded ill. Pinchot's was a rigorous standard, to be sure, as his professional colleagues discovered when they prioritized technical fixes or industry-friendly solutions to the ongoing and rapid devastation of America's forests. "Every forester in the country must face a clear-cut issue," he confirmed in "The Lines Are Drawn" (1919). "He must act with foresters in the public interest, or with lumbermen with a special interest." Naturally, there was only one acceptable answer, "if he is to call himself a forester in the finest sense of that fine word."

A decade later, Pinchot reiterated that his peers must return to the fold. "Failure to grapple with the problem of forest destruction threatens the usefulness of our profession," he and his coauthors wrote in "A Letter to Foresters" (1930). They called on foresters to abandon "apathy and doubt." Through a "rebirth of faith in forestry and a reawakening of all [their] moral and mental energies," foresters could reclaim the profession's "high ideals and great purposes." Even the exigencies of war did not release foresters from their obligation to protect the lands under their care. Furious that Pennsylvania was plundering the state forests he had helped regenerate while serving as governor, in 1942 Pinchot castigated those foresters managing Penn's Woods. "If the war needed every last tree in Pennsylvania, we should give it, of course. But the war does not need it." Instead, the swift and indiscriminate harvesting of these forests was robbing them of their future productivity and thus stealing from subsequent generations. "I say [this] is not forestry at all," an aggrieved Pinchot thundered, "but tree butchery."

That he felt as deeply about forestry's idealistic claims in the 1940s as he had when he first embraced them in the 1890s, and that he worked so diligently and for so long to embed this moral vision into the institutions he helped create, says a great deal about his commitments. Despite his enduring record of achievements as chief executive of the Commonwealth of Pennsylvania, he pledged his allegiance to forestry: "I have since been a Governor, every now and then, but I am a forester all the time—have been, and shall be, all my working life."[1]

---

1. Pinchot, *Breaking New Ground*, 137.

Government Forestry Abroad

Pinchot traveled to Europe in 1890 to buy some books on forestry and then return home. He stayed for the better part of a year; studied forestry in Nancy, France; and met with every significant forester in England, France, Germany, and Switzerland. The ever-ambitious young man, with his future career in mind, established his presence by writing a series of articles about his experiences overseas for the lead journal in the United States, *Garden and Forest*. His reflections about the prospect of "planting" forestry in the New World made him its primary advocate, a status he coveted and nourished.

Originally published in *Garden and Forest* 4, no. 150 (January 7, 1891): 8–9; no. 151 (January 14, 1891): 21–22; and no. 152 (January 21, 1891): 34–35.

. . . All forest management may be said to rest on two self-evident truths: (1) that trees require many years to reach merchantable size; and, (2) that a forest crop cannot be taken every year from the same land. From the last statement it follows that a definite, far-seeing plan is necessary for the rational management of any forest, from the first; that forest property is safest under the supervision of some imperishable guardian; or, in other words, of the State. . . .

To begin with Germany, we find that about two-thirds of the forests are under more or less complete control of the State. It will not be necessary when dealing with forest policy in the German Empire to treat independently the different States of which it is composed because one principle lies at the root of forest policy in each of them, and may be fully illustrated by reference to any one. This principle, special to no country or form of government, holds that "the State is the guardian of all public interests." It is in its interpretation that, for the purposes of this paper, its chief interest lies. From this point of view "public interests" must be taken to mean all interests other than private ones. So understood, this maxim may be said to sum up the forest policy of nearly all the nations of Europe, as well under republican as under governments of a distinctly paternal character. For its illustration I will describe in a few words the forest-organization of the Kingdom of Prussia.

Covering an area of some 20,000,000 acres, the forests of Prussia occupy 23.4 per cent of the total surface of the country. Their ownership, a point of capital importance in relation to our subject, is divided as follows:

To the State belong nearly 6,000,000 acres, or twenty-nine percent; to towns, village communities and other public bodies, sixteen percent; and to private owners rather more than half the total area, fifty-five percent.

The relation of the State to the forests which it owns is simple and rational. Holding it as a duty to preserve the wood lands for the present share which they take in the economy of the nation, the State has recognized also the obligation to hand down its forest wealth unimpaired to future generations. It has recognized and respected equally the place which the forest holds in relation to agriculture and in the economy of nature, and hence feels itself doubly bound to protect its woodlands. It has, therefore, steadily refused to deliver its forests to more or less speedy destruction, by allowing them to pass into the hands of shorter-lived and less provident owners. Even in the times of greatest financial difficulty, when Prussia was overrun and nearly annihilated by the French, the idea of selling the State forests was never seriously entertained.

But the government of Prussia has not stopped there. Protection, standing alone, is irrational and incomplete. The cases where a forest reaches its highest usefulness by simply existing are rare. The immense capital which the state woodlands represents is not permitted to lie idle, and the forest as a timber producer has taken its place a permanent feature on the land. The Government has done the only wise thing by managing its own forests through its own forest officers.

The organization of the Forest Service is briefly as follows: At its head stands the Department, or more correctly, the Ministry of Agriculture, State lands and forests, which exercises general supervision over forest affairs through the medium of the (Oberlandforstmeister) chief of Forest Service. Next in authority is the Bezirksregierung, a council in charge of one of the thirty-five minor divisions of the Prussian State, which has full control over forest business within its sphere of action. The members of the controlling staff, the Oberförstmeister and the Forstmeister, are also members of this council. Their duties lie in the inspection of the officers of the executive staff, of whom there are 681 in Prussia. These officers, styled Oberförster, are charged with the actual management of the public forest lands, and it is on them that the security of public interest in the forest chiefly rests. Upon their selection and education the utmost care and forethought are expended.[1]

---

1. "As one who has suffered from the lack of it," Pinchot notes in a longer version of this article, "I may perhaps be permitted to bear my testimony to the value of a custom which is unfortunately less widely extended than its merits deserve; but which I hope to see one day established in the forest schools of our land." He and his family would make good on this promise, underwriting the creation of the Yale Forest School in 1900.

Such is in outline the organization of the Prussian forest service. The principles upon which it rests are thus stated by Donner, now Oberlandforstmeister, in a work which carries all the weight of an official document. He says:

"The fundamental rules for the management of State forests are these: First, to keep rigidly within the bounds of conservative treatment, and secondly, to attain, consistently with such treatment, the greatest output of most useful products in the shortest time."

And again:

"The State believes itself bound, in the administration of its forests, to keep in view the common good of the people, and that as well with respect to the lasting satisfaction of the demand for timber and other forest produce, as to the numerous other purposes which the forest serves. It holds fast the duty to treat the Government wood lands as a trust held for the nation as a whole, to the end that it may enjoy for the present the highest satisfaction of its needs for forest produce and the protection which the forest gives, and for all future time, at least an equal share of equal blessings."

. . . In closing this brief sketch of forest policy in Prussia, you will perhaps allow me to refer for a moment to the erroneous ideas of German forest management which have crept into our literature. They have done so, I believe, partly through a desire of the advocates of forestry, because they tend to make forest management ridiculous in the eyes of our citizens. The idea has arisen that German methods are exaggeratedly artificial and complicated, and not unnaturally the inference has been made that forestry in itself is a thing for older and more densely populated countries, and that forest management is inapplicable and incapable of adaptation to the conditions under which we live. It is true, on the contrary, that the treatment of German forests is distinguished above all things by an elastic adaptability to circumstances, which is totally at variance with the ironclad formality with which a superficial observation may believe it sees. It is equally true that its methods could not be transported unchanged into our forests without entailing discouragement and failure, just as our methods of lumbering would be disastrous there; but the principles which underlie not only German, but all rational forest management, are true all the world over. It was in accordance with them that the forests of British India were taken in hand and are now being successfully managed, but the methods into which the same principles have developed are as widely dissimilar as the countries in which they are being applied. So forest management in America must be worked out along lines which the conditions of our life will prescribe. It never can be a technical imitation of that of any other country, and a knowledge of forestry abroad will be useful and necessary rather as matter for comparison than as a guide to be blindly obeyed. Under these conditions I do not believe that forest management in the United States will present even serious technical difficulties. It only asks the opportunity to prove itself sound and practical.

Switzerland is a country where the development rather than the actual condition of forest-policy may best claim our attention. The history of forestry in the Swiss republic is of peculiar interest to the people of the United States because in its beginnings may be traced many of the characteristics of the situation here and now, and because the Swiss, like the Americans, were confronted with a problem of a concrete forest policy extending over the various states of a common union. The problem has been brilliantly solved, and not the least important result of its solution is the fact that the people of Switzerland have recognized the vast significance and importance of the forests in so mountainous a country, and a full and hearty appreciation and support of the forest policy of the Confederation is in every nook and corner of the land. . . . As the example set by a republic to a republic, as the brilliant result of a few devoted men, crowned by a public opinion which they created, and rewarded by the great and lasting blessing which they brought to their country, our country can find no worthier model, no nobler source of encouragement and inspiration.

"Our forest laws," Professor Landolt [observes], "are intended to work more through instruction, good example, and encouragement than by severe regulations. This method is somewhat slower than one that should involve more drastic uneasiness, but the results achieved are more useful and lasting. Our laws require the same treatment for the forests of the state, the communes, and other public bodies."

It hardly needs to be added that the present condition of forestry in Switzerland is admirable. Systematic forest management has probably been known here as long as anywhere in Europe, and nowhere can finer individual examples be found.

In France, which stands with Germany at the head of the nations as regards the thoroughness of forest-policy, the large extent of Government and other public forests is in excellent condition. The training of French foresters, and, to some extent, the treatment of French forests, differ widely from those that distinguish Prussia, as indeed the genius of the people would naturally lead us to expect. That this training extends over two years instead of the six to eight spent by the Prussian candidates, cannot help but make the task of national forest management seem lighter, especially in view of the admirable, and very often the wonderful, results which the

French forest officers have achieved. Perhaps their most brilliant work has been accomplished in the correction in the torrents in the Alps, Pyrenees, and Cevennes, in the course of which 350,000 acres have been rewooded under difficulties which seem almost insurmountable. Of the total cost to the French Government, some 50,000,000 francs, about half were consumed in engineering works whose direct object was to make the replanting of the drainage areas of torrents possible. . . . The disappearance of this forest may be traced, in most cases, directly to mountain pasturage, and the whole story of reboisement in France is of the deepest interest in comparison with the past history and probable future of our mountain forests.

Perhaps the closest analogy to our own conditions in the magnitude of the area to be treated, the difficulties presented by the character of the country and the prevalence of fire, and the nature of the opposition which it encountered, is to be found in the forest administration of India, and that in spite of the tropical climate with it has to deal. . . .

Systematic forest-management was begun in India about thirty-five years ago, under difficulties not unlike those which confront us now. An insufficient or wrong impression of the interests involved, the personal bias of lumbermen, the alternating support and opposition of the men in power, were the chief difficulties with which it had to contend; and against them were pitted the splendid perseverance and magnificent administrative powers of one man. The victory was brilliant, conclusive, and lasting, and India has to thank Sir Dietrich Brandis for benefits whose value will go on increasing from age to age.

These forests have been gradually brought under simple, but systematic, methods of management, which aim at effective protection, an efficient system of regeneration and cheap transportation, the whole under well considered and methodical working plans. . . . The results of this enlightened policy are conspicuous, not only in the great fact that forests yield, and will permanently yield, the supply of timber and forest produce which the population requires but also in the beginning which has been made toward regulating the water supply in the mountains, and in the increasing capital value and the annual net revenue of the state forests. This last has reached the verge of half a million sterling, and it is believed by the men best fitted to judge, that the forest revenue will increase at least four times during the next quarter of a century.

There are two other facts resulting from the forest policy of India which are of special significance to us as citizens of a country where any interference by the Government with private rights would be so vigorously resented, and where private enterprise must consequently play so conspicuous a part: First, a body of experienced and efficient officers of all grades has gradually been formed in the state forests whose services are available for the management of private forests, and of communal forests when the time shall come to form them; secondly, the example set by the well managed state forests, and the steadily increasing revenue which they yield have induced native and other forest proprietors to imitate the state. . . .

. . . The destructive tendencies of private forest management in India might with equal truth have been made as a general proposition. It is the salient fact which the history of the forests of the earth tends to teach; but nowhere have the proofs of its truth taken such gigantic proportions as the United States today. Even in Germany, where the state has done its utmost to surround them with every possible safeguard, the wood lands of private proprietors are steadily decreasing both in area and in quality. A second great fact, which is of equal and immediate significance to us in America, is that the countries which have been successful in forest preservation have been so along the lines of forest management. The first and most evident function of the forest is to produce wood, and no scheme which leaves out of account the imperative and legitimate demand for forest produce is likely to meet with the support of a people as practical as our own. The forests which are more profitably used are the forests which are best preserved. These truths have never had the currency with us that their importance has deserved, and as a result we have been hastening along a road whose end is painfully apparent. We are surrounded by the calamitous results of the course we are now pursuing. In fact, it seems as though there were no civilized or semi-civilized country in either hemisphere which cannot stand to us as an example or a warning. To this great truth they bear witness with united voice: The care of the forests is the duty of the nation.

The Forests of Ne-Ha-Sa-Ne Park in Northern New York

Pinchot's first major work of forestry was on George Vanderbilt's Biltmore estate in North Carolina, a job he secured through his connections to the estate's landscape architect, Frederick Law Olmsted. Networking brought additional work. In his memoir, *Breaking New Ground*, Pinchot notes, "On a visit to George Vanderbilt, his brother-in-law, Dr. W. Seward Webb, saw the work at Biltmore and was impressed by it. He was the owner of a superb tract of 40,000 acres in the Adirondacks in Hamilton County, New York, which he named Ne-Ha-Sa-Ne Park. October of 1892 found me there making an examination with a view to the practice of sound forest management."[1]

Originally published in *Garden and Forest* 6, no. 268 (April 12, 1893): 168–69.

———————————
———————————

Except for local variations and the greater proportion of soft timbers in the [site's] western and northern part, the forest over the whole park is approximately the same. The high ground is covered by magnificent growth of hardwood timbers, thinly interspersed with Spruce. Beech is here the most common tree, with Birch and Maple closely second. The swamps and low grounds are chiefly occupied by Balsam, Tamarack, Hemlock, and White Pine. To these, which are mentioned in the order of frequency, are to be added in the same order, Cherry, Poplar, Cedar, and Ash. Spruce and Pine are at present the most valuable timbers. It seems likely in future Birch will be the most important tree. The silvicultural value of the soil has been reached by the accumulation of mold from the waste of many generations of forest trees. The ground itself is rocky and not rich, and its sustained vigor depends entirely on the preservation of humus or duff, with which it is covered almost everywhere, sometimes to the depth of six feet. Humus disappears gradually upon free exposure to light and air, and may be entirely consumed by forest fires. Hence fire and reckless cutting are especially destructive to Adirondack forests, entirely apart from the important loss which they occasion in standing timber and the growth it would have made during the years when the burnt area is slowly reclothing itself with forest.

. . . [Y]oung trees are almost always seriously retarded in their growth by the heavy cover of the older specimens. For this reason the rings of

1. See Pinchot, *Breaking New Ground*, 74–76.

annual growth formed during early life are much closer together than the later ones. In endeavoring to count the rings of stumps standing on the right-of-way near Lake Lilla, I was often unable to separate those of the first fifty or one hundred years, even with a [magnifying] glass. I found no Maple or Birch whose inner rings could be counted, and but one Beech. This tree was twenty-eight inches in diameter at four feet from the ground, and somewhat over two hundred years old. A Hemlock of seventeen inches of diameter on the stump was two hundred and ninety-two years old. Spruce stumps, on which all the rings were far enough apart to be counted, were also exceptional. One butt log, with a diameter of seventeen inches, was two hundred and eighteen years old. This tree had evidently been stunted in the shade of older hardwoods. It is remarkable that the finest Spruce, that on the hardwood ridges, must have passed through this period of repression before making its principal growth. By cutting away the merchantable hardwoods, which are suppressing the Spruces over a large portion of the park, their rate of growth may be enormously increased. For example, two young Spruces, eight inches in diameter, which had grown among others of the same age, and therefore with comparatively abundant supply of light and air, were but fifty two and sixty years old, although almost twice the diameter of another tree almost one hundred and twenty years old.

The power of natural regeneration of all the trees I have mentioned, with the single important exception of White Pine, seems to be amply sufficient for all the purposes of forest management. The presence of this reproductive power is of greatest importance. It puts aside at once the difficulty and expense of planting and insures a steady improvement in the condition and value of the forest.

The vigorous and abundant young growth makes it possible to remove mature trees without injury to the forest, and under proper handling will insure the continuation of its productive power. The constant character of the forest, even with its changes, lends itself easily to needs of forestry, while the presence everywhere of mature trees over the young growth makes it possible to cut and yet increase the annual growth of wood from year to year. The steady increase of the value of the forest under forest management is one of the strongest reasons for its introduction. Forest management will add constantly to the proportion of valuable timbers in the forest, by judicious cutting, without a corresponding abatement in the amount of lumber produced. In other words, for a few years the forest will yield slightly more under ordinary lumbering than it will under forest management, because in the latter case greater care is used, and many trees that otherwise would fall all at once must be allowed to stand. After that time the revenue from forest management will surpass that from lumbering, and will go increasing indefinitely while the returns from lumbering methods will as steadily diminish. The profits will certainly pass their lowest during the first twenty years, and probably during the first ten. Thereafter they will rise with the rise in prices and the growing productive capacity of the forest. Timberland as productive as this, as safe from fire, and as accessible from the centers of consumption by rail and water, is, in my judgment, one of the best long investments.

. . . The statement is often made it is possible to lumber the same land a second and then a third time at intervals of fifteen or twenty years, and get as good a cut from it as at first. In exceptional cases this is true. The probabilities are, however, that the second and third cuts were as good as the first in a pecuniary way, and not otherwise, since the years which intervened the diameter of merchantable trees has steadily diminished, while the price of lumber has increased. Forestry provides not merely for sustaining the proportion of the more valuable woods, but for increasing it.

The ordinary methods of lumbering are exceedingly careless of the life of all the young growth which may happen to stand under the old trees. Such carelessness is not only destructive of the future value of the forest, but also increases the danger of fire by the presence of a quantity of dry saplings which forest management would have allowed to grow. Young green trees are the greatest protection a forest can have against the spread of fire. Hence forest management tends distinctly to keep fire out, as compared with the methods of ordinary lumbering.

Lumbering yields a slightly larger revenue than forest management, but then falls far behind it. It increases the danger from fire, tends to deprive the forest of its more valuable timber and lowers its capital value. Forest management does none of those things.

A Plan to Save the Forests

The 1891 Forest Reserve Act had granted the president the authority to designate forest reserves but had not identified whether or how these lands were to be managed. As Congress, the White House, and the public debated the issue of forest management, a number of forest advocates, including Gifford Pinchot, were invited to publish their thoughts in *The Century Magazine*. Other respondents included a who's who of contemporary conservationists, among them Bernard E. Fernow, Frederick Law Olmsted, J. F. Rothrock, Theodore Roosevelt, and John Muir.

Originally published in *The Century Magazine*, February 1895, 626, 630.

―――――――――
―――――――――

The following communications were written in response to a request from *The Century* for opinions as to the general need of a thorough, scientific, and permanent system of forest management in this country, and specifically as to the plan suggested by Professor Charles S. Sargent of Harvard University, which comprises the following features:

1. Forestry instruction at West Point: the establishment of a chair of forestry at the United States Military Academy, to be supplemented by practical study in the woods and by personal inspection of foreign systems of forestry.
2. An experimental forest reservation: the purchase on the Highlands near West Point, or elsewhere, of a small territory for the use of the proposed new branch of instruction.
3. Control by educated officers: the assignment of the best educated of these officers to the supervision of the [U.S.] forest reservations.
4. The enlistment of a forest guard: a body of local foresters, to be specifically enlisted for the purpose of carrying out the principles of forestry thus taught. . . .

Professor Sargent's otherwise excellent plan appears to me susceptible of enlargement. It involves waiting for the establishment of a forestry school and the giving of its course of instruction at least once before the management of the national forests can be undertaken, and it does not provide for the best grade of trained skill. The first of these points gains its importance from the fact that management of the national forests is the most pressing need and duty of forestry in the United States. The second is more fundamental in character. A course in forestry which is merely an adjunct to a military education must fail to produce the highest efficiency as foresters in the officers who take it. Adequate training in so large a subject can be reached only be prolonged and undivided attention. This fact has been most clearly recognized in the most efficient government forest services. In Prussia the course preliminary to a state position requires six years; in France, five, of which three are preliminary; in England the candidates for the Indian forest service, who until recently spent two years at the forest school after passing competitive exams, now spend three. The addition of a proposed board of trained foresters, acting under the War Department, would, I believe, meet both these difficulties. The forest service would then include three branches, as from the nature of the work it must:

First: The protective staff, consisting of forest guards, and including private soldiers and noncommissioned officers, to whom lessons in forestry might be given at the post schools.

Second: The executive staff, composed of officers to whose course at West Point some instruction in forestry had been added, perhaps in the form of an additional term. They would have direct charge of the reservations, and would be responsible to headquarters for the guards under their orders, and for carrying out the working plans issued by the War Department for each subdivision of the forest.

Third: The administrative staff, a body of trained foresters acting under the War Department, who would determine the general policy of the forest service, prepare the working plans for each executive charge, and inspect and report to headquarters. They would come into effective touch with the executive staff only through the medium of the War Department.

Such a system could be put in operation by Congress at any time. While the army was doing protective work, the first duty of the forest service, a commission of scientifically trained men would study the reservations on the ground, outline general features of policy, recommend legislation, and do the other preliminary work which must precede the introduction of regular forest management. In the meantime a government school of forestry, established at West Point or elsewhere, would be preparing officers for the executive work soon to be required. A longer course, open to civilians, would provide the more thoroughly trained men demanded by the expanding work of continuous administration.

In the Philippine Forests

Forestry was an international force, a tool that many European empires used to manage a key resource and, by doing so, extend control over the people dependent on this resource. Many of Pinchot's mentors had been involved in such global projects, and he contributed to this process shortly after the Spanish-American War, when in 1902 he visited the Philippines and reported to U.S. colonial authorities that management in the archipelago's tropical rainforest was possible and necessary.

Originally published in *Forestry and Irrigation* 9, no. 2 (February 1903): 66–72.[1]

———————————

———————————

October 30, 1902.—Up early in the morning, as we were coming into Paluan Bay. We landed about 8.30, on the left bank of the Paluan River, near its mouth, where we found Company L, Thirtieth United States Infantry, quartered in an old church—a smart, neat, and efficient looking body of men in thoroughly good health and spirits. The commissary was in an old convent at one end of a town of nipa huts. There were a few better houses, but nearly all with nipa thatch and walls.

Scattered through the village were palai pounders; heavy wooden mortars used for hulling rice (palai). Sometimes there were two mortars in a single block of heavy, dark-brown, coarse grained wood. Usually the mortars were round, about 20 inches to 2 feet off the ground, 18 inches in diameter, and the hole from 8 to 12 inches deep. The pestles were double-ended, about 1 inch thick in the middle and 3 inches at each end, and perhaps 20 to 30 inches long. Under several of the houses were huge brown cylinders, perhaps 3 to 4 feet in diameter and 3 to 4 feet high, for holding palai, apparently made of the inner bark of some tree.

Instead of being supported on bamboo, nearly all these houses were raised off the ground on heavy, round, upright logs. The smaller ones consisted of one room, with a sort of uncovered piazza. The better houses have, in most cases, nipa partitions, in a few cases wooden ones. Where the floors are not of bamboo strips, the usual material, they are finely polished woods.

1. The journal editor's note reads, in part: "Mr. Pinchot, as announced in the January number of *Forestry and Irrigation*, recently returned from a trip to the Philippine Islands taken at the request of Secretary [of State Elihu] Root. The text of the accompanying article is taken from notes made by Mr. Pinchot during several days spent exploring the forests of the island of Mindoro."

On the right bank of the Paluan, which we reached across a flimsy bridge of bamboo and other poles, were the same nipa huts, none as good as the best of those on the left bank. On the beach were several deep and narrow fishing boats in process of construction. The wood used was Lauan, in long, clear boards.

While this is evidently in part a fishing village, there were no remains of fish or other trash on the shore, and the streets were as neat as possible. Behind the town, in the valley of the Paluan, were extensive rice fields, the crop from which is 20,000 cabanes (90 pounds in one caban) a year. These fields are irrigated by water from the Paluan River, thrown into the fields by a small diversion dam.

We took with us ten Filipinos engaged by Don Mariano, who is interested in forest work because he holds a license now and hopes to get others later on. These men carried light loads. We started about 11.30 and traveled across the rice and grass fields for about two miles to the edge of the forest. The rice fields were of rich clayey, micaceous, alluvial soil, and in the river bottom were loose, flat, round stones of schist, with some quartz. In the flat before reaching the woods were low scattered trees, branching and twisted not unlike apple trees at home and resembling them in leaf. In the edge of the woods the soil was gravelly, but altogether without humus. This absence of humus lasted throughout the day, except on the tops of the flat ridges and on northerly exposures in the dense forests. It was apparently caused in part by the rapid decomposition of the leaf mold through the action of the sun and in part by the removal of the dead and fallen wood by termites and other insects. Nowhere was the humus more than one-fourth inch thick, and it was present at all but seldom, although the soil on the slopes and ridges was a clayey loam, well suited to its retention.

The lower part of the forest, after passing the stunted trees at the edge, was composed chiefly of old timber, but usually with an abundance of young seedling growth. I was too unfamiliar with the trees to get a very correct idea of the distribution of the timber, but I remember that two or three trees of Tindalo (*Afzelia rhomboidea*), of moderate size, were found not far from 1,000 feet above the sea, and that Lauan (*Anisoptera thurifera*) was, for considerable stretches, the principal lumber tree, growing tall, cylindrical, and clear-boled to a great height. Above the greater number of Lauan, Boc-boc (*Streblus sp.*) was plentiful, while Taloto (*Sterculia campanulata*) was frequent along the lower edges of the Lauan belt. The Yango, growing to great size, occurred with the Lauan and the Dungon (*Heritiera silvatica*). At somewhat over 1,000 feet a change in the character of the forest gave far greater numbers of low and high saplings and low poles, while the mature trees were smaller in size, of less height, and evidently younger than below. I do not attribute this to the altitude, but to the usual accidental variation in the distribution of species in virgin forest.

The impression which this tropical forest makes is less unlike the forests of the temperate zone than I had expected. While intolerant trees are manifestly rare, still light has much to do with distribution. The relations of seedlings to seed trees are of the familiar type, and many, both of the younger and older timbers, resemble distinctly in general appearance, certain species at home.

With the exception of Lauan and a species of Diospyros, the bark of nearly all the trees was colored in shades of yellow, sometimes very light, or of light brown. In addition to the buttresses, their most conspicuous external features were the smoothness of the bark, the almost uniform presence of little knobs, evidently lenticelles, dotting the bark often very thickly, and the remarkable thinness of the latter. I saw no tree except Lauan of which the bark seemed to me over one-half inch in thickness, and usually it was far less. It is common for irregular plates, usually not more than six inches long, to drop from the bark of various species of these trees, leaving slightly sunken scars, which, however, do not differ in color from the adjacent surface. Horizontal, and more especially vertical, rifts, very delicate and small, occur in the outer surface of many trees, and in some there is a marked scaly or fibrous character. The trees are usually tall, seldom cylindrical, except the Lauan, and very generally crooked. They are better on the slopes than in the bottoms, as I saw them, and far taller, as well as of better form. The mixture of species is an intimate one, although here and there two or three trees of one kind are found close together.

Most of the slopes seen today were of south and southwest exposure; consequently less humus was to be expected.

October 31, 1902.—Returning to Paluan, some of us left the main trail and followed the steep valley of a dry torrent down to the Calauagan River. On the way we saw Dungon. In the river bottom were the trees of Banaba (*Lagerstroemia Flos-Regina*) and an occasional Molave (*Vitex littoralis*). In bark the two species resemble each other considerably, Molave being darker in color, except for the black lenticelles which dot the bark of the Banaba. The latter has a large single leaf, while the Molave leaf is composed of three leaflets and greatly resembles that of the hickory.

November 1, 1902.—We landed at the mouth of the Dioso River, on the northwest shore of Mindoro, north of Paluan, about half past seven. The shore was lined with Bitog (*Calophyllum spectabile*), Palo Maria (*Calophyllum inophyllum*), Apalaya, and a palm with long narrow leaves, sharply serrated on the edges, light colors, and extremely twisted, and other tropical vegetation. The forest looked more like the tropical forest of my imagination than anything I had yet seen. Near the mouth of the river was an abandoned native hut once occupied by loggers, who had been getting out Calantas (*Cedrela Toona*). I brought back a chip hewed off in squaring a log to show the waste. Near a second camp a hole, apparently to pound palai in, had been cut in a horizontal trunk of a tree. The ground was covered with fruits of various shapes and parts of a beautiful flower, consisting of a cluster of filaments wide at the base and pink at the extremity, about 5 inches long, and with a delicious odor.

The Dioso River, at present a mere trickle of water, has an extremely precipitous and rather extended watershed. Near the shore it had transported logs of large size and piled them in heaps 3 or 4 feet high along and across the channel. The rock it brought down was but little eroded, having been so short a time in transit, for the whole length of the stream is probably less than 3 miles. The alluvial cone is large and fine, and near the present river course is cut by many channels, each one bordered, as in the case of the one now used, by piles of rocks higher than the surrounding land. On the bank of the river, we found a small stump of Calantas cut by Hareford three months ago. From two branches, which already existed at that time, it had sent out sprouts perhaps 18 inches long, but there was no evidence of sprouting from the stump itself. Because of the difficulty of finding rings, this was the only tree Hareford had been able to analyze in four months on this island.

As we left the river, going east we found immediately considerable quantities of Molave, of good size. Hareford showed me what he thought might be a Molave seedling in the crotch of the first tree of that kind. Examination showed many similar seedlings on the ground, but did not confirm the opinion that they were of Molave, which seemed unlikely from Hareford's statement that the Manyans had been unable to show him Molave seedlings, although he had looked carefully for them.

With the Molave was associated the Ditaa tree, (*Alstonia scholaris*), which has a thin bark from which exudes a white sap with a taste almost exactly like quinine, for which it is said to be an excellent substitute. The tree is of fine size and shape, with smooth, yellowish brown bark dotted with frequent lenticelles. The timber, however, is said to be of but moderate value. We found also Boc-boc and numbers of large specimens of the Yango tree, with gray brown fibrous bark, easily rubbed off with the hand. This tree is said to furnish a poor construction timber, probably of about the value of the third group. It has not yet been assigned to any group.

The Tindalo appeared on the upper slopes in considerable numbers and of fine size and shape. So did the Amuguis (*Odina speciosa*), which I had not seen before. It has moderately dark brown bark and large but-tresses, and the reproduction is fairly good. I should judge the tree was most plentiful above 100 feet. There were some specimens of other timbers of fine size, but of kinds which Hareford did not know. This is part of the forest which Hareford and Clark found to contain, between the Dioso and Calansan rivers, an average of 4,000 cubic feet to the acre.

As at Paluan, the increase of size and height of the timber on the slopes was very striking. There were more vines and creepers here than at Paluan, more humus, and a generally richer and more tropical appearance of the forest. Young growth was exceedingly plentiful, especially of the seedling and sapling sizes, but poles and young standards of the valuable trees were scarce. There was more humus than at Paluan, and at places far more trash on the ground. On the upper slope especially there was much fallen dead wood of very small sizes.

We saw few butterflies to-day, or other insects, except ants, which were everywhere. There were few birds in the forest, but we heard iguanas call-ing from the trees repeatedly, and once or twice a noise which was prob-ably from a monkey. The call of the iguana is like a repetition of the word "Gecko" or "Tuckoo," with the two syllables well apart.

Along the beach, although we traveled it for perhaps half a mile, I saw no single scrap of fish, although Seymour found some cuttle bone of very large size. There were few shells, most of them of small size, and occupied by hermit crabs, which were even common at some distance in the forest. Little land crabs seemed to be everywhere, even several hundred yards back from the shore.

We got back to the ship about four, and started east along the Mind-oro coast. From Mt. Calavita to Puerto Galera, steep hills come close to the shore. There are some cliffs immediately above the water, but of small height. In spite of the steepness of the country, I could see nothing to prevent successful logging, although it is true that I had only a distant view; but it is equally true that the timber in the country I traveled over was perfectly accessible. Near Abra de Olog there is a good deal of clear-ing on the hills, presumably for the camote (sweet potato) fields of the natives. At Puerto Galera is a good harbor.

Although we did not go over a half a mile back from the northern seacoast or more than 100 feet above tide, Hareford said that we had seen the characteristic forest. . . .

Dear Forester

Because there had never been a chief forester in the United States, and never been a Forest Service that such an individual would direct and thereby manage millions of acres of national forests, Secretary of Agriculture James Wilson was at pains to lay out Pinchot's new responsibilities. In this important task, Pinchot was a great help, writing the letter reprinted below for his boss to sign.[1]

Source: U.S. Forest Service History Collection, Forest History Society.[2]

Department of Agriculture
Office of the Secretary
Washington, D.C.

February 1, 1905
The Forester, Forest Service.
Sir:

The President has attached his signature to the following Act:

"An Act Providing for the transfer of forest reserves from the Department of the Interior to the Department of Agriculture.
   "*Be it enacted by the Senate and House of Representatives of the United States of America in Congress assembled,* That the Secretary of the Department of Agriculture shall, from and after the passage of this Act, execute or cause to be executed all laws affecting public lands theretofore or hereafter reserved under the provisions of section twenty-four of the Act entitled 'An Act to repeal the timber-culture laws, and for other purposes,' approved March third, eighteen hundred and ninety-one, and Acts supplemental to and amendatory thereof, after such lands have been so reserved, excepting such laws as affect the surveying, prospecting, locating, appropriating,

---

1. As Pinchot notes in *Breaking New Ground*, "That letter, it goes without saying, I had brought to the Secretary for his signature. Being a Departmental letter it had been prepared with care in Departmental style. . . . In the four decades between, this letter has set the standard for the Service, and it is still being quoted as the essence of Forest Service policy" (260–62).
   The quotation marks within the quoted Act appear in the original letter.
2. The letter can be accessed online at http://www.foresthistory.org/ASPNET/policy/Agency _Organization/Wilson_Letter.aspx.

entering, relinquishing, reconveying, certifying, or patenting of any such lands.

"Sec. 2. That pulp wood or wood pulp manufactured from timber in the district of Alaska may be exported therefrom.

"Sec. 3. That forest supervisors and rangers shall be selected, when practicable, from qualified citizens of the States or Territories in which the said reserves, respectively, are situated.

"Sec. 4. That rights of way for the construction and maintenance of dams, reservoirs, water plants, ditches, flumes, pipes, tunnels, and canals, within and across the forest reserves of the United States, are hereby granted to citizens and corporations of the United States for municipal or mining purposes, and for the purposes of the milling and reduction of ores, during the period of the beneficial uses, under the rules and regulations as may be prescribed by the Secretary of the Interior and subject to the laws of the State or Territory in which said reserves are respectfully situated.

"Sec. 5. That all money received from the sale of any products or the use of any land or resources of said forest products shall be covered into the Treasury of the United States, and for a period of five years from the passage of this Act shall constitute a special fund available, until expended, as the Secretary of Agriculture may direct, for the protection, administration, improvement, and extension of Federal forest reserves.

"Approved, February 1, 1905."

By this Act the administration of the Federal forest reserves is transferred to this Department. Its provisions will be carried out through the Forest Service, under your immediate supervision. You have already tentatively negotiated the transfer with the Commissioner of the General Land Office, whose powers and duties thus transferred I assign to you. Until otherwise instructed, you will submit to me for approval all questions of organization, sales, permits, and privileges, except such as are entrusted by the present regulations to field officers on the ground. All officers of the forest service transferred will be subject to your instructions and will report directly to you. You will at once issue to them the necessary notice to this effect.

In order to facilitate the prompt transaction of business upon the forest reserves and to give effect to the general policy outlined below, you are instructed to recommend at the earliest practicable date whatever changes may be necessary in the rules and regulations governing the reserves, so that I may, in accordance with the provisions of the above Act, delegate to you and to forest officers in the field, so much of my authority as may be essential to the prompt transaction of business, and to the administration of the reserves in accordance with local needs. Until such revision is made, the present rules and regulations will remain in force, except those relating to the receipt and transmittal of moneys, in which case Special Fiscal Agents of this Department will perform the duties heretofore rendered by the Receivers of Local Land Offices in accordance with existing laws and regulations. The Chief of Records, Bureau of Forestry, is hereby designated a Special Fiscal Agent, and you will direct him at once to execute and submit for my approval a bond for Twenty Thousand Dollars.

On December 17, 1904, the President signed the following order:

"In the exercise of the power vested in the President by section 1753 of the Revised Statutes and acts amendatory thereof:

"IT IS ORDERED, That all persons employed in the field and in the District of Columbia in the 'protection and administration of Forestry Reserves in or under the General Land Office of the Interior Department' be classified and the civil-service act and rules applied thereto, and that no person be hereafter appointed, employed, promoted, or transferred in said service until he passes an examination in conformity therewith, unless specifically exempted thereunder.

This order shall apply to all officers and employees, except persons employed merely as laborers, and persons whose appointments are confirmed by the Senate."

This order classifies the whole forest reserve Service, now transferred, and places it under the Civil Service Law.

In the administration of the forest reserves it must be clearly borne in mind that all land is to be devoted to its most productive use for the permanent good of the whole people, and not for the temporary benefit of individuals or companies. All the resources of forest reserves are for use, and this use must be brought about in a thoroughly prompt and business-like manner, under such restrictions only as will insure the permanence of these resources. The vital importance of forest reserves to the great industries of the Western States will be largely increased in the near future by the continued steady advance in settlement and development. The permanence of the resources of the reserves is therefore indispensable to continued prosperity, and the policy of this department for their protection and use will invariably be guided by this fact, always bearing in mind that the conservative use of these resources in no way conflicts with their permanent value. You will see to it that the water, wood, and forage of the reserves are conserved and wisely used for the benefit of the home builder first of all, upon whom depends the best permanent use of lands and resources alike. The continued prosperity of the agricultural, lumbering, mining, and livestock interests is directly dependent upon a permanent and accessible supply of water, wood, and forage, as well as upon the present and future use of their resources under businesslike regulations, enforced with promptness, effectiveness, and common sense. In the management of each reserve local questions will be decided upon local grounds; the dominant industry will be considered first, but with as little restriction to minor industries as may be possible; sudden changes in industrial conditions will be avoided by gradual adjustment after due notice; and where conflicting interests must be reconciled the question will always be decided from the standpoint of the greatest good of the greatest number in the long run.

These general principles will govern in the protection and use of the water supply, in the disposal of timber and wood, in the use of the range, and in all other matters connected with the management of the reserves. They can be successfully applied only when the administration of each reserve is left very largely in the hands of the local officers, under the eye of thoroughly trained and competent inspectors.

Very respectfully,

James Wilson
Secretary

The Proposed Eastern Forest Reserves

The national forests were a western phenomenon because that was where the federal government owned millions of acres. But forest reformers in the east were as convinced as their peers in the west that national forests could play a vital part in protecting watersheds and forest health. To develop such management, however, required the purchase of private property from willing sellers. In 1911, Congress passed the Weeks Act, which would provide the requisite funds to purchase forested headwaters across the region. Pinchot was among those promoting this possibility, as reflected in his talk to the Appalachian Mountain Club in 1906.

Originally delivered to the Appalachian Mountain Club on January 20, 1906, and published in *Appalachia* 11, no. 2 (May 1906): 134–43.

———————————

———————————

. . . A number of years ago it was first suggested that forests should be preserved in the Southern Appalachian Mountains. The attention of thoughtful men had been drawn to the fact that great injury was being done to the streams, great damage was accruing from floods, and great forest destruction was going on in the Southern Appalachians, and agitation began to interfere with the progress of destruction. Then far-sighted men at this end of the great chain took up the matter; and now coming from North and South these two movements have met, and the last stage of the two is the amalgamation of the two bills for the two Reserves in a single measure (so far as that could be done without Congressional action) by the American Forestry Association, acting for all who are interested in both of them, and what we are hoping to see is the passage of a single bill carrying to success the two measures which have been advocated by two entirely different sets of men.

It is a curious thing that these two bodies of mountains, so different geologically, so different in their forest conditions, yet may be treated with precisely the same argument for their preservation, almost throughout.

Before I say a few words as to just why I think this thing ought to be done, I want to show you a very few views illustrating on the ground just what the condition is with these forests. I am going to begin in each case near the tops of the mountains, follow them down, and indicate very briefly some of the reasons why they should be preserved.

First is a typical timberline forest in the White Mountains, showing the condition of that high forest before it was touched by fire. The second view shows a somewhat familiar forest on Sugar Loaf Mountain after being devastated by fire; and I call your attention particularly to the absolutely barren condition of the rock after the fire has run over it. The replacing of the forest under conditions such as this is a matter of tens and perhaps hundreds of years. The damage done is not absolutely irrevocable, but from the point of view of those of us who are here upon earth it comes very near to being so. Fire is the great scourge we have to fear in the White Mountains. When a fire runs through the forest, what is left by the lumbermen goes instantly, so far as we are concerned.

Another view illustrates a somewhat different state of affairs. Here a forest, not quite so high, has been cut over first, and then the few trees which were left, and which should have provided the second growth, have gone by way of fire, and now there is nothing on the ground but a tangle of dead wood, with a few hard woods coming through them—the whole a perfect fire-trap which, under the circumstances, is almost sure to be burned over again. For it is not only a single fire, in many cases, that does the damage: it is a continuous succession of fires. And if there is anything clearly proven, so far as forest fires is concerned, it is the difficulty in such a region of protecting forests against fire when the forest is subject to the vicissitudes of changing ownership.

As we descend the slopes of these high mountains, gradually we come to the lower benches where the forest is level and where the effect of lumbering is less severe.

There is a good deal of mountain land through New England—medium mountain land, so to speak—which, while it is not absolutely forest land, is yet capable of producing more effectively under forest than it is under any other crop. Much of that land will be held by the lumbermen themselves under the enlightened ideas which are coming to them so widely, and need not therefore be taken by the Government in order to be safe. Such timber as this produces rapidly, grows well, and is of value to the lumbermen. Many of these mountain forests in New Hampshire contain not only spruce, the most valuable tree, but also hardwood trees.

In the attack on the New Hampshire forests that has been going on for many years, much of the best of the forests has already been destroyed, great areas have been cut, and even now the most important of the mountain forests that remain are threatened. It is a critical question, whether those of the White Mountain region are to be treated as in these pictures, or whether they are to be taken under the protecting wing of the Government and handled as they ought to be.

I find it difficult to convey an impression to any audience, however intelligent, of the tremendous destruction that takes place through forest fires; and for that reason I have chosen for the pictures of the White Mountain region this evening mainly pictures showing destruction by fire. For, however serious the lumbering may be, the great question there is not the need of conservative lumbering instead of destructive lumbering, but first and foremost the protection against fire. The results are so bad, and the length of time during which they continue to inflict injury on the people who come after those who did the harm is so great, that no impression I can give you of the damage by fire is too strong.

These pictures show you soil of no value whatever except for the growth of trees and it has been rendered of almost no value whatever for that purpose since fire has completed the work of destructive lumbering. Much of the land once cleared, if it had been possible to protect it adequately, would have come back again to second growth; but much of the land which has been trying to come back to second growth has been treated like this white pine thicket, where young trees twenty feet high have been destroyed to make more pasture. I am distinctly for the utilizing of any piece of land for that purpose for which it will produce the most good; but there are many parts of the earth where that purpose cannot be achieved under private ownership.

Now I am going to ask you to pass for a moment with me to the Southern Appalachian region, where I will show you a few views of a different kind of destruction. In the North, fire; in the South, agricultural destruction for a while, and then erosion—these are the great forces that are doing the harm.

This is a timberline forest on Grandfather Mountain, and, with the succeeding pictures, shows lands of wonderful beauty and of very great value for purely economic reasons; for however much we may each of us value the sentimental view of the forest, nevertheless it is the business view that must control if we are to succeed in doing the thing we have set out to do. Throughout this region of the Southern Appalachians the small farmers have taken up here and there a little bit of land. For example, here a farmer has settled and cleared his land by deadening the trees. Very soon he forms a little clearing here, with the dead trees standing and a little growth coming in on a moderate slope. But I want to show you what happens when the slope is severe. The tributaries of streams which carry only a moderate amount of water, and that water always clear, after heavy rains are filled by debris coming from land such as this. And even measures to arrest erosion, such as the building of dams or brushwood fences, expensive as they are, with difficulty effect it. In other words, we get a double result from forest destruction in the Southern Appalachians: the destruction of the soil at the headwaters of the streams, and the deposition of that soil lower down, to the injury of the interests concerned.

Here is a farm in one of these rich mountain valleys; a large part of it has been washed away by the streams, and the soil replaced by stones and sand—a kind of damage which has amounted, within a comparatively short time, through that Southern Appalachian region to many millions of dollars. The official estimate of the total loss during a single twelve-month was $18,000,000, and during the year 1901 the total damage along the tributaries of streams was officially ascertained to be $10,000,000—not only the destruction of agricultural lands involving the destruction of homes, but, almost as important, the unsettling of all values along the bottom lands, the practical destruction of the values along the bottom lands, the practical destruction of the value of the farms, not only to their owners directly, but to their owners as security for loans and as valuable pieces of property for negotiation.

The reasons why these forests should be preserves, different as the conditions are in different parts of the Appalachian chain, north and south, practically meet. We have got first the fact that it is wise policy to have these lands preserved, and for many different reasons. For example, we are now using, incredible as it may seem, ten times as much timber, valued in dollars, as we were in 1850, while the population of the United States has only increased three times. In other words, the census of 1850 gave us $60,000,000 as the value of the produce of the forests, while the census of 1900 gives $566,000,000, and during the same period the population has only increased from 23,000,000 to 76,000,000.

The timber question is far more than a business question, in the sense that it is utterly impossible for us to repair the damage of forest destruction in any reasonable time. You may start a mine which has been stopped, and there is little damage; you may let a farm lie fallow and take up the cultivation of it again, and the farm is better than it was; you may begin once more fisheries that have been abandoned, when the fish have returned; but the destruction of the forest means the destruction of the growth, the productive capacity of the land, through a long series of years.

The shortest possible time in which the damage of a timber famine can be repaired is fifty years. And all the signs point to the fact that unless the people of the United States, especially the Government of the United States, wake up to the present condition, we shall have a famine in that material, which, even more than steel, stands at the bottom of the productive industry of this country. For you can operate no mines, you can operate no railroads, you can have no farms, you can conduct no fisheries, you can conduct few manufactures, in the absence of timber. In this age of steel, timber is, nevertheless, one of the great essentials of civilization, and from a timber point of view we must preserve our forests. Therefore, since forest destruction is going on in the Southern Appalachians and in the Northern Appalachians, the White Mountains, it is a wise policy for us to stop that destruction, and to let the lands that are better capable of producing timber than anything else produce that timber crop.

Now, secondly, it is wise policy from a business point of view. This that I have been speaking of is a larger question than any of business, but it is wise for the Government, from a business point of view, to take possession of these forests and handle them. For example, when this movement first started for a reserve in the Southern Appalachians, it was very conservatively estimated that we could get all the land that we wanted, including the timber, for $2.50 an acre. Now I happen to know of one large tract in the Southern Appalachians which was bought for $2.50 an acre at about the time that this movement began, and other owner of it, within the last year, has given an option on the timber alone, without the land, many tens of thousands of acres. That timber can be cut under the rules of conservative forestry, just as it would be by the Government, at $15 an acre; and much of the land has sold at higher prices. That is to say, through delay we have reached a point throughout the South where we can get only the land, without the best of the standing timber.

It is perfectly clear that as an investment it would pay the Government to create these reserves. This has been the first year of the organization of the Forest Service, and the national forest reserves have this first year met nearly half the total charge for Forest Service; and it is the confident expectation of those of us who are handling the matter that within from three to five years the Forest Service will be self-supporting, and a permanent source of revenue to the Government. And precisely the same method of handling will in the end give us the same sort of revenue from these forests. In other words, the purchase which is asked for is a purchase which in the very nature of things is bound to be a profitable one. Therefore, it is good statesmanship and it is good business to buy these forests. That is regarding it purely from a lumber point of view.

Now let us consider it for a moment from the point of view of water supply; and here is the nut of the question, North and South. It is estimated that there are 2,700,000 horse-power used for manufacturing in New England; and in the Southern States more than half a million horse-power (of which 180,000 are produced by water) are already in use, and not less than a million horse-power are capable of being developed. Now what happens, of course, in any region rich by nature, is that men coming in first of all use the natural resources, cut the forests, open the mines, over-crop the farms, skim the cream. Whatever the virtues of our race may be, and they are very many, it is a fact that wherever the white man, and especially the Anglo-Saxon, sets his foot, the first thing he does is to take the cream off the country, and after that he settles down definitely and quietly to develop it along more rational lines. Now we have taken the cream from our forests North and South, from our rich agricultural lands in the West, from our mines, from all the other natural resources that we have, as fast as possible.

But following the destruction of natural resources comes the era of manufacturers. Now that era is wonderfully well developed here in Massachusetts, and is just about at its most rapid growth in the South; and it would be nothing less than suicide, from the commercial and manufacturing point of view, for you here, and for those in the South, to allow the destruction of the forests from which comes the water that turns your wheels. Not only is it necessary for you to protect yourself against floods—one single flood at Holyoke some time ago cost $100,000—but it is fair for you and for the South to look forward to the maintenance and the increase of the means of wealth which you have at hand. It is a direct question of self-preservation in business for you, whether or not you are to allow the destruction of the sources from which so much of your wealth has sprung in the past, and from which, under proper conservation, still more will spring in the future.

Now, granted for the sake of argument that these forests ought to be saved, the reply very many times is: "Yes, that's true, but this is not a national question; the States in which these forests lie ought properly to take care of them, and we may fairly leave that matter to them." And it is cited that the State of New York has bought 700,000 acres, and so on—the plea being that in New Hampshire and North Carolina, Georgia and South Carolina we may ask the States also to make these provisions for the safety of the forests.

That argument in general is good, and it is good here, except for a single reason. There are two great regions east of the Mississippi River in which waters center, from which waters rise: the Southern Appalachians, which feed streams tributary to the Ohio, and to the Mississippi, streams which flow into the Gulf, and also streams which flow eastward to the Atlantic, through Georgia, South Carolina, North Carolina, and Virginia—a great three quarters of a circle of living streams flowing from this single region of mountains; and the second region is the White Mountain area in New Hampshire, out of which streams flow into all the other New England States, except Rhode Island.

The reason why the United States Government is asked to take care of this matter in the South and in the North is that the benefit to be derived from forest preservation in one State is to be felt in another. It is an inter-state question, and as such is not to be handled by any other state.

Then the objectors say: "Suppose we buy a region in the Southern Appalachians and in New Hampshire, where shall we stop? Every State will be asking us to do the same thing." That would be a good objection except for one thing, and that is, that we have already the headwaters of every single stream in the United States except these of which I am speaking, protected more or less—in theory, if not in practice. All the great streams of the West take their rise in national forest reserves; and the great policy of irrigation, perhaps the largest forward step that has been made in the national housekeeping for many years, depends absolutely on the protection Forest Service may be able to give these streams. The Mississippi River takes its rise in a national forest reserve; the Hudson, which begins and ends in the State of New York, rises in a State forest reserve. But all the protection in the West, all the protection in New York State, does not cover this question that I have been laying before you; therefore the objection of which I spoke does not apply. In other words, we have eliminated the regions which might ask for further protection, and we have left simply these two regions from the Potomac south along the Southern Appalachians and in the White Mountains of New Hampshire, in which the water is an inter-state question.

Now if I am right in thinking that this is an inter-state question, and if the objection that other States will come and ask for the same thing is not valid, then why is not the thing done? Why has it not been done already? The answer is a perfectly simple one: that the people who are interested in this matter have not made themselves heard. I have lived in Washington long enough to know that, whatever any other government on the earth may be, this Government of ours is a representative one, and that what the people ask for and mean to have they will get, be it right or wrong—for no man has lived in Washington long without seeing mistaken demands enforced on congressmen and senators, as well as demands that were right. It is simply a question of how much and how earnestly the people of the New England States desire the White Mountain reserve, and how much and how earnestly the people of the Southern States desire the Southern Appalachian reserve and nothing else will secure them. President McKinley has spoken in favor of the movement; President Roosevelt has given it his hearty and his most effective support; your best men here in Massachusetts have pronounced in favor of it over and over again; we in Washington have put in our little word here and there where the occasion demanded it or where the occasion made it possible, we have spoken sometimes in season and sometimes out of season, all to no effect. The matter is purely one which rests with you.

Now you have a body of men in Congress from New England who are simply irresistible when they go after something. The Southern members united on this subject would be equally so. These two bodies of men asking for an appropriation of three millions of dollars out of total budget of six or seven hundred millions would, of course, get it without the slightest difficulty; and they will get it whenever you ladies and gentlemen in this State, in New Hampshire, in Vermont, and Connecticut and Maine, make up your minds that you really want it. And until you impress upon your representatives in Washington the fact that you really want it, I think I am perfectly safe in giving you my word that it never will be done.

Finally, if I have given you the impression that this movement does not look hopeful, I should like to correct that impression. I have been engaged in this fight since it began, and I have never seen the day when the chance of success in both these directions was anything like as bright as it is tonight.

Speech to the Denver Public Lands Convention

As a key spokesman for the Roosevelt administration's conservation agenda, Pinchot routinely traveled across the west and spoke before often hostile audiences considerably less enamored of the national forests—and the regulations that governed their use—than was the nation's chief forester. Backed by a series of Supreme Court decisions that sustained the Forest Service's right to manage these federal lands (and which debunked claims that these were state lands) and by a resolute President Roosevelt who shared Pinchot's conviction that conservation, practically applied on the ground, would be good for the land and those who made their living from its resources, Pinchot tirelessly promoted the cause. This particular address, delivered in June 1907 at a public lands convention in Denver called to dispute the president's recent designation of millions of acres of new national forests, proved especially important to dispelling some of the anger that had led to the conference. As one newspaper opined in the aftermath of his speech, and the subsequently temperate resolutions that emerged from the conference, the once-angry delegates left Denver "roaring as mildly as a suckling dove."[1]

Published in the *Idaho Statesman*, June 21, 1907.

The national forest policy as we have it now began when the people of the United States themselves began to realize that the timber was being cut faster than it was being reproduced. The American citizen uses wood more freely and depends on it for his comfort and well-being more directly than the citizen of any other nation. Ours is a civilization of wood as much as it is of coal and steel. We are using every year three times as much wood from our forests as they are growing. A great timber famine is not only in sight but is approaching with bewildering speed.

After the first national forests (called forest reserves) were created under the act of March 3, 1891, it began to appear that a few rich men were getting control of vast areas of public timber lands, often by methods I need not stop to describe. These men saw that not only was there going to be a great shortage of timber but that when the shortage came it would be enormously profitable to control what timber there was [left]. Their reasoning was good, and they went vigorously to carry it into effect. But

---

1. Quoted in Elmo R. Richardson, *The Politics of Conservation: Crusades and Controversies, 1897–1913* (Berkeley: University of California Press, 1962), 39.

President Roosevelt was awake to the situation. He saw that it would be vastly better to have some of the timber in the government's hands for the benefit of all the people, rather than have it in the hands of a few great owners strictly for their own benefit. Action was needed. He acted, and created many million acres of national forest.

In view of this action taken by the president to prevent monopoly and consequent excessive price of lumber, it is curious to find some good men honestly convinced that the creation of the national forests is a bad thing, because, they say, it is raising the price of lumber for the consumer, and this is proved by the fact that prices have risen far more rapidly in the east, where there are no national forests, than in the west, where there are many.

Another powerful reason stands behind our forest policy. It is needed to protect the watershed of streams used for irrigation, for domestic water and manufacture supply, and for transportation. No well-informed man any longer doubts the beneficent effect of the forest on the streams. No friend of irrigation, which is to be the great fundamental industry of the west, doubts the wisdom of protecting the forests, or of protecting the vegetation on the summer ranges within the forests which are almost as important in their effect on water flow as the forests themselves. If there were no other reason—and there are many—the protection of irrigation throughout the west would amply justify the president's forest policy. . . .

It is often asserted that the government is trying to make money out of the national forests. This is a profound mistake. The forest service is not in business in the ordinary sense of the word. What it is trying to do, and trying hard, is to make the national forests pay expenses by handling them in a businesslike way. As soon as possible, we hope to make the national forests self-supporting, so that they will meet the costs of ordinary administration, but also of trail and road making, bridge building, planting on important watersheds, and all other improvements to make the forests as useful to the people as possible.

The returns from the sale of timber, in the end, will be very large. We can and do give away large amounts of timber to the small man who is making his home, but there is only one safe and clean way to dispose of timber to men who use considerable quantities of it in their business, and that is by auction to the highest bidder; then there can be no question of favoritism or graft.

The case of the range in the national forests is wholly different. The charge for range amounts to but a small fraction of its market value. The range, however, is not a transportable commodity like timber.

It must be used by people who live reasonably nearby, and has been used by them. There is no insuperable difficulty in finding out who has the best right to use it without putting it up to auction. It is not the policy of the forest service to charge the full market value for range rights, unless the users of the range themselves should make that necessary. The intention is to charge merely the cost of range protection and improvement to the users of the range in the form of grazing fees.

The effect of range protection is already strikingly evident. In many localities it has been possible to increase the number of stock carried because of marked improvement of the range under more reasonable use. Very much of the range on the national forests was badly over-grazed. It is recovering on the whole, with most gratifying rapidity.

The protection of the forest and the protection of the range by wise use are two divisions of a problem vastly larger and more important than either. This is the problem of the conservation of all our national resources. This is the basic problem, and it is a very practical one and definite one. If we conserve our natural resources, we shall prosper. If we destroy them, no amount of success in any other direction will keep us prosperous. It is the question of both the present and the future.

The ABC of Conservation

Pinchot was an avid contributor to journals, magazines, and newspapers. He understood the power of the press to educate and persuade the public about the pressing need for conservation of America's natural resources. This article is an example of his conviction that the Forest Service's mission, and conservation in general, could not succeed without significant support from the American people.

Originally published in *The Outlook*, December 4, 1909, 770–72.[1]

———————

———————

1. What does Conservation stand for?
The central thing for which Conservation stands is to make this country the best possible place to live in, both for us and for our descendants. It stands against the waste of the natural resources which cannot be renewed, such as coal and iron; it stands for the perpetuation of the resources which can be renewed, like the food-producing soils and the forests; and, most of all, it stands for equal opportunity for every American citizen to get his fair share of benefit from these resources, both now and hereafter.

Conservation stands for the same kind of practical common-sense management of this country by the people that every business man stands for in the handling of his own business. It believes in prudence and foresight instead of reckless blindness; it holds that resources now public property should not become the basis for oppressive private monopoly; and it demands the complete and orderly development of all our resources for the benefit of all the people, instead of the partial exploitation of them for the benefit of a few. It recognizes fully the right of the present generation to use what it needs and all it needs of the natural resources now available, but it recognizes equally our obligation so to use what we need that our descendants shall not be deprived of what they need.

2. What has Conservation to do with the welfare of the average man to-day?
Conservation has much to do with the welfare of the average man to-day. It proposes to secure a continuous and abundant supply of the necessaries of life, which means a reasonable cost of living and business stability. It

———

1. The journal editors' note reads, in part, "The immediate interest attaching to the fundamental problems of conservation has led The Outlook to ask Mr. Pinchot, the highest American authority on such questions, to send to it for its readers such positive and clear answers as would give the average uninformed citizen the reasons for this public interest."

advocates fairness in the distribution of the benefits which flow from the natural resources. It will matter very little to the average citizen when scarcity comes and prices rise, whether he cannot get what he needs because there is none left or because he cannot afford to pay for it. In both cases the essential fact is that he cannot get what he needs. Conservation holds that it is about as important to see that the people in general get the benefit of our natural resources as to see that there shall be natural resources left.

Conservation is the most democratic movement this country has known for a generation. It holds that the people have not only the right but the duty to control the use of the natural resources, which are the great sources of prosperity. And it regards the absorption of these resources by the special interests, unless their operations are under effective public control, as a moral wrong. Conservation is the application of common sense to the common problems for the common good, and I believe it stands nearer to the desires, aspirations, and purposes of the average man than any other policy now before the American people.

3. What is the danger to the Conservation policies in the coming session of Congress?

The danger to the Conservation policies in the coming session of Congress is that the privileges of the few may continue to obstruct the rights of the many, especially in the matter of water power and coal. Congress must decide at this session whether the great coal-fields still in public ownership shall remain so, in order that their use may be controlled with due regard to the interest of the consumer, or whether they shall pass into private ownership and be controlled in the monopolistic interest of a few.

Congress must decide also whether immensely valuable rights to the use of water power shall be given away to special interests in perpetuity and without compensation, instead of being held and controlled by the public. In most cases, actual development of water power can best be done by private interests acting under public control, but it is neither good sense nor good morals to let these valuable privileges pass from the public ownership for nothing and forever. Other Conservation matters will doubtless require action; but these two, the Conservation of water power and of coal, the chief sources of power of the present and the future, are clearly the most pressing.

4. Why is it important to protect the water powers?

It is of the first importance to prevent our water powers from passing into private ownership as they have been doing, because the greatest source of power we know is falling water. Furthermore, it is the only great unfailing source of power. Our coal, the experts say, is likely to be exhausted during the next century, our natural oil in this. Our rivers, if the forests on the watersheds are properly handled, will never cease to deliver power. Under our form of civilization, if a few men ever succeed in controlling the sources of power, they will eventually control all industry as well. If they succeed in controlling all industry, they will necessarily control the country. This country has achieved political freedom; what our people are fighting for now is industrial freedom. And unless we win our industrial liberty we cannot keep our political liberty. I see no reason why we should deliberately keep on helping to fasten the handcuffs of corporate control upon ourselves for all time merely because the few men who would profit by it most have heretofore had the power to compel it.

5. How must it be done?
The essential things that must be done to protect the water powers for the people are few and simple. First, the granting of water powers forever, either on non-navigable or navigable streams, must absolutely stop. It is perfectly clear that one hundred, fifty, or even twenty-five years ago our present industrial conditions and industrial needs were completely beyond the imagination of the wisest of our predecessors. It is just as true that we cannot imagine or foresee the industrial conditions and needs of the future. But we do know that our descendants should be left free to meet their own necessities as they arise. It cannot be right, therefore, for us to grant perpetual rights to the one great permanent source of power. It is just as wrong as it is foolish, and just as needless as it is wrong, to mortgage the welfare of our children in such a way as this. Water powers must and should be developed mainly by private capital, and they must be developed under conditions which make investment in them profitable and safe. But neither profit nor safety requires perpetual rights, as many of the best water power men now freely acknowledge.

Second, the men to whom the people grant the right to use water power should pay for what they get. The water power sites now in the public hands are enormously valuable. There is no reason whatever why special interests should be allowed to use them for profit without making some direct payment to the people for the valuable tights derived from the people. This is important not only for the revenue the Nation will get. It is at least equally important as a recognition that the public control their own property and have a tight to share in the benefits arising from its development.

There are other ways in which public control of water power must be exercised, but these two are the most important.

6. Does the same principle apply to navigable streams as to non-navigable? Water power on non-navigable streams usually results from dropping a little water a long way. In the mountains water is dropped many hundreds of feet upon the turbines which move the dynamos that produce the electric current. Water power on navigable streams is usually produced by dropping immense volumes of water a short distance, as twenty feet, fifteen feel, or even less. Every stream is a unit from its source to its mouth, and the people have the same stake in the control of water power in one part of it as in another. Under the Constitution the United States exercises direct control over navigable streams. It exercises control over non-navigable and source streams only through its ownership of the lands through which they pass, as in the public domain and National forests. It is just as essential for the public welfare that the people should retain and exercise control of water power monopoly on navigable as on non-navigable streams. If the difficulties are greater, then the danger that the water powers may pass out of the people's hands on the lower navigable parts of the streams is greater than on the upper non-navigable parts, and it may be harder, but in no way less necessary, to prevent it.

These answers to your questions will, I hope, give you the information for which you wrote. It must be clear to any man who has followed the development of the Conservation idea that no other policy now before the American people is so thoroughly democratic in its essence and in its tendencies as the Conservation policy. It asserts that the people have the right and the duty, and that it is their duty no less than their right, to protect themselves against the uncontrolled monopoly of the natural resources which yield the necessaries of life. We are beginning to realize that the Conservation question is a question of right and wrong, as any question must be which may involve the difference between prosperity and poverty, health and sickness, ignorance and education, well-being and misery, to hundreds of thousands of families. Seen from the point of view of human welfare and human progress, questions which begin as purely economic often end as moral issues. Conservation is a moral issue because it involves the rights and the duties of our people—their rights to prosperity and happiness, and their duties to themselves, to their descendants, and to the whole future progress and welfare of this Nation.

Mr. Pinchot on Forest Fires

Although he was no longer the Chief of the Forest Service when the Great Fires of 1910 erupted, Pinchot understood intuitively the threat these conflagrations posed to the Forest Service. Their destructive force consumed lives and land-scapes as well as challenging the agency's can-do reputation. He immediately released a public statement in full support of his former employees and doubled down by arguing that it was possible to prevent forest fires, even blazes of such magnitude as these that swept across three million acres in two days and killed 87 people. His successors concurred and their proactive policy of fire suppression would dominate the Forest Service's actions for the next fifty years.

Originally circulated as a press release, August 1910, and later published in *Forest and Stream*, September 3, 1910.[1]

———————————

———————————

I am proud of the splendid work the men of the Forest Service have been doing against the Western forest fires. Many of them have given their lives to protect the homes of settlers and the forests on which the prosperity of the Western people depends. To my mind their conduct is beyond all praise.

Forest fires are preventable. It is a good thing for us to remember at this time that nearly or quite all of the loss, suffering and death these fires have caused is wholly unnecessary. A fire in the forest is the same kind of thing as a fire in the city. There is only one way to fight either. The fire department of every city is organized with the prime idea of getting to the fire when it is young. So with forest fires. The time to conquer them is before they grow strong. If a forest is equipped with roads, trails, tele-phone lines and a reasonable number of men for patrol, there is no more likelihood that great fires will be able to get started than there is that great conflagrations like the Chicago fire will get started in a city with a modern fire department. Under rare circumstances they may, but the chances are against it.

The Forest Service has done wonders with its handful of devoted men. It has put out every year many thousands of small fires, any one of which

1. Journal editor's note: "In an interview at Washington Aug 26, Gifford Pinchot, former United States Forester, issues a statement which takes the same ground recently expressed by *Forest and Stream* as to where the responsibility rests in part for the great loss of life and property in the recent forest fires of the West."

under favorable conditions might have developed into a conflagration which 10,000 men could not stop. This year, because of the great drouth, the worst in much of the West for more than twenty years, there were too many fires and too few rangers.

The lesson from these forest fires is perfectly clear. When a city suffers from a great fire it does not retrench in its fire department, but strengthens it. This is what the nation must do on the National Forests. If even a small fraction of the loss from the present fires had been expended in additional patrol and preventative equipment, some or perhaps nearly all of the loss could have been avoided. I believe our people will take this lesson to heart and insist that the settlers and their wives and children, the lumbermen and the miners and the $2,000,000,000 worth of National property in the National Forests shall be adequately protected.

Roosevelt's Part in Forestry

Close friends and devoted conservationists, Gifford Pinchot and Theodore Roosevelt forged a tight bond as a result of their shared work in and out of government. They hunted and hiked together; Pinchot was a key member of TR's "Tennis Cabinet" and an essential speechwriter and adviser during Roosevelt's 1912 Bull Moose campaign; Roosevelt was among the small party at Pinchot's wedding. The forester was rocked by news of Roosevelt's death in January 1919, and he quickly composed this compelling eulogy for his friend and mentor.

Originally published in *Journal of Forestry* 17, no. 2 (February 1919): 122–24.

———————————
———————————

Instead of a formal article from me describing in a balanced way President Roosevelt's service to forestry, will you accept this discursive letter, which neither surrounds the subject nor lays measured stress upon its different parts, but just talks about the man and the leader whom we all loved. Just at the moment I am deep in an effort to defend the Roosevelt policies as to coal, oil, and phosphate, and that comes first.

Some men belong to all people and all time. I suppose it is true that Theodore Roosevelt was loved and trusted by more men and women in more lands during his lifetime than any other man who ever lived. Certainly more men and women followed him in spirit to the grave than ever did the like before for any other man in human history.

Very much of the work that Roosevelt started is yet unfinished. As his great soul goes marching on, we know that at the very heart of the goal to which it marches is that greatest of Roosevelt policies—the planned and orderly development and conservation of the natural resources of America—by no means forgetting the forest, which in a true sense is the mother of all the rest.

No matter how or where you touched him, you could not long delay in finding that Roosevelt was an outdoor man. Gifted in the highest degree with the forester's master qualities of hardiness, judgment, self control, and the power of observation, Roosevelt brought with him to the White House so deep a sympathy with the foresters' viewpoint that it gave color and direction to all he did touching the great central problem of conservation.

There was no forester but would have liked to have him on the hardest of his trips. There was no time when his mind was not alert for the protection and advancement of the forests. His sympathy with foresters as such was well shown when he broke all Presidential precedents to attend, at a private house, a meeting of the Society of American Foresters, to address its members and to meet them all personally. Roosevelt's sympathy with forests and his genius for administration made him from the first an active and powerful supporter of the proposal to transfer the National Forests from the General Land Office to the old Bureau of Forestry, and thus to unite the forest work of the Government under a single head. For more than three years, as I remember it, his recommendations for the transfer were made to Congress, while the personal pressure which he exerted was by far the strongest factor in our final success. Without him it would have been wholly impracticable to bring the transfer about. It was Roosevelt who made the Forest Service possible.

It tells but little of the story to say that Roosevelt saved for us more National Forests than all other Presidents put together. He not only created but defended and preserved them, and when Congress finally took from him the power to add to their number, at the last moment he saved to the people of the United States some 16,000,000 acres more of mountain forest lands. He did it by using the method which has meant so much to forestry and conservation in America, by out-thinking the opposition.

It was William T. Cox, now State Forester of Minnesota, who came to me with the suggestion that Roosevelt should save this forest land before the objectionable provision had passed both houses. When I took Cox's suggestion to him, the President approved it with enthusiasm; the Forest Service was ready; the necessary field studies had been made; the maps had been drawn; we knew what we wanted and we knew how to get it. It remained only to prepare the official proclamation for each addition to the existing National Forests.

For 48 hours the drafting force of the Forest Service worked night and day. As fast as they prepared the proclamations they were taken to the White House. As fast as he received them the President signed them, and sent them at once to the State Department for safekeeping. Thus Roosevelt saved from destruction and set aside for all the people an area more than half as large as the State of Pennsylvania, and did it in the short interval while the bill was passing and before it passed.

No other President has ever been, and doubtless no other ever will be, as practically familiar both with the forest and the range as was President Roosevelt. It was in the early part of his administration that the forest and grazing problem in the Southwest became the livest question before the Bureau of Forestry. To the huge gain of the nation as a whole, Roosevelt was thoroughly equipped to handle it. At the recommendation of the Secretary of the Interior, as I recall it, President Roosevelt made, soon after he came to the White House, a decision as to grazing on National Forests in Arizona which I thought to be unwise. Representatives of the grazing interests of that territory, including, I believe, the present Associate Forester of the United States Forest Service, came to me and set forth their objections to the President's decision. I agreed with them, and I suggested that, although the President's action had been made public, we might nevertheless put the case before him. We did so, very briefly. With his usual lightning grasp of a situation, Roosevelt saw that he had followed the wrong trail, and without the slightest care that he would be reversing himself in public, he set the matter right. I knew then that he was a great man.

It was the endless good fortune of forestry in America that while it was still young it should have had in the White House so firm, sympathetic, and understanding a friend. How much it owes to him it will never be possible accurately to determine; for the debt of forestry to Roosevelt is not to be counted only in the great things he did for it, but also in the thousands of small advances and advantages which came to American forestry because it was known to be dear to the heart of the first citizen, the greatest driving force, and the most powerful influence in America.

Forestry is firmly established among us today because Roosevelt stood behind it like a stone wall when there was little to it except hope and good intentions.

National or State Control of Forest Devastation

As the founding president of the Society of American Foresters (SAF), Pinchot was deeply involved in the association's affairs from its launch in 1910 until his death thirty-six years later. He was among a group of foresters who pressed for an ever-larger federal role in the management of all forested acres in the United States—not an easy sell in a society that believed private property was the foundation of democracy. Convinced that only Washington could compel the lumber companies to better manage their lands, this article in SAF's lead publication, the *Journal of Forestry*, was one of several that Pinchot would contribute that laid out his conviction that all natural resources, regardless of ownership, were public assets, and that they would be most effectively and productively managed at the national, not state, level. His arguments—at once political and historical in nature—powerfully counter twenty-first-century demands on the part of some western states, and their congressional representatives, that national forests, parks, and grasslands should be under local control.

Originally published in *Journal of Forestry* 18, no. 2 (February 1920): 106–9.

The plan suggested of by the advocates of State control and that of the Committee for the Application of Forestry both hold that the owners of commercial forest lands should be required by law to prevent the devastation of their properties. The spirit and purpose of both are the same. Both agree as to the facts, the fundamental principles, and the remedies. Each provides for both State and National action. The plans differ only in this—that the one looks to the separate States for the chief executive control, and the other to the Nation.

This is a difference in method only. If I believed that forest devastation could be promptly, permanently, uniformly, and efficiently prevented through State control, I should be perfectly willing to accept it. The means are unimportant. The result is everything.

Conflicts in Jurisdiction.

Objection is made that National control involves a division of authority leading to conflicts of jurisdiction. I have observed that such anticipated conflicts seldom materialize. Under the smoothly working Reclamation Act, for example, the Nation builds works for the distribution of water controlled or owned by the State (a vastly more complicated problem), and both the States and Nation are actively concerned with regulated grazing. But if the avoidance of chances of conflict is so important, let us remember that the plan for State control, with standardization, supervision, and inspection by the National Government, is far more likely to breed friction than the simple and workable division between silviculture and slash disposal on one side, and fire patrol and fire-fighting on the other.

American and Safe.

It is suggested that National control of this National question is un-American. The same objection was made against National control of transportation, corporations, irrigation, migratory bird life, and many other matters now seen to be rightly assigned to the National Government. I cannot recall a case in which any matter so assigned has been sent back to the separate States, while it is easy to name many cases in which affairs once in State control have been transferred to the Federal Government, from which no one now suggests they should be removed.

If it be urged that the defeat of a single Federal appropriation might endanger the whole plan, I reply that the danger and the argument apply equally to the National Forests. Said Pudd'nhead Wilson, "Put all your eggs in one basket and watch that basket." By that method the National Forests have been preserved hitherto and today are safer than ever.

Participation by the States.

The Committee's plan does not exclude the States, but proposes that they shall share with the National Government in preventing forest devastation. No plan could succeed which overlooked the vital necessity of creating and maintaining genuine local interest in the care of local forests. The States, and later on municipalities also, must of necessity have an important share in preventing forest devastation, and State forest forces must necessarily form essential parts of the nation-wide organization.

Subsidies Ineffectual.

Under the State control plan each State must enact and maintain certain standards of law and administration in order to receive financial assistance from the National Government. Is it likely that the great lumber States would do so? It has been my experience that a Legislature can seldom be induced by considerations from outside to take action against the opposition of interests dominant in the State. The States where the lumbermen are strongest are, moreover, just those where forest devastation must be stopped. It would only be necessary for the lumber interests, when the time was ripe, to prevent the passage of bills in the three or four great lumber States in order effectually to cripple the whole plan of State control.

Theoretically, if the National Government were contributing to a State, and should discover that the conditions were being broken, it could withdraw its aid. Practically, if the attempt were carried beyond a mere threat, it would throw the whole question into politics, and would succeed, if at all, only against all the political pressure the State could apply. If it failed, the State's control would probably collapse, with the net result of time and money thrown away.

Pressure on the States.

Just as the waterpower monopolists and grazing interests formerly clamored for State control, well knowing they could themselves control the States, so now the lumbermen will be found almost without exception against Federal and for State control, and for the same reason.

In their fight to ward off governmental control the lumber interests will be joined by other interests engaged in exploiting the country's natural resources whose influence is nation-wide. States are seldom able to resist such pressure. *Under the plan for State control the public must attack the lumber interests in the lumbering States, where they are strongest; and without help from the deforested and treeless States, where the sentiment for conservation is most alive. The lumber interests would be fighting in their strongest trenches, the public from its weakest ground.*

It is obviously improbable that the several States will enact simultaneous and parallel legislation in the face of the fact that the lumbermen of any State that refuses to pass such legislation will have a material advantage in competition against lumbermen in the States that do.

National Control Saved the National Forests.

During the years when the National Forests were being created and the Forest Service established, what saved them both was that both were free from State control. The opposition controlled practically all of the legislatures of the Western States, so they passed resolution after resolution denouncing the forests and the Service. Time and again the Forests and the Forest Service were saved in Congress by the support of the Central and Eastern States. We have National Forests and the Forest Service today only because they were supported by forces which the State control plan now proposes to eliminate from the critical points in the fight.

Weakness of State Control.

Many of our State forest departments and commissions have done good work. A few States have excellent laws, but in how many are the laws efficiently applied? How many States have started out with a definite policy and held to it? In how many has the forest work escaped serious injury from changes in politics and administration? In more than one State the forest departments are sterilized; in some, to my personal knowledge, positively bad. Success in keeping forest lands productive calls for unity and stability in policy and management. To scatter the control among the States would be to subdivide and distribute it among numerous comparatively weak and frequently changing hands. A variety of State jurisdictions over what is distinctly one problem, nation-wide in scope and in effect, in my judgment cannot but fail. Moreover, there is no argument for State control which does not advocate with equal force the transfer of the National Forests to the States, with similar standards, supervision, and inspection by the Nation.

The Nation Only Can Succeed.

Once more, the kind of executive machinery we use to keep trees growing on forest lands is simply a question of how best to get the desired results. I am clear that only the National Government can do what the situation demands. To try State control first would, I think, be merely to lose time. The problem is National, and the Nation alone is strong and steady enough to handle it.

A Letter to Foresters

As the Great Depression bore down, and lumber companies began to fail, Pinchot and his like-minded peers agitated for greater federal control over the nation's forests to prevent their destruction. The signers of this letter in the *Journal of Forestry* were all closely associated with Pinchot and constituted the progressive wing of the forestry profession. In addition to Pinchot himself, other signatories included George P. Ahern, Robert Marshall, E. N. Munns, Ward Shepard, W. N. Sparhawk, and Raphael Zon. Their missive sparked a several-months-long debate in the journal about whether foresters should be engaged in politics, an engagement that Pinchot believed was essential to foresters' public responsibilities. Not all his peers agreed.

Originally published in *Journal of Forestry* 28, no. 4 (April 1930): 456–58.[1]

—————————
—————————

The destruction of the forests of America has been a long-drawn out tragedy of waste. Now we face the danger of a moral tragedy also: that the foresters of America will accept that destruction and by silence condone it.

Forest devastation is the heart of the forest problem. Yet on this vital issue we are drifting. Some of us are lured by the illusion that forest owners will voluntarily end forest devastation in spite of the overwhelming evidence, after half a century of public protest, that the progress in this direction is almost negligible. Some of us are lulled to inaction by a lack of faith in the possibility of remedying the evil. And now, to justify failure to meet the real issue, comes the excuse that after all timber is not going to be much needed. If the grapes cannot be reached, it is consoling to think they are sour.

It is not too late to adopt a policy of mastery instead of drift. But the first step is to recognize that the fate of our forests depends in large measure on the mental attitude of foresters, here and now, toward the problem of forest destruction. The profession must squarely face the problem of forest devastation. In every field of human activity, failure to meet responsibility is implacably punished by spiritual decay. Failure to grapple with the problem of forest destruction threatens the usefulness of our profession.

---

1. Journal editor's note: "This letter was originally circulated with the notation 'not for publication.' It is now printed, together with several replies, at the request of many members of the Society of American Foresters and with the permission of all of the signers."

We must cleanse our minds of apathy and doubt; and through a rebirth of faith in forestry and a reawakening of all our moral and mental energies, we must set the forestry movement on the path to its goal.

The profession of forestry in America was born with high ideals and great purposes. It has fought many a bitter fight against heavy odds. It has won magnificent victories. From the very first its guiding spirit has been that of public service. The profession can be proud of its history.

Today foresters are confronted with as great a challenge as any they have met in the past. Will they meet this new challenge in the old spirit? There was never a more compelling call for constructive leadership in forestry than now. The forests of America were never more in peril than at this moment. We are headed toward forest bankruptcy. What forestry there is on private lands is too little to exert the slightest effect on the vast problem of our future forests.

Today, after fifty years of exhortation and protest, the bulk of our forests are still being slashed and ruined, the second growth even more disastrously than the old growth. They are being stripped of their timber with no provision for regrowth. This is forest devastation. Our public forests excepted, forest destruction holds unchecked sway.

The duty of the foresters of America, with faith in the forest and in the nation, is clear before them. It is to destroy forest destruction in the United States.

For the safety and prosperity of our country, forest devastation must be stopped.

There exists today no program for dealing on a large scale directly with forest devastation. Except for the creation of public forests, the main attack on forest destruction has hitherto been indirect. It consists chiefly in encouraging private forestry by forest fire protection, research, and tax reform.

We recognize the splendid work done in these fields. But we also recognize the obvious truth that these efforts are not enough. The forestry movement must now be reinforced by an organized nation-wide program on the part of public agencies and of forest owners and industries to abolish destructive logging.

The cure of deforestation must be sought along two main lines; public measures to prevent forest devastation and a greatly increased program of public forests.

With such a background of control to assure forest renewal, the whole forestry movement would acquire a new vitality and energy. Today with the general prevalence of destructive logging many of our forestry activities are kept from full fruition. To what end a vast and expensive system of fire control if the forests it protects are to be destroyed by the axe? To what end a great program of forest research if the forests to which it should minister are to be destroyed? The future of our forests, of our forest industries, of organized forestry agencies, of education in forestry, and of the profession itself is all dependent on stopping forest destruction.

World-wide experience shows that in the absence of public control few private forests escape destruction. Most of the older countries have public control of private forests, from the well-nigh complete control of Sweden, Japan, and Switzerland, to the partial control of France and Germany. In most countries, public control of forests needed for protecting mountain and river systems is taken for granted.

When private property is so used as to lead to public injury, public regulation must be invoked. In the United States, public regulation is exercised over many forms of property, such as railroads and other public utilities, urban buildings, and interstate commerce. When the very existence of a great resource like our forests is at stake, and the results of present abuse may be felt for centuries, it is even more necessary to declare the public interest supreme.

The forest problem is a national problem. It cannot be solved without federal regulation. There is a wide and unquestioned field for state regulation, but it is idle to rely on independent action by forty or more states in time to save our forests. A great nation can and must invoke the powers necessary to save itself from the disaster of forest destruction. The Supreme Court of the United States in the recent Migratory Bird case has said: "It is not lightly to be assumed that in matters requiring national action, a power which must belong to and somewhere reside in every civilized government is not to be found."

The silvicultural basis for control has already been laid by the Forest Service in the nation-wide "Timber Growing and Logging Practice" study. The original purpose of that study was to define the simplest measures necessary to prevent forest devastation. The next step in forestry is to put these measures into effect in every forest region of the United States.

The forests needed for the protection of our mountain and river systems are in need of special attention. Ultimately they should be largely in public ownership, but meanwhile their devastation must be prevented by public control.

Public regulation to prevent devastation is the most urgent need in forestry. Nevertheless public regulation would not in itself be a complete or in the long run a wholly satisfactory remedy for devastation. We need a great expansion of public forests. Among the many reasons for such a program we must give special attention to the pressing tendencies in forest land ownership. Private cut-over lands are being abandoned on an immense scale. They are coming back on the public whether it wants them or not. The breakdown of private ownership is creating a new public domain. If these lands are to be saved from complete devastation and from becoming an increasing burden on the community, they must be definitely organized and handled as public forests.

There must be not only more national forests, but especially more state, county, and town forests. The problem of forest acquisition is altogether too big for any one public agency. There is room to spare for all, without conflict or overlap. But to prevent conflict and to stimulate public ownership of every character the federal government and the states should work out a joint program nation-wide in scope and amply financed.

It goes without saying that all other current forestry work should be properly developed. Public support of forestry should be proportionate to the greatness of our forest resources and the vastness of the problem of their preservation.

This statement is not a forest program. It is a discussion of a few principles which, in our opinion, are basic to the real advancement of forestry. In brief, we believe that:

Forests are now and always will be indispensable to civilization.

Forest devastation goes on unchecked. Forest devastation cannot and will not be stopped by voluntary effort of forest owners and industries.

The only way to stop forest devastation is by public control.

Both federal and state governments have ample power for such control.

Forest devastation must be stopped.

It is the duty of the foresters of America to stop it.

Old Evils in New Clothes

Never one to shy away from a fight, in the 1930s Pinchot battled with Interior Secretary Harold Ickes. The source of their brawl was Ickes's decade-long attempt to move the Forest Service from Agriculture to Interior as part of a super-agency devoted to conservation. President Franklin Roosevelt had folded this concept into his wider effort to reorganize the executive branch. The White House muzzled the Forest Service, so Pinchot stepped in to challenge the administration's efforts; the essay below is one of many he crafted to rebut Ickes. That the Forest Service remains in Agriculture is a signal of which man prevailed.

Presented at the meeting of the Allegheny Section, Society of American Foresters, Harrisburg, February 26, 1937, and later published in *Journal of Forestry* 35, no. 5 (May 1937): 435–38.[1]

—————————
—————————

In this world of ours old evils are constantly turning up in new clothes. That exactly describes the proposal of Secretary [Harold] Ickes to return control of the National Forests to the Interior Department (to be renamed the Conservation Department) from which they were taken some thirty years ago.

Before that time the Forest Reserves were horribly mishandled by the Interior Department. How horribly will appear when I tell you that at one time not a single man in Washington engaged in handling these vitally important forest lands had ever set foot on one of them.

On the other hand, what foresters there were in the government service were in the Department of Agriculture. The forest work of the United States was hamstrung because it was split up.

Research—the study of our forest resources and what to do with them—was entirely separated from their administration, with the result that both of them fell far below the public need.

Then, in 1905, research and administration—knowledge and its application—were brought together in the Forest Service of the Department of Agriculture. The result was the handling of the work in a way for which no one need ever apologize.

1. Journal editor's note: "Every forester in America, despite his personal beliefs or political faith, will find the following paper by Governor Pinchot of intense interest."

Why in the Department of Agriculture? Because the forest is a crop. That is the very essence of forestry. It is a crop grown from the soil. Forestry is a part of agriculture. It belongs by its very nature in that Department which deals with production from soil.

The Department of the Interior does not have charge of production from the soil. The Department of Agriculture does have. Then why should forestry be separated from the production of all other crops that grow from the soil? That question answers itself.

In spite of all that, now comes the proposal of Secretary Ickes to return to that same indefensible situation of thirty years ago dressed up in a new name. Under the smokescreen of establishing a Department of Conservation, Mr. Ickes proposes to split up and hamstring the forest work of the government all over again. He proposes once more to take the publicly owned National Forests out of the Department of Agriculture, where they have been admirably handled for a generation, and return them to the re-named Interior Department, whose treatment of them was a national scandal.

The Interior Department has regularly mishandled every public natural resource of which it has had charge, with the possible exception of the National Parks, the forest in which is not treated as a crop. And I do not except grazing on the public lands, of which it has recently taken control.

Here again is the old proposition of Secretary Fall, and it is no more worthy of respect now than it was when that distinguished enemy of the whole conservation policy was pushing it.

Under Secretary Ickes' plan, which proposes to return the forest work of the government to the bad old days of dual control, much of the old jealousy, division, and inefficiency would inevitably return. It would leave forestry on private lands in the Department of Agriculture and put forestry on public lands in the Department of Interior—Conservation.

Thus forestry on one side of a fence would be handled by one Department, and on the other side of the same fence by another Department.

Right now there are more than thirty million acres of private lands inside the boundaries of National Forests. So far as forestry is concerned, the Ickes proposal would simply bring back the old confusion in a futile effort to remove confusion which does not exist. Confusion there is, and plenty of it, but not in forestry.

In a speech delivered in New York in February, the Secretary of the Interior spoke of "the administrative branch of the government as it now exists, with its overlappings, its inconsistencies, its inefficiencies, and its sheer wastefulness in time and effort, as well as in money." So far I agree with him completely.

Then, after claiming that the Department of the Interior "now administers the majority of our natural resources" (a statement which can only be described as ridiculous), he asserts that "there should also be an orderly and logical arrangement of conservation activities"—obviously under the new Department of Conservation which he advocates. Then in another part of the same speech he shows us what is in his mind—what, according to him, an "orderly and logical arrangement" should be. I quote:

> "We must realize the close relationship between the problem of the farmer on the banks of the Ohio or the Mississippi Rivers whose land is periodically flooded, with the result that his rich top soil is rapidly being carried down into the Gulf of Mexico; the problem of the stockman of the West whose diminished flocks are hard put to it year after year to support themselves on a wasted range that only a comparatively few years ago produced ample forage; the problem of the husbandman in the 'dust bowl' whose top soil is spared the fate of being washed away by raging floods only to be blown away by the mighty winds that prevail in that area; the problem of the lumberman whose transcontinental pursuit of our vanishing timber resources has already brought him stark against the shore line of the Pacific Ocean; the problem of the owner of rich soil that can support him and his family in generous comfort if only he can get water from irrigation dams for it; the problem of the farmer whose land is not exposed either to abnormal flood or abnormal drought conditions but who watches his water table vanishing under him; the problem of the outdoor man who finds the wilderness areas in which he loves to tramp and camp becoming more restricted year by year; and the problem of those who delight to go forth with rod or gun to track down the elusive game or to lure the wary trout with cunningly contrived bait."

Mr. Ickes, unquestionably without intending to do so, has given us a perfect picture of what he would like to do. The 'one common problem' which he sees in conservation includes the problem of the farmer; the problem of the stockman; the problem of the husbandman in the dust bowl; the problem of the lumberman; the problem of the owner of rich soil; the problem of the farmer who watches his water table vanish under him; the problem of the outdoor man; the problem of those who delight to go forth with rod or gun.

I quote again: "The particular problems I have enumerated, and others like them, are only variations of one common problem."

Either Mr. Ickes doesn't mean that "there should be an orderly and logical arrangement of conservation activities," and that "the particular problems that I have enumerated and others like them are only variations of one common problem"; or else we have here the picture of a gentleman so befuddled by the lust for power that he actually sees himself handling the problems of the farmer, the stockman, the dust bowl victim, the lumberman, the victim of erosion, the hunter, the fisherman, and the forester—all under his new and unnecessary Department of Conservation.

Undoubtedly Mr. Ickes would deny any such purpose. Undoubtedly he did not intend that any such meaning should poke its head out of his speech. But it is equally beyond question that his own statement shows how impossible is the attempt to confine the conservation activities of the government within a single department.

Conservation is the use of the earth and all that therein is for the permanent good of the human race. Thirty years ago its purpose was defined as the greatest good of the greatest number for the longest time. It is the greatest question of all, for upon its solution depends the future of civilization and the very continuance of human life.

Applied at first only to natural resources, it has come to include human resources as well. Conservation is as universal as the air we breathe, and in the long run just as necessary. No one Department, though it were as far flung as Mr. Ickes' dream, can ever include the whole of conservation. Then why transfer the Forest Service?

I defy Mr. Ickes or anybody else to mention a single specific benefit of any sort, kind, or description that could be obtained for the people of the United States, or for their work in forestry, by returning to the old split-up of that work between the Department of Agriculture and the Department of the Interior, that would compare in any way with the benefits and advantages of leaving the Forest Service where it is now so well administered.

And incidentally, what Bureau in the Interior Department today is better and more intelligently handled, more generally clean, fine, and admirable than the Forest Service in the Department of Agriculture? Then why make a change? Mr. Ickes' answer probably will be that the transfer is in the interest of "an orderly and logical arrangement of conservation activities." In that case, according to Mr. Ickes' own showing, an "orderly and logical arrangement of conservation activities" would equally require the transfer of the conservation activities that have to do with farmers, stockmen, lumbermen, and "others like them."

The fact is that the Interior Department is Uncle Sam's real estate agent. Without regard to how well or how badly it has performed that function, you do not let your real estate agent keep house for you. And there is no reason why you should. Or why that part of national house-keeping which has to do with the National Forests should be taken from where it is so well done, and transferred and split up in order to put part of it back where it was so badly handled before.

I object to Mr. Ickes' proposal to bring back the evils of thirty years ago in a new suit of clothes. In spite of the fact that he has set his mind upon it, and to my personal knowledge has been working for it during much or most of his term as Secretary of the Interior, I am against it for the simple but sufficient reason that the public interest lies the other way.

This proposal is not sugarcoated for me by Mr. Ickes' unconscious revelation that he would like to take possession of a large section of the rest of the government at the same time. Too much power is bad for some people, and this case is no exception.

PART TWO

WAR AND PEACE

Gifford Pinchot was an internationalist. Maybe even a born internationalist. After all, his grandfather and great-grandparents had emigrated from France, so that the family into which he was raised was bicultural and bilingual. As a child he spent more than a year in Paris immersed in the language, a fluency he maintained for the rest of his life. An emblem of the family's continued ties to the patrilineal *patrie* remains embedded in the eastern face of Grey Towers, their Norman-style chateau in Milford, Pennsylvania: a bust of Lafayette oversees the grounds that slope east toward the Delaware River Valley.

Being a Francophone shaped Pinchot's forestry education, too. Between 1889 and 1890, he studied at the École nationale forestière in Nancy, France, using his linguistic skills (including a working knowledge of German) to his advantage while taking every opportunity to travel and tramp across portions of France, Prussia, and Switzerland. Among the many foresters with whom he met and studied, most crucial was Sir Dietrich Brandis, who was knighted for his pioneering work of introducing European principles of forestry to the Indian subcontinent on behalf of the British Empire. By his biography, if nothing else, Brandis taught Pinchot that the profession this young American was pursuing was global in its aspirations and impact.

The impressionable Pinchot would extend Brandis's lessons to other corners of the world. He helped inaugurate forestry management in the new American colony of the Philippines, traveled the Trans-Siberian Railroad so as to assess that region's boreal forests, and later would write about the deleterious impact that American-funded rubber plantations were having on the Amazon's rainforests, a pattern of exploitation he knew well from his studies at home and abroad. A signal of his internationalist credentials was the confidence that Theodore Roosevelt placed in them: it was rumored that had the Bull Moose candidate won the 1912 presidential election, he would have tapped Pinchot to be his Secretary of State.

Roosevelt and Pinchot shared a deep commitment to linking conservation and America's growing presence in world affairs; in step with the chief executive, Pinchot believed the nation's future in good measure lay outside its borders. "One of Pinchot's urgent tasks," notes historian Ian Tyrrell, "was to rise to the challenge presented by [the] American encounter with the tropics and its potentially abundant natural resources, a new and momentous stage in the development of national and global power." This ambition is nicely reflected in the February 1909 North American Conservation Conference. Pinchot not only helped underwrite the event but also drafted Roosevelt's keynote address to its delegates. "In international relations the great feature of the growth of the last century has been the gradual recognition of the fact that instead of its being normally to the interest of each nation to see another depressed, it is normally to the interest of each nation to see the others elevated," argued the Nobel Peace Prize–winning president. After calling upon those gathered to closely cooperate for the common good of all, and challenging his audience to think about the global threat posed by the too-rapid consumption of natural resources, Roosevelt concluded, "I believe that the movement that you this day initiate is one of the utmost importance to this hemisphere and may become of the utmost importance to the world at large."[1]

The 1909 conference succeeded in focusing attention on the need for conserving timber, coal, and water resources in North America, and the president was eager to expand this concept globally, committing the U.S. to organizing a world conservation conference to be held in the Netherlands in September 1909. Once again, Pinchot was one of its chief organizers, and during the waning days of the Roosevelt administration and the early months of William Howard Taft's, he received commitments from thirty nations to attend what would have been the largest, most inclusive conservation conference yet. President Taft did not share his predecessor's support and, in Pinchot's words, "killed the plan." For the next thirty years, driven in part by the furies that World War I had unleashed (and about which he wrote extensively), Pinchot buttonholed every subsequent president about the need for a world conservation conference. Finally, the second President Roosevelt—Franklin—listened. Their conversations began in 1939 as World War II erupted, which is when Pinchot began arguing that conservation was the only route to a "permanent" peace.[2]

This concept was threaded throughout his 1940 article in *Nature* that closes out this section. Although war had long been "an instrument of national policy for the safeguarding of natural resources or for securing them from other nations," this need not be the inevitable fate of human society, Pinchot observed: "International cooperation in conserving, utilizing, and distributing natural resources to the mutual advantage of all nations might well remove one of the most dangerous of all obstacles to a just and permanent world peace." Well aware of the precarious balance that conservationists had to maintain as they fought to preserve natural resources and the human communities that depend on them, he was convinced that the "conservation of natural resources and fair access to needed raw materials are steps toward the common good to which all nations must in principle agree." At war's end, FDR reengaged with Pinchot and encour-

---

1. Ian Tyrrell, *Crisis of the Wasteful Nation: Empire and Conservation in Theodore Roosevelt's America* (Chicago: University of Chicago Press, 2015), 36, 209–210.
    2. Pinchot, *Breaking New Ground*, 367.

aged the State Department to follow up on the plan, planning that carried on after Roosevelt's death. President Harry S. Truman picked up the torch, and just days before Pinchot himself died in 1946 submitted a request to the newly formed United Nations that it host such an international gathering. It was held in 1948, a posthumous celebration of Pinchot's internationalist commitments.

Declaration of Principles: North American Conservation Conference

This document underscores the powerful place that international affairs held in the Theodore Roosevelt administration, and of Pinchot's role in setting some of the agenda. Moreover, these declarations of principles—which Pinchot signed as the American representative to this innovative conference on conservation— reveal as well the array of issues that Progressive conservationists like Pinchot believed were critical. Leading off the list was not the usual resources of water, forests, and minerals, but "public health." This focus, which Pinchot would later call "human conservation," reflects his broad understanding of what constituted the environment.

Source: Gifford Pinchot, Robert Bacon, James Rudolf Garfield, *Commissioners Representing the United States.* Sydney Fisher, Clifford Sifton, Henri S. Béland, *Commissioners Representing the Dominion of Canada.* Rómulo Escobar, Miguel A. de Quevedo, Carlos Sellerier, *Commissioners Representing the Republic of Mexico.* E. H. Outerbridge, *Commissioner Representing the Colony of Newfoundland.* Attest: Robert E. Young, Thomas R. Shipp, *Secretaries of the Conference.* Washington, D.C.
February 23, 1909

———————————

———————————

We recognize the mutual interests of the Nations which occupy the Continent of North America and the dependence of the welfare of each upon its natural resources. We agree that the conservation of these resources is indispensable for the continued prosperity of each Nation.

We recognize that the protection of mutual interests related to natural resources by concerted action, without in any way interfering with the authority of each Nation within its own sphere, will result in mutual benefits, and tend to draw still closer the bonds of existing good will, confidence and respect. Natural resources are not confined by the boundary lines that separate Nations. We agree that no Nation acting alone can adequately conserve them, and we recommend the adoption of concurrent measures for conserving the material foundations of the welfare of all the Nations concerned, and for ascertaining their location and extent.

We recognize as natural resources all materials available for the use of man as means of life and welfare, including those on the surface of the earth, like the soil and the waters; those below the surface, like the minerals; and those above the surface, like the forests. We agree that these resources should be developed, used and conserved for the future, in the interests of mankind, whose rights and duties to guard and control the natural sources of life and welfare are inherent, perpetual and indefeasible. We agree that those resources which are necessaries of life should be regarded as public utilities, that their ownership entails specific duties to the public, and that as far as possible effective measures should be adopted to guard against monopoly.

Public Health

Believing that the Conservation movement tends strongly to develop national efficiency in the highest possible degree in our respective countries, we recognize that to accomplish such an object with success, the maintenance and improvement of public health is a first essential.

In all steps for the utilization of natural resources considerations of public health should always be kept in view.

Facts which cannot be questioned demonstrate that immediate action is necessary to prevent further pollution, mainly by sewage, of the lakes, rivers and streams throughout North America. Such pollution, aside from the enormous loss in fertilizing elements entailed thereby, is an immediate and continuous danger to public health, to the health of animals, and, when caused by certain chemical agents, to agriculture. Therefore we recommend that preventive legislation be enacted.

Forests

We recognize the forests as indispensable to civilization and public welfare. They furnish material for construction and manufacture, and promote the habitability of the earth. We regard the wise use, effective protection, especially from fire, and prompt renewal of the forests on land best adapted to such use, as a public necessity and hence a public duty devolving upon all forest owners alike, whether public, corporate or individual.

We consider the creation of many and large forest reservations and their permanent maintenance under Government control absolutely essential to the public welfare.

We favor the early completion of inventories of forest resources, in order to ascertain the available supply and the rate of consumption and reproduction.

We recommend the extension of technical education and practical field instruction in forest conservation, afforestation and reforestation, so as to provide efficient forest officers whose knowledge will be available for necessary public information on these subjects.

Believing that excessive taxation on standing timber privately owned is a potent cause of forest destruction by increasing the cost of maintaining growing forests, we agree in the wisdom and justice of separating the taxation of timber land from the taxation of the timber growing upon it, and adjusting both in such a manner as to encourage forest conservation and forest growing.

We agree that the ownership of forest lands, either at the headwaters of streams or upon areas better suited for forest growth than for other purposes, entails duties to the public, and that such lands should be protected with equal effectiveness, whether under public or private ownership.

Forests are necessary to protect the sources of streams, moderate floods and equalize the flow of waters, temper the climate and protect the soil; and we agree that all forests necessary for these purposes should be amply safeguarded.

We affirm the absolute need of holding for forests, or reforesting, all lands supplying the headwaters of streams, and we therefore favor the control or acquisition of such lands for the public.

The private owners of lands unsuited to agriculture, once forested and now impoverished or denuded, should be encouraged by practical instruction, adjustment of taxation and in other proper ways, to undertake the reforesting thereof.

Notwithstanding an increasing public interest in forestry, the calamitous and far-reaching destruction of forests by fire still continues, and demands immediate and decisive action. We believe that systems of fire guardianship and patrol afford the best means of dealing adequately with fires which occur, whether from natural causes, such as lightning, or in other ways; but we affirm that in addition thereto effective laws are urgently needed to reduce the vast damage from preventable causes.

Apart from fire, the principal cause of forest destruction is unwise and improvident cutting, which, in many cases, has resulted in widespread injury to the climate and the streams. It is therefore of the first importance that all lumbering operations should be carried on under a system of rigid regulation.

Waters

We recognize the waters as a primary resource, and we regard their use for domestic and municipal supply, irrigation, navigation and power, as interrelated public uses, and properly subject to public control. We therefore favor the complete and concurrent development of the streams and their sources for every useful purpose to which they may be put.

The highest and most necessary use of water is for domestic and municipal purposes. We therefore favor the recognition of this principle in legislation, and, where necessary, the subordination of other uses of water thereto.

The superior economy of water transportation over land transportation, as well as its advantages in limiting the consumption of the nonrenewable resources, coal and iron, and its effectiveness in the promotion of commerce, are generally acknowledged. We therefore favor the development of inland navigation under general plans adapted to secure the uniform progress of the work and the fullest use of the streams for all purposes. We further express our belief that all waterways so developed should be retained under exclusive public ownership and control.

We regard the monopoly of waters, and especially the monopoly of water power, as peculiarly threatening. No rights to the use of water powers in streams should hereafter be granted in perpetuity. Each grant should be conditioned upon prompt development, continued beneficial use and the payment of proper compensation to the public for the rights enjoyed; and should be for a definite period only. Such period should be no longer than is required for reasonable safety in investment. The public authority should retain the right to readjust at stated periods the compensation to the public and to regulate the rates charged, to the end that undue profit or extortion may be prevented.

Where the construction of works to utilize water has been authorized by public authority and such utilization is necessary for the public welfare, provision should be made for the expropriation of any privately owned land and water rights required for such construction.

The interest of the public in the increase of the productiveness of arid lands by irrigation and of wet lands by drainage is manifest. We therefore favor the participation of the public to secure the complete and economical development and use of all water available for irrigation and of all lands susceptible of profitable drainage, in order to ensure the widest possible benefit. Special projects should be considered and developed in connection with a general plan for the same watershed. In the matter of irrigation public authority should control the headwaters and provide for the construction of storage reservoirs and for the equitable distribution and use of the stored water.

Lands

We recognize land as a fundamental resource, yielding the materials needed for sustaining population, and forming the basis of social organization. Increase in the productivity of the soil is a growing need, and the possession of the land by the men who live upon it not only promotes such productivity, but is also the best guarantee of good citizenship. In the interest of the homemaker, we favor regulation of grazing on public land, the disposal of public lands to actual settlers in areas each sufficient to support a family, and the subdivision of excessive holdings of agricultural or grazing land, thereby preventing monopoly.

The preservation of the productivity of the soil is dependent upon rotation of crops, fertilization by natural or artificial means, and improved methods in farm management. The quantity and quality of crops are also dependent upon the careful selection of seed. We therefore favor the distribution by Government bureaus of scientific and practical information on these points, and we urge upon all farmers careful attention thereto.

The national importance for grazing of non-irrigable public lands too dry for cultivation, and the public loss occasioned by overgrazing, are generally acknowledged. We therefore favor Government control of such lands in order to restore their value, promote settlement and increase the public resources. The first requisite for forest or other covering which will conserve the rainfall and promote regularity of water flow is the retention of the soil upon watersheds. We therefore favor the construction of such artificial works as may effect this purpose and the encouragement thereof by remission of taxes, Government cooperation or other suitable means.

Minerals

We recognize the mineral resources as forming the chief basis of industrial progress, and regard their use and conservation as essential to the public welfare. The mineral fuels play an indispensable part in our modern civilization.

We favor action on the part of each government looking towards reduction of the enormous waste in the exploitation of such fuels, and we direct attention to the necessity for an inventory thereof. Such fuel should hereafter be disposed of by lease under such restrictions or regulations as will prevent waste and monopolistic or speculative holdings, and supply the public at reasonable prices.

We believe that the surface rights and underground mineral rights in lands should be separately dealt with so as to permit the surface of the land to be utilized to the fullest extent, while preserving Government control over the minerals. Regulations should be adopted looking to the most economical production of coal and other mineral fuels and the prolongation of the supply to the utmost. We favor also the substitution of water power for steam or other power produced by the consumption of fuel.

Great economy in the use of fuel has resulted in the past from the application of scientific inventions and the use of improvements in machinery, and further progress can be made in the same direction. We therefore recommend that all possible encouragement and assistance be given in the development and perfecting of means whereby waste in the consumption of fuel can be reduced.

The loss of human life through preventable mining accidents in North America is excessive. Much needless suffering and bereavement results therefrom. Accompanying this loss there is great destruction of valuable mineral property and enhancement of the cost of production. The best method of eliminating these known and admitted evils lies in the enactment and strict enforcement of regulations which will provide the greatest possible security for mine workers and mines. We therefore favor the scientific investigation of the whole subject of mine accidents by the governments participating in this conference, the interchange of information and experience and the enactment and enforcement of the best regulations that can be devised.

Mineral fertilizers should not be monopolized by private interests, but should be so controlled by public authority as to prevent waste and to promote their production in such quantity and at such price as to make them readily available for use.

Protection of Game

We recognize that game preservation and the protection of bird life are intimately associated with the conservation of natural resources. We therefore favor game protection under regulation, the creation of extensive game preserves and special protection for such birds as are useful to agriculture.

Conservation Commissions

The action of the President of the United States in calling this first conference to consider the conservation of the natural resources of North America was in the highest degree opportune, and the proceedings which have followed, and the information mutually communicated by the representatives assembled, have, we believe, been conducive to the best interests of the countries participating. To derive the greatest possible benefit from the work which has already been done, and to provide proper and effective machinery for future work, there should be established in each country a permanent Conservation Commission.

When such Conservation Commissions have been established, a system of intercommunication should be inaugurated, whereby, at stated intervals, all discoveries, inventions, processes, inventories of natural resources, information of a new and specially important character, and seeds, seedlings, new or improved varieties, and other productions which are of value in conserving or improving any natural resource shall be transmitted by each Commission to all of the others, to the end that they may be adopted and utilized as widely as possible.

World Conservation Congress

The conference of delegates, representatives of the United States, Mexico, Canada and Newfoundland, having exchanged views and considered the information supplied from the respective countries, is convinced of the importance of the movement for the conservation of natural resources on the continent of North America, and believes that it is of such a nature and of such general importance that it should become worldwide in its scope, and therefore suggests to the President of the United States of America that all Nations should be invited to join together in conference on the subject of world resources and their inventory, conservation and wise utilization.

England in War

Like former President Theodore Roosevelt, Pinchot was an early promoter of the U.S. entry into World War I, chiding President Woodrow Wilson for delaying the inevitable. "War is not the worst of evils," he wrote Senator Henry Cabot Lodge; "righteousness and justice are the only foundations of enduring peace." But this article, written after Pinchot visited England to check in on his sister, Lady Antoinette Johnstone, and to get a better sense of how her adopted country was adapting to wartime exigencies, was not framed around domestic politics. Instead, Pinchot offered a person-on-the-street perspective, an impressionistic approach that humanized the English experience of the global conflict.

Originally published in *Harper's Weekly*, April 17, 1915, 364–65.

———————————

———————————

What a great war is and means it is not easy for an American born after the Civil War fully to understand. Before landing at Liverpool, I had, of course, read everything I could about the war. Like everyone else, I knew what enormous battles had been fought and what vast losses had been sustained. But still I did not realize the gigantic fact of war. Most of my countrymen, I do not doubt, are in the same mental position. So little, indeed, do our people realize what war implies that the American legation at Brussels has had to provide itself with rubber stamps which read: "A state of war exists in Belgium," because men and women constantly write over and ask for things which are wholly impossible because war does exist.

The actual fact of war was the strangest impression made upon me during the first few days in England. The outward evidences of a nation at war are plentiful in London. Soldiers are everywhere. Columns of armed men and columns of recruits still in civilian clothes march through the streets. Drilling goes on in the parks and other places every day. The shop windows are full of articles for use at the front. War fills the papers and monopolizes conversation. But all this fails to make war really felt. None of these, nor the posters calling for enlistment which cover every wall, appear in every shop window, flash across whole blocks of buildings, and decorate every taxi cab, not the darkened streets at night, nor the supply of candles in the house against the time when a Zeppelin raid may require the cutting-off of the electric light, are sufficient to bring home completely the actual fact of war. What finally does it are the faces and the talk of the women.

There is no parade of suffering whatever. I have scarcely seen a crepe veil since I landed. Talk goes on about the men who have been killed, or are wounded, or prisoners, or (worst of all for the women) who are missing, and it goes on as much as possible in the ordinary tone and way. Complaint is altogether absent. Every woman appears to be doing all she can to help, and everyone is giving what she has. For in this war every family, at least among the richer classes, has given its men to the service of the nation.

After two weeks in England, during which I have taken pains to inquire, I have learned the name of but one single Englishman of the so-called leisure class and of military age who is not engaged in the war. As soldiers, or, when they cannot pass the physical examination, as civilians, all of the men of prominence and position are doing what they can. Two British admirals of seventy years, long since retired on their pensions, have, for example, taken to the sea again, not as admirals in the active service of the Navy, for that is evidently impossible, but as lieutenants, and both are engaged in the dangerous work of sweeping for mines.

But it is far from true that the leisure class alone shows this temper toward the war. The bone and sinew of England, you hear on every side, is in Kitchener's army. Mechanics, clerks, small businessmen, the successful in all the active occupations which lead to success, are the men who fill the ranks. What strikes the casual observer about the bodies of troops who pass in the streets is the obvious high level of physique and intelligence both.

Such spirit among the men of England is admirable, but even more so is the spirit of the women. Over and over again I have heard women say of their men, "We can stand it if they go, but we could not stand it if they stayed at home."

At the end of a recent call upon an American lady, during which no word was said of her bereavement, an English woman advanced in years replied to an inquiry about her eldest son: "My husband and I have been highly distinguished. Our son has died for his country."

To me by far the most striking fact in England is the total lack of bitterness against the Germans, either as a people or as individuals. Full discussion of German methods of warfare I have heard daily, almost hourly, and strong condemnation, but no bitterness or abuse. Full and generous recognition is everywhere given to German courage and German efficiency. Although the whole nation is profoundly convinced that it is fighting for its liberties and its economic existence against a system of military absolutism, there seems to be no bitterness at all. At least I have found none. There can be no stronger evidence than this that the English believe that their quarrel is just.

There is another phase of the situation in England which deserves special mention. It is this: No Englishman of influence desires anything but strict neutrality on the part of the United States. Although they believe themselves to be fighting the fight of democracy against the effort of a military autocracy, to control, if not rule the world, and although they believe this to be in the last analysis our fight as much as theirs, their faith in democracy being the same as ours, still there is no desire on their part that we should take upon ourselves any active share of the burden of the war.

But there is bewilderment, and not a little sense of regret, over what the average intelligent Englishman regards as our failure to realize the facts. He says:

England went into this war on a great question of principle, much as you Americans went into the war with Spain. We went to war to insure the safety of small neutral states in the future, and to force respect for the obligations of treaties. We cannot understand why America did not lend the enormous weight of her influence to the cause of international [morality] by protesting against the violation of Belgium.

But let that pass. What seems incredible to us now, is that you in America apparently do not see how England is fighting to prevent democracy from being overwhelmed in Europe. We have nothing against the German people, but we cannot permit the Prussian system of military bondage to set the pace for the whole world. If we are beaten, the United States will be next in the way of German expansion and will have to surrender or fight. Of course you will not surrender. That being so, England has a right to the whole-hearted sympathy of the American people.

In general you Americans understand that we are right, but you do not realize what we are giving to the cause of liberty. We do not see why you Americans should not be willing for a time even to lose a little trade in this great war, which we English are fighting to protect and establish your own principles, and in which you are losing nothing."

This is the Englishman's point of view, and the fact that he is backing his convictions with an army of two or three million fighting men gives weight to his words.

Preparedness and Common Sense

Hoping to increase public support for World War I, Pinchot chose to position himself in the center between two poles; he dismissed those who too easily bellowed for war just as he rejected the pacifists' arguments. The middle ground that he occupied led him to urge his readers on the basis of their common sense and practicality to demand that Congress and the White House accelerate the nation's preparations for the conflict to come.

Originally published in *Journal of Education* 83, no. 24 (June 15, 1916): 649–50.

———————————
———————————

Along with thousands of our citizens, I am deeply interested in the question of National defense. Like them, I am anxious to know the facts and to use whatever common sense I have in reaching a wise conclusion as to what we ought to do for our own protection. I am not stampeded, and I do not propose to be, but I do want the United States to take what precautions are reasonable in view of the facts. The situation looks to me like this:—

Certain pacifists assure us that Preparedness is useless because there is no danger of war. Do they know, or are they merely asking us to accept their guess in a matter which vitally concerns the safety and welfare of the nation? Millions of pacifists in the past have given the same assurance, and have been mistaken. Wars have come in spite of them. England was full of people who affirmed that the present war was impossible up to the very moment of its breaking out, and who opposed with all their might any increase in armament until war actually began.

The United States has already had five wars, each one of which was undesired and unexpected by great numbers of our people. For a year past our state department has been occupied with questions which might lead to war. What if our present pacifists should in their turn prove to be wrong, and war should come and find us unprepared? It is a serious chance for any nation, this gamble on their opinion, which the pacifists are asking us to take.

Preparedness is insurance against war. It is not militarism, and must not be confused with it. Militarism is making ready for aggressive war. Anyone who believes that the people of the United States can be driven or dragged into aggressive militarism must have forgotten the whole trend of our history, particularly our recent retirement from Cuba.

It is nonsense to say that our people will plunge into militarism because they prepare themselves in order to discourage aggression. On that theory, no citizen should be allowed to own a gun, because guns can be used to kill people, or to insure his house, lest insurance should bring on fire.

Here and there an extremist will make ridiculous proposals for Preparedness or against it. Such proposals should not be permitted to upset our judgment. They lead nowhere. We waste our time discussing them. For us the extremes of militarism and of non-resistance are equally out of the question. In sober fact, our final choice will lie not between any fantastical extremes, but between reasonable National defense and an imitation of it that will fail in the day of trial—between moderate genuine Preparedness and a sham. We may prepare too little, but there is no danger whatever that this country will rush to the other extreme.

The pacifists assure us that such military training as the Swiss people are giving themselves endangers democracy, and that our young men will be hurt by learning to obey. But neither democracy nor personal independence has been injured in Switzerland, which is the most democratic country in Europe. Universal military service in New Zealand and Australia goes hand in hand with the most thorough-going labor-controlled democracy on earth.

France, whose military training is far more thorough than ours will ever be, is the living proof that an army can be a great democratic institution, and that citizens trained in arms may possess the highest personal initiative and intelligence. Germany cannot be offered as an example of what military training does to democracy, because Germany has never been democratic.

But even if all of this were true, it would still be idle to make a bogey of universal military service, because even those who believe in it most heartily understand that it has not the slightest chance of being adopted. No National leader in any political party is asking for its adoption. It is not an issue, and nothing less than the pressure of actual invasion could make it an issue for the United States.

The American people have a way of reaching common-sense decisions after long and often bitter discussion. There is hope that this is about to happen in the present case. The reasonable advocates of National defense and the reasonable pacifists seem to be on the verge of a reasonable agreement of views. For example, the papers of April 23 report that Henry Ford said, in an interview given in New York: "I wouldn't object to an army of 250,000 men." Less than a week before this statement of Ford's, I asked

Colonel Roosevelt what he would consider reasonable Preparedness. He replied: "The second navy in the world and an army of 250,000 men."

In this case, pacifist and advocate of Preparedness are in agreement as the size of a reasonable army. An army of 250,000 men means one soldier to about 430 people. There is one policeman for every 416 people in Philadelphia, and one to every 429 people in New York. To me at least an army of that proportionate size carries no threat that militarism is about to overwhelm democracy.

As to the navy, from 1905 to 1909 our navy was second in the world. Having it second did not endanger democracy then. I see no reason why it should endanger democracy now.

So far as I am aware no one who is familiar with naval affairs believes that submarines and mines at sea and guns on land, without a fleet, can be depended on to defend a coast like ours. The whole teaching of the present war shows that it cannot. German submarines, it is true, have succeeded in preventing any increase in the British merchant marine by destroying vessels about as fast as tonnage could be added. They have not even threatened, much less endangered, the supremacy of the British fleet. It is the British fleet which keeps England safe from invasion, just as our fleet must keep us safe.

It will not do, however, to forget that genuine Preparedness includes far more than arms. A navy and an army are not enough. In modern war nations fight not alone with weapons, but with all the natural resources, with their industry and transportation, and above all with the patriotic devotion of their citizens.

Rounded National Preparedness on modern lines works not only toward securing peace, but also toward making this country a better place to live in for all of us when peace has been secured. The great natural resources, like coal, iron, copper and waterpower, are the raw materials of prosperity as well as the raw materials of National defense. They must be made available for the use of the people both in peace and war. But above and beyond all else, we must have a country defended against attack from within and without by equal opportunity and social justice—a country whose people will stand by it because it has stood by them.

I recognize that in the manufacture of munitions and supplies for war excessive profits are often found. I am in favor of eliminating them with a strong hand. But it seems to me as foolish to decide against National defense because there is graft as it would be to abolish the police force in any city because there is graft. The thing to do is to drive out the graft, and yet maintain the protection which is so necessary to all our people.

You and I are protected by our laws because behind the law there is force. International law has not force behind it. Someday, we hope and intend, it will be made unsafe to break the law of nations. As yet, however, each nation must still go unprotected or protect itself. Until the nations unite together to enforce international law, our best hope for peace lies in making it dangerous for any nation to attack us.

You and I belong to a great peace-loving people. We hate war and desire peace. We seek with earnestness any means that will hasten the coming of permanent peace. We are ready to do everything that is just and honorable to secure it. Doubtless we join with every lover of peace in looking forward to the day when reason and understanding will settle or prevent disputes among nations. But the road to peace does not lie through flabby weakness, as the history of China proves, but through self-respecting strength. That is why I believe in National defense. The mere desire for peace, and the best intentions on our part, cannot always secure peace. Among nations, as among men, it often takes but one to make a quarrel.

Last year I was in Belgium. What I saw there I shall never forget. No sacrifice can be too great to prevent our people or any part of them from being ruled by foreign bayonets. Talk is always cheap, but never cheaper than when it sets guesses and wishes against the tremendous facts of the world war.

Guessing and wishing are no defense. Guessing and wishing cannot even keep the peace between our citizens. The force behind the law does that. How then can we trust them to keep the peace between the nations? I am for Preparedness because I believe it offers the best chance to escape war. It is cheap insurance at the price.

An Agricultural Policy for the United States in War Time

The moment the United States entered the war in April 1917, Pinchot cast aside his earlier and sharp disagreements with the Wilson administration's cautious diplomacy and offered his services to the government. Within three months, he was working under Herbert Hoover in the Food Administration, the goal of which was to accelerate the production of all foodstuffs to feed the American troops and the civilian populations overseas. Pinchot's task, as he notes below, was to increase the number of livestock on farms and ranches—and to do so through market incentives, promising producers top dollar to increase their stocks, a strategy that was in line with Bernard Baruch's efforts as chair of the War Industries Board but which ran afoul of Hoover's managerial vision. The two men's arguments about strategy reached such a level that by the time this article appeared in print, in November 1917, Pinchot had already resigned his post.

Source: Box 943, Gifford Pinchot Papers, Library of Congress; a revised version appeared in *Annals of the American Academy of Political and Social Science* 74 (November 1917): 181–87.

———————————

———————————

One of the outstanding facts which is least recognized among the great facts that this war is gradually forcing upon the attention of the world—perhaps the outstanding fact of all—is that the world will never be the same again; in fact the change has already been made. We have passed already into a new world order which has laid the foundations of a new point of view not only in world affairs but in national and civic affairs as well.

I do not mean by a "new point of view," a view that has never been advocated before, but a view that has never before been widely adopted; and that view, if a conservationist may say so, is the point of view of the conservation policy. It is the point of view of planned and orderly development to reach distant ends.

Hitherto, in all our national affairs, we have gone where the pressure was least. I do not say that as a criticism; I state it as a fact. It is necessarily so in the early stages of any civilization. We have yielded to the thrust that sent us this way or that way without accepted plan or definite conception of where we were going, and this has led us, as it necessarily has led every other nation in a similar stage of development, to haphazard excursions in this direction and in that. The condition which we have now reached, not only in agriculture but in every phase of our national life, is a result far more of the action of forces which we did not count upon in advance than it is of any planned and definite effort to reach any definite condition by following any definite line.

Is it desirable to reverse this national habit of mind? The answer is that perhaps this is an academic question, for we have been forced into a set of circumstances which compel us to adopt a new point of view. We have reached a situation in which the indispensable basis of national survival is a higher degree of national efficiency than we have yet sought and a more conscious pursuit of distant aims than has ever been characteristic of the American people. We are thrown into a world order molded upon a plane of efficiency such as we in the United States, efficient as we have been in many respects, have, in my judgment, never conceived to be possible.

We shall find ourselves, after the war, forced into competition for commercial survival with nations, driven by the pressure of debts unimagined before into an absolute necessity for conquering foreign trades as the first means, after food, of self-preservation. In order to hold our position we shall be compelled, in my judgment, to reorganize our national point of view and plan where we mean to go, instead of allowing ourselves to drift where it is easiest to go, as we have done about so many things in so many directions.

If that is true, have we reached a stage where the adoption of a definite agricultural policy for the United States is demanded? Is such a policy possible? It seems to me to be inevitable in view of the known facts of the world's situation.

The essential consideration, as I see it, is the change in the direction of agriculture in the nations that are at war, because of facts brought about by the war. What I mean is this:

The world is short of livestock. Mr. Hoover's figures give us a world deficiency of 28,000,000 cattle, 32,000,000 hogs and 54,000,000 sheep; or a total shortage of livestock in the world of about 115,000,000 head. The submarine warfare means that we can no longer supply to the nations of Europe the additional feeds required in the past to keep their supply of domestic animals up to its normal point.

For example, an embargo has just been placed on cotton-seed cake, of which we have been shipping abroad a million tons a year. That means a reduction in cattle abroad. We can no longer ship corn as we used to do. That fact is reflected in the English government's decision to reduce English cattle on a very considerable scale.

The French supply of livestock is short already. Since the beginning of the war, it has fallen below the pre-war average 16 per cent in cattle, 33 per cent in sheep, and 38 per cent in hogs; and similar figures might be adduced for other countries.

The first fact then, as I see it, is the large shortage, and the necessity for an increase, in livestock abroad.

The second fact is that after the war, European farmers will be forced in the direction of grain production. They will have less stock to eat their feed; therefore they will grow less feed. They will have a larger demand for grain for human food; therefore they will grow more grain. In other words, the agricultural policy of the European nations, from the very nature of the situation, will be driven in the direction of grain rather than livestock.

What then ought we to do both in relation to what they are going to do and to our own situation here?

Our first great contribution to the war is food, and of food, wheat first of all. We shall doubtless produce next year a crop of wheat so large that it may reach even a billion bushels. In other words, our own coming increase in wheat, coupled with the certainty of larger European production of wheat after the war, fairly re-moves the wheat question from the debatable field.

But not livestock. What is our own situation in livestock? The first great fact is—and it is true also of grains—that our per capita production has dropped. There has been within the last year or two, however, no decrease—indeed, a slight increase—in absolute numbers. For example, we have 102 per cent this year of the cattle that we had last year, and 103 per cent of dairy cows. There has been a slight decrease, amounting to only 300,000, in the number of hogs.

In addition, then, to considerations arising from the European nations, we find ourselves faced in this country with a situation which leads to the belief that we shall have a very alarming shortage of livestock in the near future.

Take, for example, the question of hogs. In Iowa, the greatest hog producing state, estimates show there are 20 per cent less hogs now than there were a year ago; in Missouri, 18 per cent less, in the United States, as a whole, about 7,000,000 fewer hogs than a year ago.

Why? Because of a doubt on the part of the farmer that it will pay to raise hogs. The high price of grain, coupled with the uncertainties of the market, has persuaded the farmers of a large part of this country that it is not worth their while to raise more pigs. The result appears in an immediate decrease, which will be reflected in a shortage in supply later on, just when the war demands a very large increase.

The question is not merely one of keeping our normal amount of livestock or producing our normal amount of meat and especially of pork products. It is a question of very largely increasing that supply, just exactly as it was in the matter of wheat, because it is necessary in order to win the war. Without it we handicap our allies and we endanger the winning of the war. Yet as things stand today we face the probability not merely of no increase in pork products, but in the face [of] a tremendously enhanced demand, we face an actual decrease.

Take now the matter of beef cattle in the west. Last winter was a very hard one. The losses were very large. In Texas the drought of this summer has resulted in sending prematurely to market large numbers of cattle and in the death of very many others; and such examples might be multiplied. So in beef cattle also, we find ourselves threatened with a decrease, both because of bad seasons and because of the farmers' doubts. Will it be worthwhile, for example, for the man in Nebraska to buy "feeders" from the west, feed them on corn and ship them to the Chicago market as fat stock? There is doubt whether that operation will pay, and that doubt is reflected now in the difference on the Chicago market between the price of finished cattle and the price of feeders and stockers, because the demand for the latter is abnormally small for this time of year.

Again, take the matter of dairy cattle. We have some 22,000,000 dairy cattle in this country. Nearly a fifth of the dairy herds, on the average all through the country, go to the slaughter every year. The exact figure in New York State seems to be 17 per cent. In New York it was found that between April first of this year and April first of last year, the number of dairy cattle going to the slaughter, in addition to the normal 17 per cent, amounted to an extra 14 per cent, due, in brief, to the high cost of production. A still more serious situation was revealed when it was found that where a year ago there were 300,000 heifers being raised for dairy use, this year there are in round numbers, only 225,000 or one-quarter less.

In sheep the losses have been very heavy from the hard winter in the west; and a great majority of the sheep, about two-thirds of them, are west of the one hundredth meridian. The crop of lambs, roughly speaking, is said to be about 50 per cent of the normal, and in addition to that very large numbers of the lambs have gone under contract into the hands of feeders, so that fewer of them will be raised than usual. We have fewer sheep in the United States, and at the same time an enormous rise in the price of wool and in the necessity for wool for war purposes.

All this seems to me to point to a simple conclusion, which is that the world situation, the American situation, and the demands of the war all point to the necessity for a very large emphasis upon livestock production as against grain production in the United States.

It is true, of course, that the various parts of the country must produce what their physical conditions prescribe. You cannot raise peanuts in North Dakota nor truck in the Panhandle of Texas. But there is an enormous area in the country in which one product or another can be increased as the needs arise; and in that area, which is abundantly sufficient to supply all we need in the way of increased livestock production—in that area, as I see it, the need for more livestock is greater than the need for more grain.

In spite of early frosts we are likely to have in our corn crop the largest crop of any grain ever raised in any country at any time since the world began. The estimate of three and one-quarter billion bushels allowed, I am informed, for a certain amount of damage from frost, and the chances were if there had been no frost the total crop might have amounted to 3,800,000,000 or even 4,000,000,000 bushels.

There is likely to be a very considerable surplus. Feed for livestock will be in excess of animals to consume it. Thus it is estimated by a man who ought to know that the south will produce this year, beyond the supply required to feed all its livestock, feed sufficient for 500,000 head. In the south, in the corn belt, and elsewhere, we shall have an exceedingly heavy corn crop and roughage enough to supply and more than supply all the livestock we can put upon it.

Obviously, then, the situation points to that form of agriculture which, in addition to all the considerations I have mentioned, has this other striking advantage in time of war, that it can be handled with a smaller expenditure for labor than any other. You can raise more agricultural products in the form of livestock with less man power than you can grain, as everyone knows.

So the elements which indicate strong emphasis on an agricultural policy of promoting livestock production are briefly: abundance of feed, insuring relative cheapness; shortage of agricultural labor, necessarily resulting in a premium on meat products rather than on grain; a shortage of all kinds of livestock as measured by the certain demand, which means good prices for the producer; the demand for a large increase in exports of meat (we have been exporting 200 or 300 per cent more pork products than we did before the war, and we must export still more, which furnishes additional reason why prices should be high); and the fact—and it is a very important one—that even if there were no war, to export meats is vastly wiser than to export grains. For when you export wheat, you export soil fertility with it. When you export meats you create fertility and keep it at home; so that the future richness of the land argues likewise for livestock as the trend which we ought to follow in our agricultural policy.

The essential lesson of the war, as I have tried to indicate, seems to me to be that team play, to a degree hitherto unknown, has become the indispensable condition of national success. If, then, we are to stimulate agriculture in the United States, and if the trend of our agricultural policy looks toward livestock rather than toward grain, then it is absolutely essential to bring to that stimulation this same point of view of team play. Therefore the organization of American farmers has become indispensable. The spread of cooperation among the producers of livestock and of grains on the farm is an essential factor in winning the war.

The farmer is a business man like any other. He is in business to support his family. It is true that he earns a very much smaller return than any other business man—probably less than $400 a year in money for his work. He has, in addition, a house to live in and produce from the farm worth perhaps a couple of hundred dollars in cash.

The farmer, like anybody else, will remain in the business, or in any particular part of the business, just in proportion to the chance he has of making a living. He will be guided in his business, like any other business man, by his chance of profit and success. He will trend toward grain, livestock, truck, other conditions being equal, according to his belief that there is in any one of these lines a reasonable return for his labor and his investment.

We have dealt with the farmer for years as if he were a fixture that could not move away; as if he were a mere maker of agricultural products, and not a man with a family to whom the ordinary human considerations are just as important as they are to anybody else. Now we have come to the time when the nation as a whole must recognize the dominating position which has come to the man who produces food from the soil. Although our population is but one-third agricultural and two-thirds industrial, still the emphasis today is on the man who grows things out of the ground rather than on the man who makes things in a factory.

If it is true that the general lines of policy I have tried to outline are sound, then the time has come when a reconstruction of the national point of view about agriculture is absolutely essential. Not less so is the reconstruction of the farmer's point of view about himself. The introduction of cooperative methods among producers is absolutely vital to success in our agricultural policy.

An integral part of the success of any agricultural policy we may adopt must be the recognition of the dominant part the farmer is playing in the affairs of this country and of the world. He has been set aside. He has not had his fair share of influence in the government, nor his fair share in the benefits of government, and he is beginning to understand it and to consider what he shall do about it.

If we are to meet the obligations that have been imposed upon us by the war, the first of which is the production of food on a large scale, we must do three things: first, direct our efforts mainly toward livestock rather than mainly toward grain; second, convince the agricultural producers of this country that their efforts in producing livestock will be met by a fair remuneration when that livestock comes to be marketed; and third, see to it that the farmer has what he has never had sufficiently before, his fair and reasonable share and part in determining the plans and policies of the country, of which he forms the underlying and most essential part.

A Forest Devastation Warning

Even during his first term as governor of Pennsylvania, Pinchot kept a sharp eye on issues affecting forests and forestry. One that particularly caught his attention, and that remains a key concern to this day, was the deforestation of the Amazon. Knowing that unchecked harvesting had devastated U.S. woodlands, he urged his fellow citizens to remember that "common sense tells us, if selfish interests do not, that the welfare of the world depends to a vital degree upon the wise handling of forest resources."

Originally published in *Pan American Union Bulletin* 59, no. 2 (February 1925): 165–69.

The forest plays a leading role in the every-day life of all the civilized nations of the world. In some countries the relationship between the forest and human welfare is more obvious and direct than in others, but in all of them the standard of living is greatly influenced by the condition and value of local forest resources.

The average citizen knows that the population of the world is increasing, but most of the people have overlooked the vital fact that the forest wealth of the world is being depleted rapidly. There are now approximately 1,710,000,000 people and 5,500,000,000 acres of productive forest land in the world. This means that there are about 3 acres of forest land for each inhabitant.

There need be no alarm about the world acreage of forest land, for if properly handled it will satisfy the wood needs of all the people for many years to come. But much of this forest land is in a deplorable condition. There are vast areas of poorly stocked forest land and extensive stretches of barren wastes. In the United States alone are 81,000,000 acres of forest land that are nothing more than forest deserts.

In addition to this enormous acreage of idle forest land there are 250,000,000 acres stocked with stands of inferior trees, all below saw-timber size. In its present condition this land can produce little or nothing of value. Similar conditions exist in many other countries of the world. In fact, forest depletion has gone forward so far that 50 of the important nations of the world must be classed as wood-importing countries.

The wood situation of the world demands prompt and serious attention. It can no longer be said that the forest problem is a local, a State, or a national problem, for it is actually a world problem. The forests of no restricted part of the world can be considered solely by themselves, for a survey of the world's wood trade shows an intricate interrelationship in wood exports and wood imports. We cannot dispute the fact that the forest conditions in any one country do not limit their influence to that country alone, but extend to other countries, and in some cases to very distant lands.

In my opinion forest conservation is a common enterprise in which all the people of the world must sooner or later participate, and the sooner this point of view prevails the better it will be for everybody.

In the long course of events no country can afford to maintain an abnormal timber level. If the timber level is kept too high, an accusation of hoarding may be justly filed, and if too low, the more serious offense of gross negligence in the handling of a heritage given to us for wise use, but never for willful and wasteful exploitation, can be rightly charged.

The nation that lives unto herself alone is not even worthy of a good name. Common sense tells us, if selfish interests do not, that the welfare of the world depends to a vital degree upon the wise handling of forest resources. No nation, regardless of her size, condition, or position, can afford to overlook her forest problems.

Just as the forests of Europe have pointed the way for the development of the forests of the United States, so the present forest conditions of the United States should serve as a warning to Latin American countries. I am aware of the fact that vast areas of tropical forests await exploration, and I am confident that tropical America is approaching an era of great development. Many of the tropical forests are still beyond the commercial touch of man, but they will gradually take their place among the commercial forests of the world.

In most of the tropical forests that are being worked to-day only a few of the many different woods are utilized. Some of the countries of Central America boast of 900 different species of trees, of which less than a dozen are now of commercial importance. At the present time lumbering operations are limited largely to accessible regions, and especially to such special or precious woods as mahogany, cedar, rosewood, and the dye woods.

With so large a percentage of inferior trees and so small a percentage of important timber trees, and with the consequent ultra-selective method of logging, it is important that the countries of Latin America take a chapter from the forest experiences of the United States.

The people of the United States are just awakening to the fact that the virgin forests, once supposed to be inexhaustible, are now nearly all cut over. For centuries we have permitted the lumberman to rove over our country and pillage our forests. He is now nearing the end of his run in virgin timber, for most of our original forests are gone.

The lumberman did not consider the land. All he wanted was the wood, and he took only the best. If he could not get it at one place he moved to another, and as a result of this blundering and pillaging we to-day have areas of desolation where we should have promising and orderly forests of thrifty trees.

We do not know the wood situation down to the last acre or to the last cord, but we do know it well enough to be convinced that it is vitally serious. When the first settlers arrived, the United States was covered with about 62 per cent of forests, 8 per cent of brush land, and the remaining 30 per cent was open country. To-day only 28 per cent remains in forest, the brush land has already increased to 30 per cent, and much of the land that is now classified as forest is actually covered with a very sparse growth of inferior trees.

These vast areas of idle land are a serious menace to our national life. Idle forest land has no place in a well-balanced economic program. It is an economic crime to maintain these unproductive areas at a time when a serious wood shortage actually exists.

Conservative estimates show that we have left 745,000,000,000 cubic feet in the forests of our country. The annual drain upon these forests is approximately 25,000,000,000 cubic feet, and the annual growth is only 6,000,000,000 cubic feet. These few figures are enough to show whither we are drifting, and it now remains for us to work out a practical program of forest restoration.

The State of Pennsylvania, which was first in lumber production among all the States of the Union in 1860, and even as late as 1900 produced 2,321,280,000 board feet of lumber, now imports 80 per cent of her lumber, 74 per cent of her pulp wood, and enormous quantities of wood for both the anthracite and bituminous mines. The Pittsburgh district alone uses more wood than the State is now producing. The unavoidable wood importation into Pennsylvania means an annual freight bill of $25,000,000, and an average haul of imported lumber of 1,250 miles. To be compelled to pay this enormous freight bill is most unfortunate, but what is far more tragic is the fact that as a result of destructive lumbering methods and no provision for forest renewal, there are now great stretches of barren waste land producing nothing of value, although if given proper attention, these wastes are capable of yielding valuable crops of timber.

Unless better methods of harvesting the products of tropical forests are used than were employed in the United States, I foresee an enormous unnecessary waste and vast stretches of barren land. To permit such a condition to develop in the light of forest experiences in Europe and the United States will be little short of criminal. To say the least, it will be economic suicide.

The right time to begin forestry is before the forests are gone. The United States is laboring under the handicap of having started her forest work too late. We must expel the false notion, still too prevalent, that forest conditions can be corrected in a few months. Forest restoration at best is a slow process. The nation is fortunate that does not delay in establishing a sound forest conservation policy. Countries that still retain a large part of their forests, and this holds for many of the Latin American countries, will do well if they take a leaf from the book of experience of older countries and make provisions for a forest policy that will safeguard them against the evils of forest devastation. Each nation owes it to her people and to those of other lands to work out a sound and broad-based forest policy. If we give way to short-sighted selfishness in our attitude toward the forest, and if we fail to have a worthy goal, we must expect nothing short of economic disaster and social distress.

The nation is indeed fortunate whose statesmen are wise enough and whose people are willing to establish a wise and foreseeing forest policy. I hope that the countries of Latin America will not postpone the enactment of effective forest laws. The more quickly this is done the sooner will good results make themselves felt.

It would doubtless be extremely unwise for the forest program of tropical countries to concern themselves only with the few precious woods that now find a ready market. The trees that now have little or no commercial value should also be considered, for experience of other countries shows conclusively that many of the despised trees of to-day will be prized to-morrow. Provision should be made for the handling not only of the few species that are now marketable but also for the many others that have commercial possibilities.

I am hopeful that the period of forest devastation through which we are now passing in the United States is the forerunner of better years. If, as in the Old Testament, the seven lean years of wood scarcity through which we are passing and are to pass can be followed by seven fat years of wood plenty produced by forest conservation, we shall be fortunate. For years to come we shall have lean wood years, but if we do our part well in fashioning a sound forest program we shall have our reward.

The central thing for which the conservation policy stands is to make the country to which it is applied the best possible place to live in, both for the present and future. It keeps constantly in view the permanent prosperity of the human race. It works for good and aims to overcome evil. It promotes wise use and operates against needless waste and destruction. It brings benefits to those who promote it and blessings to future generations.

Conservation as a Foundation for Permanent Peace

This is arguably Pinchot's most far-reaching essay. Published on the eve of World War II, it is a plea for a new approach to global resource management that if enacted, he believed, would prevent the outbreak of World War III. Building on his initiatives during the waning years of the first Roosevelt administration, once again Pinchot proposed holding an international conservation conference that would resolve the pressing need of all nation-states for an equitable share of the planet's resources—and for a regulatory agency that would ensure that these resources would be sustainably utilized so that subsequent generations would also benefit. Without such commitments, there would be no end of war, an argument that social critics such as William Vogt and Fairfield Osborne would expand in the aftermath of the war.[1]

Source: Box 943, Gifford Pinchot Papers, Library of Congress; a revised version appeared in *Nature* 146, no. 3693 (August 1940): 183–85.

_____

_____

Thirty-two years ago there was held in Washington a conference which was the first of its kind. It was the first not only in America but in the world. It was also the first conference in the history of this country of the Governors of all the States and Territories with the President of the United States. Since it included also the Congress, the Cabinet, the Supreme Court, scientific experts, representatives of national associations, and outstanding citizens, it was one of the most distinguished gatherings ever brought together in the United States.

But no one of these was the essential reason for its epoch-making importance. The reason why the meeting of the Governors with President Theodore Roosevelt in the White House in May, 1908, may well be regarded by future historians as a turning point in human history, the reason why it exerted and continues to exert a vital influence on the United States, on the nations of the whole world, is this: it was called to introduce, and it did introduce, to mankind the newly formulated policy of the conservation of natural resources.

---

1. Miller, *Seeking the Greatest Good*, explores the connections between Pinchot's ideas and those of Vogt and Osborne. Osborne was, in fact, one of the founders of the Pinchot Institute for Conservation in 1963.

Even at that time the profound significance of conservation was beginning to make itself felt. In announcing his intention of calling the Conference, the President said: "The conservation of natural resources is the fundamental problem. Unless we solve that problem it will avail us little to solve all others . . . It (the Conference) ought to be among the most important gatherings in our history, for none has had a more vital question to consider."

This conference set forth in impressive fashion, and it was the first national meeting in any country to set forth, the idea that the protection, preservation, and wise use of the natural resources of the earth is not a series of separate and independent tasks but a single problem. As the President [Theodore Roosevelt] said: "The various uses of our natural resources are so closely connected that they should be coordinated, and should be treated as parts of one coherent plan."

The Conference asserted that the conservation of natural resources is the one most fundamentally important problem of all. It drove home the basic truth that the planned and orderly development of the earth and all it contains is absolutely indispensable to the permanent prosperity of the human race. It spread far and wide the new proposition that the purpose of the conservation of natural resources is the greatest good for the greatest number for the longest time. It taught the people of the United States, and other peoples, the new meaning of the word conservation, which in its general application to natural resources was then generally unknown.

By defining, describing, and making known the new word and the new policy, by endowing it with the approval and support of the leaders of all the States, of the great industries, and of the nation itself, the Governor's Conference put conservation in a firm place in the knowledge and the thoughts of the people. From that moment conservation became an inseparable part of the national policy of the United States.

It is worth mention that this brilliant example of national foresight occurred not in a time of scarcity, not in a depression, but in a time of general abundance and well-being. The unanimous declaration of the Governors ended with this discerning admonition: "Let us conserve the foundations of our prosperity."

The conception which we know as conservation originated and was formulated in the United States Forest Service in the early winter of 1907. Conservation grew out of forestry. Thus, conservation was born without a name. But it had to be given a name before it could be introduced to the people.

After discussion among perhaps a half a dozen men, the name conservation was tentatively decided on. Thereupon it was submitted to and approved by Theodore Roosevelt, and the infant was christened accordingly. We know the growing youngster, thirty-three years old but growing still, by the same name today. The hold conservation has gained in these thirty-three years upon the civilized peoples of the world is little less than amazing. Today the soundness of the conservation policy is everywhere accepted as a matter of course.

The Conference of Governors recommended and was followed by the appointment of conservation commissions by a majority of the states, and of the National Conservation Commission, which later in January of 1909 submitted to the President the first national inventory of natural resources ever made. In February of the same year the North American Conservation Conference, the first international conference to consider the policy of conservation, met in Washington at the invitation of President Theodore Roosevelt.

In his address to the Conference in the White House the President made this highly significant statement: "In international relations the great feature of the growth of the last century has been the gradual recognition of the fact that instead of its being normally to the interest of one nation to see another depressed, it is normally to the interest of each nation to see the others elevated . . . I believe that the movement that you this day initiate is one of the utmost importance to this hemisphere and may become of the utmost importance to the world at large."

The North American Conservation Conference declared that the movement for the conservation of natural resources on the continent of North America "is of such a nature and of such general importance that it should become world-wide in its scope." Therefore it suggested to the President "that all nations should be invited to join together in conference on the subject of world resources and their inventory, conservation, and wise utilization."

What the Conference thus recommended was, however, already under way. The President had foreseen that the North American Conference would be the precursor of a world conference. Accordingly, to quote Elihu Root, then Secretary of State: "By an aide-memoir in January last (1909), the principal governments were informally sounded to ascertain whether they would look with favor upon an invitation to send delegates to such a conference. The responses so far have been uniformly favorable, and the conference of Washington has suggested to the President that a similar general conference be called by him. The President feels, therefore, that it is timely to initiate the suggested world conference for the conservation of natural resources, by a formal invitation."

With the concurrence of the Netherlands, invitations were sent out to fifty-eight nations to meet at the Peace Palace in The Hague in September 1909. Thirty of the nations, including Great Britain, France, Germany, Canada, and Mexico, had already accepted when President Taft, who succeeded President Roosevelt on March 4, 1909, killed the plan.

Two attempts have been made to revive it. At the end of the War of 1914–18, President Wilson, at the suggestion of Colonel House, took steps toward securing world-wide cooperation in the conservation and distribution of natural resources. Unfortunately, nothing came of it.

During President Hoover's administration a group of nearly two hundred leading citizens from all parts of the United States urged him in a public petition to take action along the same general line. Again nothing came of it.

But these checks notwithstanding, the conservation problem remains the fundamental human problem. Without natural resources, no human life is possible. Without abundant natural resources civilized life can neither be developed nor maintained. To the human race, land is the basic natural resource. The demand for new territory, made by one nation against another, is a demand for additional natural resources; and it is not necessary to point out how many times this demand has plunged nations into war.

In view of the forgoing, I have a definite plan to suggest—a plan for the permanent peace through international cooperation in the conservation and distribution of natural resources.

National life everywhere is built on the foundation of natural resources. Throughout human history the exhaustion of these resources and the need of new supplies have been among the greatest causes of war.

A just and permanent world peace is vital to the best interests of all nations. When the terms which will end the present war are considered, the neutral nations should be in a position to assist in finding the way to such a peace. That being so, it would be wise to prepare in time.

The proposal is that the nations of the Americas prepare now for an endeavor to bring all nations together, at the right moment, in common effort for conserving the natural resources of the earth, and for assuring to each nation access to the raw materials it needs, without recourse to war.

In all countries some natural resources are being depleted or destroyed. Needless waste or destruction of necessary resources anywhere threatens, or will threaten, sooner or later, the welfare and security of people everywhere. Conservation is clearly a world necessity, not only for enduring prosperity but also for permanent peace.

No nation is self-sufficient in essential raw materials. The welfare of every nation depends on access to natural resources which it lacks. Fair access to natural resources from other nations is therefore an indispensable condition of permanent peace.

War is still an instrument of national policy for the safeguarding of natural resources or for securing them from other nations. Hence international cooperation in conserving, utilizing, and distributing natural resources to the mutual advantage of all nations might well remove one of the most dangerous of all obstacles to a just and permanent world peace.

The conservation and fair access to needed raw materials are steps toward the common good to which all nations must in principle agree. Since the American nations are less dependent on imported natural resources than European nations, and since they are already engaged in broadening international trade through negotiated agreements, their initiative to such ends would be natural and appropriate.

The problem of permanent peace includes, of course, great factors which the foregoing proposal does not cover. But it does cover that fact which is certainly, in the long run, the most potent of them all.

If the forgoing proposal is adopted, facts in support of it will be needed, and a plan for assembling them. The formulation of a general policy and a specific program of action would follow.

Facts of each nation separately, for groups of nations, and for the whole world might well be assembled under the general classes of forests, waters, lands, minerals, and wild-life. In very brief outline they should include: resources in existence; consumption; probable duration; waste; conservation, if any; necessary reserves; available surplus; present interdependence of nations in natural resources (raw materials), with the origin, destination, and quantities of imports and exports; present barriers to "fair access"; and sources of pressures upon nations to acquire natural resources.

The information just outlined undoubtedly exists in sufficient detail for the present purpose, and can be put together without original investigation. It could be done through the creation of a Commission appointed for that purpose representing all the American nations. . . .

Formulation by the Commission of a plan and of recommendations to the American governments for a general policy and a specific program of action, including the presentation of the plan when prepared to neutral and belligerent nations, would follow.

Such a Commission would be of immense and lasting value to the American nations. It could not but advance their interests, both individual and mutual, in addition to opening a road toward a workable basis for permanent peace.

Finally, the situation in Europe and in Asia suggests that action for the purpose outlined above was never more necessary than at present.

PART THREE

GOVERNING THE KEYSTONE STATE

Gifford Pinchot did not suffer fools gladly, and he was delighted to let them know that he did not. Certainly that is how it must have sounded in January 1927, when in the final days of his first term as Pennsylvania's Governor, he stood before the General Assembly and denounced it in no uncertain terms: "After four years in a position to learn the facts, I am going out of office with the most hearty contempt not only for the morals and intentions, but also for the minds of the gang politicians of Pennsylvania."[1]

The audience gasped, but the pugilistic Pinchot was just warming up. The "gangster is no wizard. He is powerless to play any game but his own." Such myopia played into Pinchot's hands: "Because it never occurs to him to tell the people the truth, it never occurs to him that anyone else will tell the truth. From the beginning the most effective thing I could do to deceive the gang was to lay all my cards on the table and say precisely what I meant. They never got used to it."

His opponents had never gotten used to the fact that he had won the governorship in 1922 or that he would sweep into office once more in 1930. Blunt, ambitious, and charismatic, the maverick Pinchot loved nothing more than to prove his critics and enemies—and he had a goodly share of both—wrong. Those qualities were among the reasons why voters supported his candidacy. There are others. However scorching his rhetoric, however moralistic his temperament, Pinchot was an adept administrator, an innovative thinker, and an engaging personality. These qualities led his maternal grandfather, Amos Eno, a mega-developer in New York City, to urge his grandson to join the family business and make a fortune.

Gifford's parents had other ideas: they encouraged their talented child, who loved tramping in the woods, to become the nation's first trained forester. By the time he was forty, Pinchot had created an entire profession. Yet to bring these administrative chops to Harrisburg required a fight. As an ally of Theodore Roosevelt, for whom he had worked as the nation's chief forester, Pinchot, like his mentor, ruffled lots of Republican feathers during the bruising 1912 Bull Moose presidential campaign. As payback, for the next decade the state GOP blocked this radical upstart's political aspirations. Pinchot learned this reality the hard way: When he ran for the U.S. Senate in 1914, the Old Guard crushed his inaugural foray into state politics.

Pinchot realized he needed to build his own base. Drawing on his considerable skills as a forester, in 1919 he joined the Pennsylvania State Grange and served as chair of the farm organization's conservation com-

---

1. Message of Governor Gifford Pinchot, January 4, 1927, 52.

mittee. This gave him a platform from which to speak about forest-related matters and, not incidentally, on behalf of farm families. After a series of inspections of the state's forests—whose condition he found lacking—Pinchot issued a series of criticisms of the State Forestry Commission and its management ethos, and most especially of its politically appointed commissioner, Robert S. Conklin. While tweaking Conklin's lack of forestry knowledge, he also argued for a rapid expansion of the number of state forests through the issuance of bonds and a ramping up of the department's firefighting capacity. His criticism engendered a swelling controversy that ultimately led Conklin to resign and Governor William C. Sproul to tender an offer to Pinchot to become the new head of the commission. In March 1920 he accepted, leading Sproul to exult, "I have commandeered Mr. Pinchot's services. We have in him a citizen, who is the foremost figure in forestry in the United States, and I thought we should have the benefit of his services at home. Mr. Pinchot has been used to handling national problems but Pennsylvania is an empire in itself."[2]

Pinchot made good on his promise to reconstruct the forestry commission and the lands it managed, generating reams of positive press about his bureaucratic reforms, the establishment of an updated fire-protection system, and a marked uptick in employee morale. He knew what he was doing, and the state forests and those who made use of them benefitted from his expertise.

That success had a political payoff—Pinchot was no longer an outsider but someone with a demonstrable record of achievement on the Commonwealth's behalf. This did not endear him to the Republican Party, however, and it closed ranks against him after he announced his candidacy for governor in April 1922. This intense opposition forced Pinchot and his wife, Cornelia Bryce Pinchot, to develop a remarkable work-around. Using Cornelia's statewide contacts among women's groups, building a network of other disadvantaged voters—Prohibitionists, laborers, African Americans, Jews, and farm families—and stumping in every county but one, Pinchot shocked the establishment by winning the primary. Because Pennsylvania was essentially a one-party state, this victory ensured that he would win the general election that November.

The shock waves reverberated across the next four years. Pinchot slashed the budget, pulled the state out of debt, funded an old-age pension program, and bolstered support for K–12 education. He also negotiated the nation's first multistate clean water compact. A teetotaler, Pinchot

2. Sproul quoted in Harold T. Pinkett, *Gifford Pinchot: Private and Public Forester* (Urbana: University of Illinois Press, 1970), 136.

rigorously enforced Prohibition and confronted the public utilities industry, a "power monopoly" he blamed for corrupting Pennsylvania politics.
The "gang" could not wait for Pinchot to leave town.

They were in luck, if only briefly. Because at that time governors could
not succeed themselves, Pinchot had to step down in January 1927, but
not before blasting the powers-that-be in his final message to the Assembly. Then he came back, once again winning the Republican gubernatorial
primary in the spring of 1930 and the general election in November. Huge
challenges awaited him during his second term. The Great Depression was
hammering Pennsylvania particularly hard, due to its heavily industrialized economy, leaving more than two million people unemployed and
destitute. The Pinchot administration responded fast: innovative schemes
such as rebuilding roads and reforesting clear-cut landscapes gave people
work and inspiration. New York governor Franklin Roosevelt took note,
and after winning the 1932 presidential election asked Pinchot how to scale
up these projects nationally. The now legendary Civilian Conservation
Corps owes much of its origins to Pennsylvania's "Little New Deal."

Pinchot also deserves considerable credit for his tough assessment of
the Depression's political impact. "The millions are tired of being at the
mercy of the over-rich," he thundered in his 1935 message to the General
Assembly, asserting that they had rejected the "cruel, selfish, and hateful
doctrine of each man for himself." At long last, Pinchot said, "humanity
is coming into its rights."

He knew that that struggle would be a long one—reason enough that
Pinchot's energetic and controversial political career still captivates.

The Reclamation of Pennsylvania's Desert

Forestry gave Pinchot a platform in Pennsylvania, a critical boost to his political ambitions. There were a number of problems with the state's once-thick woods, and in this 1920 essay Pinchot applied many of the ideas that he had employed while chief of the U.S. Forest Service to the need to restore Penn's Woods.

Originally published in *Cornell Forester* 1 (1920): 7–8.

————————————
————————————

Pennsylvania was once covered with large, dense, and extremely productive forests. The large have become small, the dense have become open, and the productive have become waste. Today there are five million acres of idle mountain land in Pennsylvania too rough and rocky for the plow. This is the Pennsylvania desert.

Many agents helped create these vast stretches of idle land, but man played the leading role. It took him but a few generations to remove the original forest, which required many years of Nature's best efforts to build up. Where once stood the best stands of timber in the United States east of Idaho, there remain today only wide stretches of bare and barren mountain land. This is our meager heritage. It has little present value, but many fruitful possibilities, if handled in a constructive manner.

To let the land lay idle is an economic crime. It is the duty of Pennsylvania to restore these vast areas of desolation to productive value. This is the work of the Department of Forestry, which began in 1893 as a division in the Department of Agriculture, and is now 27 years old.

The first thing I did after taking charge was to ask members of the field force to give me a plan for the reorganization of the Department. They did it promptly and well. These recommendations resulted in a complete recasting and marked simplification of the entire organization of the Department, the effect of which shows already, for the morale of the personnel is improving and the output is increasing. This is important, for there is much work ahead and only a few men, little money, and meager equipment available with which to do it.

Four bureaus will handle the executive work. They are Protection, Operation, Silviculture, and Lands. In addition the Forest Academy and the offices of Maintenance and Information have their special work.

The most important duty ahead is the suppression of forest fires. Every other kind of work must give way to it while the fire season is on. The entire state has been divided into forty fire districts, each in charge of a trained forester who has direct charge of fire wardens, patrolmen, observers, and other employees. Forest protection is needed in every section of the state, for there is no part of the Commonwealth of Pennsylvania without forest land.

We are doing our best to eliminate fire hazards, and to hold responsible all persons, including companies and corporations, who through carelessness or negligence, cause forest fires. The forest fire laws in Pennsylvania are in many respects good and strong, although not yet complete. They will help do the work, but we are trying to get results through friendly cooperation, rather than by costly lawsuits. Public attention has been widely called to the need and value of forest fire prevention, and conferences are being held with forest land owners and representatives of railroads, mining companies, and other organizations interested.

To stop forest fires is a large order, but even a few men who mean business can do a lot to overcome them and to restore a green and growing cover of valuable forest trees upon the barren hillsides of the Keystone State.

A budget for the Department and each individual forest has been prepared. A re-grouping of State Forests into units of about 50,000 acres each is now under way. The present area in charge of a forester averages about 20,000 acres. This increase will permit a more economical and efficient use of the working force and reduce overhead charges. A new system of inspection is in operation, which will help to systematize the various forest activities, promote efficiency, and prevent misunderstanding.

As yet, only a good beginning has been made, but the outlook is promising. Much important work will be done at a summer meeting of all State Foresters, which will be held on one of the State Forests. A committee of Foresters has been appointed to revise the rules and regulations of the Department, and will submit its report at the summer meeting.

Pennsylvania's Desert ought to be bought as an investment by the State, for that is the only sure way to reclaim the five million acres which are now producing nothing of value.

Hitherto, the policy of the Department has been to consider the purchase of those lands only which were offered for sale by their owners. Now it is proposed to locate by actual investigation on the ground the forest land which is producing nothing, so that when funds become available, the Forest Commission will be ready to proceed to purchase.

The purchase of the Pennsylvania Desert will be an investment, not an expense. The million acres of forest already purchased by the State at an average price of $2.28 per acre has already more than doubled in value.

In a preliminary draft of the new constitution there is a provision that authorizes bonding the Commonwealth for $25,000,000 for the purchase of such forest land. If, when the time comes, serial bonds are issued for the purpose, the interest, before many years are past, will be carried by the lands bought, and before the whole series has been paid off, the purchase will represent a net gain for the state.

The Influence of Women in Politics

Perhaps more than any other male politician in the United States in the 1920s, Pinchot benefitted from and spoke eloquently in support of the power of women in the voting booth. Female voters were an important constituency in his two successful runs for the governor's mansion, and while he acknowledges their impact on his success in this article, he also speaks to the larger question of women's transformative role in the nation's civic life. He assumed that it would be profound; he was right.

Source: Box 950, Gifford Pinchot Papers, Library of Congress; a revised version appeared in *Ladies' Home Journal*, September 1922, 12, 116.

To speak of the influence of women in politics is misleading. Women have a part in political affairs, not a mere influence upon them. They are neither outsiders nor mere onlookers at the political game. Yesterday that was not true. Yesterday women were in fact outsiders and spectators, who sometimes amused themselves with a mild partisanship or external participation, and occasionally took part in the dinner-party and teacup political maneuvering whereby, according to romantic historians, momentous political issues were sometimes determined. They do not have to be content with that today. The devious times of indirection are over-past. Woman today exerts a power, not a mere influence, in politics—an independent power co-equal with the power of man. She has stepped out of her orchestra seat and become the leading woman in the play.

It may well be asked in what manner the new player is conducting herself, how apt she is to seize the spirit of the piece, and how effective in carrying out her part. How does she compare individually with the veteran leading man, and what is the relative merit of his work and her work in the company?

To change the simile, one fact has been demonstrated beyond peradventure, which is that women in politics play an absolutely clean game. They have brought the highest standards into a contest that has commonly been sullied by shady and evil practices. They are not only opposed to everything that is underhand and questionable, but ready to take the field actively against it. That is the first and perhaps the most fundamental of all the facts about women in politics.

If the advent of women into politics means the purification of political methods and the application of moral principles to government her advent is an unmixed blessing. The foundation of health and efficiency in all human affairs is honesty and courage, and these are the very qualities which women have brought and will continue to bring into American public life.

The World War was followed by a widely recognized letdown in morale all over the world. We have had and we still have our share in this inheritance of debilitated character. Many remedies have been proposed, and relief has been sought in many quarters. My own conviction is that deliverance is coming to the American people mainly through the agency of American womanhood.

My conviction is based on the striking contributions lately made by women to political progress not only in Pennsylvania but in many other states. Women like to clean the political house as much as they do the physical house in which they live. If they are given half a chance, and they are extremely likely to take that chance whether they are given it or not, I am inclined to think they will end by cleaning up the politics of the whole earth.

I do not mean that the function of mere man will be or should be reduced to zero. As a member of that sex I insist that we are not yet obsolete; but at this stage of the world's history it is certainly fair to recognize that man as a political leader is floundering about and needs even more than 50 per cent of cooperation from womankind.

The part played by women in the Republican primary contest in Pennsylvania this spring, which resulted in my nomination for governor, furnishes an apt illustration of how women handle political questions. No one, I hope, will take offense if I describe what happened as nearly as may be from the point of view of the historical record and with an honest effort to avoid all bias or ill will.

Senator Penrose, the veteran leader of the Republican Party in Pennsylvania, died December 31 [1921]. He left behind him a number of small yet powerful groups contesting among themselves for the Penrose mantle. The time was therefore ripe for a new deal among the politicians. It was also ripe for a new deal in the politics of the state—time for the people to take a hand and put new blood into the party organization.

When it was suggested that the Chief Forester of Pennsylvania should become a candidate for governor at the primary election it was seen at once that the only way to win was to bring to his support the majority of the women voters.

The Republican women had not been thoroughly amalgamated into the various parts of the old machine, because they could not be held in any organization merely for the organization's sake. They demanded a definite purpose—the nearer to a crusade the better. They wanted something to do in which they could believe with all their hearts and for which they could work and work hard, and they found it in the promise of one candidate to let in the light and clean up the mess at Harrisburg. The primary interest of women in politics, so far as my experience goes, is in moral issues. The keynote of the Pennsylvania campaign was such an issue—to restore our political standards to an honorable plane. It was worth fighting for, and the women threw themselves heart and soul into the fight.

When the candidacy of the writer was announced on March thirteenth [1922] he was wholly without organization support. The old Progressive movement, in which he ran for United States senator in 1914, was quiescent. The Republican party was reunited, although there were no less than four regular candidates for the governorship, each representing a different faction of the machine.

In order to eliminate the newcomer, who represented no faction of the machine, the opposition tried to unite on a single candidate, and in the end succeeded in doing so, although one of the retiring contestants, himself representing the demand for better things in politics, threw his influence away from the regular choice and toward the independent candidate.

From the beginning women had a most important part in the fight. Mrs. Barclay H. Warburton led the way. In her capacity as vice chairman of the Republican State Committee, she led the vice chairmen of most of the county committees, who are women, against the machine candidate. With a liberal-minded and courageous woman as leader of the Republican women, they had from the beginning a controlling part in the campaign. It is no secret that the wife of the candidate [Cornelia Bryce Pinchot] was among the most active and effective of all the workers who enlisted the aid of the women voters.

Most of the women were interested not in a political fight as such, but in a cause that was pre-eminently moral. They knew that the old-time politicians were more than indifferent to humanitarian laws affecting children and women. On the other hand, they knew the long-held position of the independent candidate on these questions. You do not have to debate such issues with women. It is enough for them to know the facts.

The opposition could find hardly a single woman prominent in civic and club life among its supporters, while literally thousands of such women rallied to the independent banner.

The Women's Christian Temperance Union of Pennsylvania gave its official endorsement on the ground that the independent candidate favored the strict enforcement of the Prohibition law along with all other laws upon the statute books. This body of women is well organized throughout the state and became a powerful factor in the final result. They worked most effectively as an organization, and as individuals as well.

This was the first primary campaign for the governorship of Pennsylvania in which women had the right of ballot. They had voted in the last presidential election and in minor political battles. But they had been treated contemptuously by the machine, and they were properly resentful.

The machine politicians had as low an estimate of the political strength of women as they had of their intelligence. They ignored what they called "the petticoat vote" and employed tactics against the independent candidate which would have thrown the women to his support in overwhelming numbers if they had not been for him already for other reasons. The use of mud and poison gas is not regarded by women as a part of civilized methods of political warfare. The elimination of such gross, cheap and unimaginative methods from political campaigns will be one of the effects of the entrance of women into politics. We shall have to thank them for that, and it will be a great thing to thank them for.

In striking contrast with the stand of the machine, the independents frankly addressed much of their appeal directly to the women, realizing not only that they formed potentially a full half of the voting strength, but that their whole tendency was to set right above expediency and a moral issue above loyalty to the machine.

We had many very able women organizers, natural leaders, who toured the counties throughout the state, speaking everywhere and using every legitimate means of persuasion, and so far as mere activity was concerned, the women surpassed the men; but there was this important difference, unusual if not unique in American politics, that the vast majority of the women were not paid workers, but volunteers actuated solely by a lofty desire to serve the cause in which they believed. This was true not solely of the women who could afford to give their time and effort, but of very many of those who could not. No one can know the facts without deep admiration for what they did.

A new thing in politics was the telephone campaign carried on by women all over the state. These women called up on the wire not only their neighbors, but in many cases every woman whose name in the telephone book indicated that she was the head of a household. They went through the phone book alphabetically. It was a most effective method, especially when used, as it was, in conjunction with house-to-house visits.

The primary election was held May sixteenth. About one million votes were cast, or something approaching one-half of the possible total Republican vote—a fairly large percentage when compared to the usual primary contest. What proportion of women took part cannot be estimated with any approach to accuracy, but we know that in many counties the number of women registered was strictly comparable to the men, and the woman vote was unquestionably large.

The independent candidate for the governorship won in the primary. In Pennsylvania the Republican nomination is practically equivalent to election. The women this year have made it the first step in the political house cleaning which is yet to come.

It is time to forget, so far as the fundamental facts will permit, that there is a distinction between men and women in politics. Women are citizens first, and women only as a distinctive character in that class. The interests of men and women in government are equal. Women are equal partners in everything that concerns the state. It is true of course that as the functions of equal partners in a business enterprise are not the same and as the duties of husband and wife differ in the equal partnership of the home, so the functions of men and women are not at all points alike in their contribution to the public welfare. But they are equal partners nonetheless.

Despite the old idea, women are realists, not sentimentalists. The things that count with them, even more than the things that count with men, are the real things, not the fictions. They care for the substance and not for the shadow. No man is going to win either a state or national election hereafter who does not have the women back of him.

One of the first and most important issues of any campaign today is law enforcement. No matter whether you are wet or dry, the law is the law, and to let one statute be broken openly weakens law and order all along the line. We must clean up politics and keep them clean. We must maintain such instruments of democracy as the open primary. A return to the old convention system would tend especially to the virtual disfranchisement of women.

Perhaps the most remarkable fact about equal suffrage, one which is unexpected and disturbing to some men, is the workmanlike way in which women are entering into and taking possession of their share in public affairs. Already these newcomers are veterans in a field which has been the exclusive possession of men during the greater part of human history.

"Look," say these puzzled skeptics, "women have had no experience with public life. We know the game of politics and so did our fathers before us. But the women seem to know it without having to get us to teach them. How did it happen?"

Here is the reason, it seems to me: Politics is a part of the way we run government in America. Government is one of the arts of management. It is the assembling and handling of men, women and things for a certain purpose, which is or ought to be the general advantage. Good ideals and good management together make good government. In theory, at least, the ideals are always good, so that good government as a matter of practical fact usually comes down to a question of good management.

Why do women find themselves so much at home in the complicated questions involved in management and government? An ill-natured man, or a man less happily married, might say that women are the managing sex. The fact is that women, far more than men, are trained in the difficult art of management by the very nature of their daily lives. Most men are not in business for themselves. They earn a living by carrying out the directions of other men. They are untrained in the art of management. Nearly every mature woman, on the contrary, is a highly trained manager. Most women are mothers, and one of the essential functions of a mother is that of a manager of children. It is her daily part to make and to lead her children to take part in making that endless series of decisions which finally determines their character and position in life. A mother is the most important of all managers. Her decisions make human nature what it is.

Furthermore, most women are housekeepers, and every housekeeper is a manager, and her own boss. Most of the family expenditures pass through her hands. If the two ends meet at the end of the year it is her doing. The health of the whole family, physically and spiritually, is in her charge. The comfort and complexion of the family life are of her making. She is the manager.

Now the central fact about a manager is that he or she is responsible; and there is no educator like responsibility. Women have been carrying responsibility until it has become second nature. It is no wonder that they find it easy to extend the application of the principle they have been trained in to public life. Women take easily to public affairs because they have been drilled in management and have acquired the habit of responsibility. Moreover, a woman who has been her own boss in the affairs of daily life is extremely likely to remain her own boss in public life also.

It happens that the two things the women are especially trained to secure, namely, economy in expenditures and efficiency in getting results, are two of the great needs of our national and state governments just now.

Women are coming into full action in the public affairs of this country at just the right time. I shall miss my guess if they do not do for Pennsylvania and all other states what they have long done so well for the family, which after all is merely a state in miniature.

Inaugural Address

A seasoned administrator by the time of his election as governor in November 1922, and an astute politician (not least because he managed to get elected running against the party establishment), Pinchot delivered a tough-minded inaugural address that underscored his commitment to the issues that mattered most to those who voted for him. Pinchot's was a commitment born of Theodore Roosevelt's progressivism and fueled by the new governor's faith that he could usher in an age of "political righteousness."

Address delivered at Harrisburg, January 16, 1923. A shorter version appeared in *American Review of Reviews*, February 1923, 171–73.

———————

———————

The people of Pennsylvania have declared for a new order in the government of their commonwealth. Their decision was forecast in the primary and confirmed in the general election. Their mandate is binding and final. It has become the duty of all their public servants to carry that mandate into effect.

The decision of the people to establish a new order was made concrete in form and direction by the approval of the Republican majority given to the platform upon which I ran in the primary campaign. The program thus adopted as sound Republican policy was my public pledge, if elected, to use every power of the Governorship in an honest effort:

To drive all saloons out of Pennsylvania.

To prevent and punish bootlegging.

To maintain and secure good laws for the protection of working children, women, and men.

To safeguard the industries of Pennsylvania and promote the prosperity of the State.

To advance the interests of the farmers, who feed us all.

To give our children the best schools in America.

To check centralization and give more home rule to cities, counties, townships, and school districts.

To maintain the direct primary and protect the rights of women voters.

To meet the just needs of those who served in the World War.

To revise and equalize taxes, establish a budget system, and reorganize the State Government on a business basis.

To keep the expenses of the State within its income.

To get a dollar's worth of service for every dollar spent.

In addition I said that as Governor I would appoint no one to the public office whom I knew to be unfit, I would move to Harrisburg and be on the job, and I would earnestly strive to give due consideration and a Roosevelt square deal to every man, woman, and child in State.

The same platform, without change of any sort, became the program which the Republican Party submitted for the approval of all the voters at the general election. It was approved by the largest vote ever given to a Governor in Pennsylvania. It has thereby become the declared policy of the Commonwealth and the chart of the new order upon which the Government of this State is about to enter.

As I undertake the duties of the great office to which the people of Pennsylvania have elected me, I here solemnly repeat to them the pledge made in the primary campaign and reasserted in the general election. That pledge is not a promise to accomplish all things that are necessary or desirable for the advantage of our people. It is a solemn undertaking to use in good faith, and use to the utmost, every legitimate means to accomplish the purposes of the Republican Party and the people of Pennsylvania as they were adopted and declared by them in the recent elections.

In addition to my platform pledge, I repeat in like manner every other pledge or promise made in either campaign. I have made no pledge or promise of any sort except in public. I enter upon the Governorship completely unhampered by any private or personal engagement, understanding, or undertaking whatsoever, and wholly free to serve the Commonwealth according to the will of the people and the dictates of my own conscience.

I was elected to carry out the program briefly set forth above. That is my first duty. It has become evident, from the number of courteous and attractive invitations to speak which are daily received, that I must choose between doing that duty and talking about doing it. However hard it may be, however much I may regret to decline, there is but one choice to make. I must stick to my work and let the talking go.

State Finances and Organization

The discussion of many questions which might well be considered here must be deferred to future messages to the Legislature, but there are three matters of prime importance which require brief mention.

The first is the financial condition of the State Government.

Appropriations in Pennsylvania have exceeded revenues in the last few years. Therefore we have accumulated liabilities amounting to many millions which must be paid off before the State can meet its bills as they fall due. Neither sound business principles nor the honor of the State will permit us to delay the necessary readjustment, however uncomfortable that readjustment may be. We must return to the healthy basis of pay-as-you-go at the earliest possible moment.

In accordance with my campaign pledge, I shall submit a budget to the Legislature in the near future, and shall refuse to approve any appropriation bill, or any item in any appropriation bill, that does not fall squarely within the estimated revenues of the Commonwealth. We are going to live within our income, as every family should.

The second question is the reorganization of the State Government.

Much of the machinery by means of which the Commonwealth serves its people has become antiquated, ineffective, and wasteful of the people's money. It needs to be recast into a form that will make possible a dollar's worth of service for every dollar spent. That is impossible now. Such recasting, to be successful, will require extended study, and prolonged practical attention. It cannot be done hastily if it is to be done well. For that reason it will not be possible, in the time we have, to prepare and submit for legislative action, a plan completely worked out, but only an outline by Departments, leaving the lesser parts to be filled in by the Executive. That outline is in preparation.

Enforcement of the Volstead Act

The third question relates to the liquor traffic.

Power and responsibility for enforcing the Volstead Law rest in the Nation and also in the State. Under the Eighteenth Amendment the two have concurrent jurisdiction. Both are at fault for the intolerable situation which confronts us.

A general conviction exists throughout this Commonwealth not only that the Volstead Act is not enforced but that no vigorous effort has ever been made to enforce it. Our people have seen men known to be opposed to the enforcement of the law selected to compel obedience to it on the part of others. They are told that appointments to the position of enforcement agent are treated as political spoils, and that politicians opposed to all that the law stands for are permitted to name such agents. They believe that persons high in official place are constantly and openly violating the spirit if not the letter of the law, and winking at its violation by others. They understand that liquor is sold almost as freely and openly as it was before the passage of the Eighteenth Amendment.

With such beliefs in mind, the people are necessarily led to conclude that the law is systematically disregarded by those whose peculiar duty it is to respect or enforce it, and in consequence the general disregard for all law grows steadily worse.

I regard the present flagrant failure to enforce the Volstead Law as a blot on the good name of Pennsylvania and the United States. If allowed to continue it will amount to a serious charge against the fitness of our people for genuine self-government. I share in the belief that no determined concerted effort to enforce the law has yet been made, and I propose not only to press with all my power for the abolition of the saloon but also to make sure that the Government of this State takes its full and effective part in such an effort.

Pennsylvania must either control the criminals who are openly breaking the law or be controlled by them. With all good citizens I believe that this Commonwealth is greater and more powerful than any band of lawbreakers whatsoever, and I intend to act on that belief.

This administration will be dry. The Executive Mansion will be dry, and the personal practice of the Governor and his family will continue to be dry, in conformity to the spirit and letter of the Eighteenth Amendment.

The law is the law. It is the foundation of order, safety, and prosperity, and of the Commonwealth itself. Every State official takes oath, and is in honor bound, to obey it. I shall expect and demand from every public servant appointed by me, or subject to removal by me, from the highest to the lowest, entire and ungrudging obedience to the Eighteenth Amendment and the Volstead Law. They are part of the law of the land.

Roosevelt Progressivism

I was a follower of Roosevelt while he was living. I am his follower no less to-day, and his great soul still leads this people on the road to better things. The movement which resulted in my election is the direct descendant of the Roosevelt Progressive movement of 1912. The point of view was the same, the specific platform planks were largely identical, and the popular support came mainly from similar sources. Both were based squarely on the proposition that the public good comes first. This administration has taken that proposition as its foundation stone, and upon it hopes and intends to erect a structure of honest and effective service to all the people, without distinction of race, creed, sex, or political complexion.

A New Birth of Political Righteousness

The breakdown of law enforcement is proof enough, if other proof were lacking, that Pennsylvania needs a new birth of political righteousness.

The responsibility lies not alone at the door of the politicians. It lies also at the door of the people, who for years have tolerated in their public servants standards of conduct known to be indefensible, and under which no private business could survive. The people have suffered the Commonwealth to be badly served. This is the essential evil, and here must be the fundamental change.

Pennsylvania is too great a Commonwealth to be permanently satisfied with less than the best. Her people are too sound at heart, her resources and her industries are too commanding, her place in the sisterhood of States too high, to permit us to consider for a moment the acceptance of any standards but the highest, any procedure but the most thoroughly approved. The Government of Pennsylvania must be in detail what the Commonwealth is in general—the leader and exemplar of the Nation. Nothing inferior is good enough for the Keystone State.

My sole ambition is to help toward making our State Government what it ought to be, to serve the people honestly and with intelligence, to contribute at least by a little to the safety, honor, and welfare of our Commonwealth. I desire and earnestly entreat the good-will, the cooperation, and the support of all well-disposed citizens, men and women alike. With their assistance, and above all with the blessing of Him in whose hands are the plans of men and the fate of Nations, I shall approach my task with eagerness to be useful, with determination to be fair, and with strong confidence in ultimate success.

The Blazed Trail of Forest Depletion

During his first term, Pinchot watched with dismay as one logging town after another shut down, leaving a growing number of abandoned communities and unemployed workers whose families had depended on their wages. His criticism of industrial lumbering operations that had cut and run their way across the state—"the American lumberman has reaped, but he has not sown"—foreshadowed his efforts in his second term, during the Great Depression, to restabilize these communities by funding reforestation projects.

Source: Box 945, Gifford Pinchot Papers, Library of Congress; a revised version appeared in *American Forests* 29, no. 354 (June 1923): 323–28, 374.

———————

———————

The people of the United States are the most wasteful in the world—wasteful in living, wasteful in manufacturing, and wasteful in handling their natural resources. The annual wastage in our homes, factories, fields, and forests is enormous.

In Pioneer days, the forests were an obstacle to development. They had to be removed to make way for agriculture, which was a more necessary and profitable use of the land. Among the early settlers, the destruction of the forest by ax, saw, and fire was accepted as normal and necessary. It was good business and sound practice for them to destroy forests and open fields, but unfortunately the same clear-cutting as were used for plowland in the valleys were also employed for the woodland on the mountains. As a result, we have inherited almost endless stretches of barren mountain slopes which are producing nothing of any value. The only satisfactory crop these lands can produce is a tree crop, and it is our business to see to it that this land is kept at work at the only job for which it is fitted.

Forest depletion has wrought havoc in all parts of the world. In this country the economic consequences of forest destruction are felt chiefly in the older settled parts—that is, in the regions where the forests have been cut over again and again and the population is relatively dense.

New England, which was at one time the center of the American lumber industry, now has left but 5 per cent of her original forests. After the best and more accessible forests of the Northeast were cut out, the lumber industry moved to Pennsylvania. Here it operated for many years, but in time lumber production began to wane in the only state that embodies the word "forest" in her name. Then the Lake States became the center of lumber production. As soon as they passed the peak of production the lumber industry moved to the pine forests of the South, where the pinnacle of production was reached about 1909. Since then there has been a wholesale shift of lumbering to the Pacific coast, where most of our remaining timber is now found. The three states of Washington, Oregon, and California contain about one-half of the timber still standing in the whole country, and fully 60 per cent of the timber supply of our country occurs west of the prairies.

The original forests of Pennsylvania covered 28,650,000 acres and contained over 500,000,000,000 board feet of lumber and 286,500,000 cords of wood. Now less than 25,000 acres of original forest remain and there is left only one-twenty-fifth of the lumber and one-sixth of the cordwood that we once had. The average acre of original forest contained about 20,000 board feet of fine lumber. The forest acre that is now left in the state carries only about six cords of wood, most of which is small in size and inferior in quality. Only a small portion will make lumber.

In 1860 Pennsylvania exceeded all other states in lumber production. Now she holds eighteenth place and produces less than 2 per cent of the total lumber production of the country. Until 1890 Pennsylvania was able to supply her own timber needs and had a large balance to export. Now more than 80 per cent of the lumber she uses, 74 per cent of the pulp wood needed by the pulp mills, and 75 per cent of the timber required by the anthracite mines is imported from beyond her borders.

Pennsylvania's dependence upon outside sources for wood costs her people at least $100,000,000 a year, of which $25,000,000 is paid out for freight. The average person in the state consumes annually over 300 board feet of lumber, of which our forests are supplying only 58 board feet. In other words, the people of Pennsylvania are consuming six times as much lumber as their forests are now supplying.

During the last thirty years Pennsylvania has been depending upon other states to make up her wood deficit. It is evident now that these states cannot continue their wood-relief work much longer. Their supply is also giving out. It is clear that if the people of Pennsylvania want sufficient wood to meet their needs Pennsylvania must produce it. There is plenty of forest land in Pennsylvania—more than 13,000,000 acres—which, if handled properly, will satisfy all the wood needs of the people of the state. It is capable of producing annually at least 2,400,000,000 board feet of lumber and 4,500,000 cords of wood. This possible yield is greater than the largest annual output of the state in the banner year (1900) of lumbering in Pennsylvania.

For three centuries the American lumberman has been roving over the country. He is now approaching his end, for most of the timber has been cut. The lumberman did not consider the land. All he wanted was the wood. His business was making the wilderness yield a commodity of civilization, regardless of how it was produced or whether it could be renewed. If he could not get it at one place, he moved to another. The time is now come when he cannot move again, for he has no place to go. Where forests of great and glorious trees once stood, devastated hillsides now remain, and famished forest communities are struggling for an existence amidst the bleak stretches of unproductive stump land.

Let us not blunder along blindly with the false notion that we have no forest problem in urgent need of solution. The forest problem is at the very foundation of our national existence. The prosperity of our states, the welfare of our communities, and the lives of our citizens depend upon the products of the forest.

Let me tell you the story of a few typical lumber towns of Pennsylvania and you will see clearly the blazed trail of forest depletion.

Fifty years ago a vast and unbroken forest covered the extreme southwestern part of Tioga County, Pennsylvania. As late as 1870 only two families lived on the site that later became the busy lumbering town of Leetonia. Then lumbering was just beginning in the region and only white pine was cut. Other trees, such as hemlock, birch, beech, and maple, had no market value. As many as 10,000,000 board feet of white pine were taken out of the region about Leetonia in a single season and floated clown Cedar Run. In those days the choicest white pine brought from $3.00 to $3.50 per thousand board feet.

After most of the white pine about Leetonia had been cut out, a market developed for hemlock bark. The bark supply was so great that in 1879 a tannery, with an annual capacity of 3,000 cords, was established. Almost overnight the settlement of two families grew to a town of two hundred people. In 1882 a railroad came to town, and in 1897 a sawmill with a 6-foot band saw was added to the town's business equipment. This mill was operated continuously until 1913, when it was replaced by a larger and a better mill, with a daily capacity of 100,000 board feet.

Leetonia was at its best from 1913 to 1917. Then the town had a population of 500 people. Many men were at work in the woods preparing logs for the sawmill and peeling bark for the tannery. More men were employed at the sawmill and in the tannery.

In 1917 it became evident that the town was doomed, for the supply of wood and bark was beginning to give out. Each succeeding year the reserve supply became lower and lower. In the early winter of 1920 the bark supply was completely exhausted, and the tannery, which had been in operation continuously for more than 40 years—to be exact, since 1879—was closed down, and in 1921 the last log was cut at the sawmill.

The closing down of the only two industries of the town was the next to the last chapter in its existence. The last chapter was the sale of the whole town of seventy houses, including the tannery, the sawmill building, and 400 acres of land, for $6,500, the price of one modest city home. There was nothing left for the people to do but pack up and get out. This they did in a hurry, for in the fall of 1922—one year after the sawmill shut down—only four families remained in the town.

Three of the four families moved out in the spring of 1923. This left only one family—that of the Forest Ranger. Within a circle of six-mile radius only one other family resides. These two families are the only human inhabitants and the sole guardians of 200,000 acres of unbroken forest land that completely surrounds their modest mountain homes.

I know of no more necessary and honorable work for the citizens of any state than that of forest restoration. A bare beginning has been made at Leetonia. Just one Forest Ranger is now on the job. He has willingly separated himself from the rest of the world to assist in building up new and better forests. But he cannot handle the situation alone. More helpers will be needed as the work progresses, for vast areas of forest land are in urgent need of protection from forest fires, and a valuable forest growth must replace the scanty scrub on the hills that were formerly covered with dense stands of big trees.

Forty years ago Gardeau was a young and promising lumber town in northern Pennsylvania. The only industry the town ever had was a sawmill, which made and kept the town. It had a daily capacity of 200,000 board feet and remained in operation until 1899, when all the lumber was cut out and there was no more work for it to do. For twenty years the town was busy and prosperous. At its height 1,000 people lived there and in nearby camps.

In 1899, when all the forests around Gardeau were cut out completely, the sawmill had to close down. There was nothing left for the people to do but move. Most of them went about thirty miles northwest to Granere, where they started up another lumber town in the midst of equally fine forests. Today nothing is left of Granere and only five people live at Gardeau.

In 1893 virgin forests practically covered the hillsides overlooking the site that in a few years became the biggest and busiest lumber town that Pennsylvania ever had. It was just thirty years ago that the Lackawanna

Lumber Company broke ground for the town of Cross Fork. Then there were only five or six families in the entire valley. In 1895 a sawmill was erected. It burned down in 1897. Another one was built, which burned down in 1903. In the autumn of the same year a bigger and better mill was in full swing. Two years of lumber output of this big mill would more than encircle the globe with boards an inch thick and a foot wide. The sawmill was the heart of the town. The annual output of rough lumber was valued in the neighborhood of $1,000,000. In addition to the sawmill, a stave mill, a kindling mill, a shingle mill, and a hub factory helped to bring business to the town. Every part of the town was busy, but back beyond the town the forest was filled with men at work cutting logs and bringing them to the mills. Not less than 5,000 lumberjacks were engaged in the woods. The town itself had no less than seven hotels and its post-office was one of the few in Potter County that issued international money orders.

In the early days few people thought that the forests about Cross Fork would ever be cut out, but in April, 1909, the big sawmill was closed down, and by autumn of the same year the people were leaving the town in large groups. In the winter of 1912–13 the stave mill was closed and in the fall of 1913 the railroad discontinued service.

Almost overnight Cross Fork became a deserted village. Its decline was even more rapid than its rise. For a number of years the town was dead, but it is being resurrected again. Much of the land about the town has been purchased by the state, and forest restoration is now moving ahead. Where the lumber company left almost endless stretches of desolation, the Department of Forestry has developed valuable young forests.

For a short time the town of Norwich held a commanding place in the lumber industry of Pennsylvania. As late as 1909 the entire town site was covered with a dense stand of big hemlock trees. Individual acres were stocked with 50,000 board feet of lumber, and in addition yielded 25 cords of bark. Nowhere in the state were better stands of hemlock found. My friend and co-worker, Colonel Henry Shoemaker, who since his boyhood days has been studying the people and the forests of northern Pennsylvania, informs me that he saw the site of Norwich before the town was born, at its height, and after its death. He relates that the first chapter of the rise of this unique lumbering town was the erection of a few shacks and shanties and the building of a general store in a small opening cut out of the dense forest of big hemlocks. Late in the spring of 1910 tree-felling and bark-peeling began. Then followed the lumbering operations, the erection of the sawmill, and the building of houses. By 1912 a busy lumbering town was hard at work.

At its height the town had a population of 2,000 people. Many more men worked in the woods. They lived in shanties, shacks, and camps scattered throughout the Goodyear Lumber Company's holdings of 30,000 acres. The mainstay of the town was the sawmill, with a daily capacity of 300,000 board feet. It was regarded as the most modern and best equipped mill that ever operated in the State of Pennsylvania.

Near the sawmill was a kindling-wood plant, and beyond it was a stave mill and a hardwood distillation plant. To supply all these industries with raw material was a big job and required an enormous amount of equipment and an efficient organization. Over one hundred miles of logging railroads were maintained to bring the wood into the plants. In those days Norwich was a busy place. It turned out 90,000,000 board feet of lumber in a single year.

When lumbering operations started almost everybody believed that the timber supply was inexhaustible. The most conservative estimates made the timber supply sufficient for not less than 25 years. But that all predictions were incorrect became evident as early as 1917. Then it was seen that the town was doomed. Its active life was less than ten years, for the mill that started in the fall of 1912 closed down forever on August 20, 1921.

The story of Norwich is a forest tragedy. When the timber at Cross Fork was cut out the people went to Betula, and when no forests were left about Gardeau the people went to Granere. When the sawmill equipment was no longer needed at Leetonia, it was shipped to Kinzua; but when the supply of timber at Norwich gave out, in 1921, not a single place was left in Pennsylvania where the mill could be re-established, and the people of the town were left high and dry.

In the fall of 1922 less than twenty families remained in Norwich. All of the remaining workmen were employed in dismantling the mill, tearing down houses, and lifting railroad tracks. According to present plans, not a single human being will be left in the town after July, 1923. Discouragement and despair are written everywhere in the village—in the faces of the people as well as in the condition of tumble-down houses and grass-covered streets. The story of Norwich is the saddest chapter in the whole history of Pennsylvania lumbering.

The hillsides about Norwich today are bare. No trees of merchantable size remain, and in many places the young growth is sparse and weak. The utilization at Norwich was probably more complete than that of any other large lumbering operation in America. To use what is cut up to the last fragment is good business, but it is not enough. No provisions were made for forest renewal. Practically no old growth and only a thin sprinkling of inferior young growth is now present on the cut-over areas. The land is lying idle, although if it were given proper protection and care it is capable of producing crop after crop of valuable timber.

The best way to make this land produce wood is for the state to buy it. If handled properly, the 30,000 acres will produce annually 30,000 cords of wood or their equivalent. This amount of wood is sufficient to maintain a sawmill with dependent wood-using plants. It is easy now to see how much better and wiser it would have been if a mill with a daily capacity of 50,000 board feet had been erected at Norwich in place of the big mill, with a daily capacity of 300,000 board feet.

When operations started, in l910, it would have been possible to work out a permanent cutting plan whereby 13,000,000 board feet of lumber and 12,500 cords of wood could be cut annually. This would have insured a permanent supply of raw material not only for the sawmill, but also for the stave mill, the pulp mill, the acid plant, and the kindling-wood establishment. Had this been done, Norwich would be a busy and prosperous place today instead of an abandoned lumbering town in which poverty has come to stay.

The American lumberman has reaped, but he has not sown. Slowly but surely we are awakening as a people to the deadly errors of the past. Human life all over the world is absolutely dependent upon the forests. Without wood we could have no manufacturing, no agriculture, no commerce, and civilization, as we know it, would come to an end.

Our appetite for wood is unparalleled in the history of nations. We use raw wood in more than 1,500 ways, and we use more of it per capita than any other great nation. We must not overlook the fact that our forests have helped us to develop from a starving and struggling band of colonists to the richest and most advanced nation on the face of the earth. Wood we must have, but in order to have wood when we need it our idle forest land must be made and kept productive.

In the United States there are invested today $3,000,000,000 in manufacturing plants where the raw material is wood. One-eighth of the total population of the country—14,000,000 people—are dependent upon woodworking industries for their livelihood. In view of this bare fact, it is a serious matter to see our sawmills closing down, our lumber towns disappearing, and our hillsides and mountain tops lying bare, impoverished, and idle.

If any one doubts that trees have a profound influence on civilization, let him look at China. She offers an excellent example of what deforestation means. Nations made treeless by the hands of man are decadent nations. Under such conditions people have to spend so much time keeping alive that they cannot think much about making progress. Our problem is to avoid going the way of China. Our ancestors lived in a world of trees, we live amid acres of desolation. The hour for action is not ahead. It is here. The people of today must provide for the forests of the future. We cannot grow a crop of trees in a day or a year, or even in a generation.

Why I Believe in Enforcing the Prohibition Laws

One of Pinchot's campaign commitments in 1922 was to support fully the Volstead Act—that is, Prohibition. He did not waver in pursuit of this goal, either, a fact that did not endear him to his opponents. But the very fact of their aggrieved opposition seemed to have delighted Governor Pinchot and brought him a measure of renown across the nation, leading editors to seek his insights for magazines, newspapers, and scholarly journals. This is one of many of Pinchot's addresses on the virtue of combatting vice.

Source: Box 947, Gifford Pinchot Papers, Library of Congress; a revised version was published in *Annals of the American Academy of Political and Social Science*, 1923, 284–85.

You ask me why I am attempting to enforce the Eighteenth Amendment and the Volstead Law in the state of Pennsylvania. In the first place I recognize no distinction between the different articles of the Constitution of the United States. Washington warned us that future amendments would be as sacred as the original document. He was right beyond all question. The Eighteenth Amendment is a part of our fundamental law and anyone who breaks it breaks the fundamental law, is a lawbreaker, and should be treated as such.

Power and responsibility for enforcing the Volstead Law rest in the Nation and also in the State. Under the Eighteenth Amendment the two have concurrent jurisdiction. Both are responsible for the enforcement of prohibition laws.

A general conviction had existed throughout Pennsylvania previous to my administration, not only that the Volstead Act had not been enforced, but that no vigorous effort had ever been made to enforce it. Our people had seen men known to be opposed to the enforcement of the law selected to compel obedience to it on the part of others. They were told that appointments to the position of enforcement agent had been treated as political spoils, and that politicians opposed to all that the law stands for had been permitted to name such agents. They believed that persons high in official places were constantly and openly violating the spirit if not the letter of the law, and winking at its violation by others. They understood that liquor was sold almost as freely and openly as it was before the passage of the Eighteenth Amendment.

I regard any failure to enforce the Volstead Law as a blot on the good name of Pennsylvania and the United States. If allowed to continue it will amount to a serious charge against the fitness of our people for genuine self-government.

We must either control the criminals who are openly breaking the law or be controlled by them. With all good citizens I believe that this Commonwealth is greater and more powerful than any band of lawbreakers whatsoever and I am acting on that belief. And we are getting results.

Certain self-styled leaders of public opinion like [Columbia University] President Nicholas Murray Butler[1] have taken it upon themselves to declare that the people of the United States are opposed to an amendment to the Constitution which has been adopted by an overwhelming majority of the states, although they do not tell us what special source of information led them so to believe. They also tell us that the fundamental law of the land so adopted cannot be enforced. These two statements taken together mean, if they mean anything, that the people of the United States do not believe in the laws which they themselves pass, and that they will not obey them.

This talk is nothing more than pernicious nonsense and worthy of attention only as it demonstrates the utter incapacity of the men who make it either to realize and live up to the clear duty of an American citizen, or to understand what has been going on in the minds of the plain people of this country for the last three or four generations. As a matter of fact not even slavery itself was more thoroughly discussed in advance of a decision than this very matter of prohibition, and no decision ever taken by our people was ever more deliberately registered or more clearly in accordance with the popular will.

There are two ways to enforce the Eighteenth Amendment, both of them necessary. One is to arrest and punish lawbreakers and thereby make the risk of lawbreaking so great as to reduce its attractiveness to the criminal. The other is to bring the forces of decency and good citizenship to bear and so create a public sentiment which will not stand for lawbreaking for the sake of any drink more than it will stand for lawbreaking for the sake of plunder. The moral sense of the American people-the backbone of this Commonwealth—is overwhelmingly behind law enforcement. The actively bad, the morally lax, the self-indulgent, and the thoughtless are arrayed on the other side. What chance have they in the long run against the people who do the thinking and the voting and the producing in this

1. Butler was president of Columbia University from 1902 to 1945, and he was opposed to Prohibition.

country of ours? Precisely the same chance as a snowball in the bottomless pit and no more.

It is perfectly true that the forces of lawlessness are in some respects well organized—well organized both politically and commercially. They are, however, in the hopeless minority and it is only necessary for the forces of decency to show that they are really in earnest to have the opposition melt away. I have confidence enough in the American people to believe—and no one can shake my conviction—that when a moral issue is put squarely before them they always decide right. This is a moral issue. It is being put squarely before them, at least in the state of Pennsylvania, and I have not the slightest question about the ultimate result.

I believe that the Eighteenth Amendment will add uncountable millions to the wealth of the United States; will enormously increase the prosperity of our people and will raise happiness and welfare, especially of our women and children, to a new and higher plane. I believe, as every man does who knows the facts, that a very formidable percentage of crime, misery and misfortune flows straight out of the liquor traffic; that the moral condition of the whole community has already been enormously benefited by the Eighteenth Amendment and that it will be benefited still more when the law comes to be better enforced. As a matter of fact crime and disease have been notably reduced already by its action and that action, of course, has only begun to be felt.

I am for prohibition. I am for the enforcement of the liquor laws. I am for both because I believe that in this way lies the well-being and the prosperity of this great people.

Old Age Assistance in Pennsylvania: Righting the Neglects of Yesterday

Prior to becoming governor, Pinchot had not discussed the plight of the elderly in American society. That he expended considerable energy and political capital on their behalf once he reached Harrisburg is a reflection of how executive authority can lead to a change in focus. Issues suddenly become important simply because, as in this case, the need to resolve a contemporary concern becomes clear and pressing. This is one of many dilemmas that Pinchot had not known he would have to resolve; that he acted is a signal of his political nimbleness.

Source: "Address to Pennsylvania State Conference on Old Age Assistance," November 13, 1924, Box 777, Gifford Pinchot Papers, Library of Congress; later published in *American Labor Legislation Review*, 1924, 288–91.[1]

Pennsylvania's interest in behalf of the aged and dependent poor antedates its name and establishment as a Commonwealth of the United States.

A study of the English poor law system reveals that the laws in force in Pennsylvania today are identical in principle, and almost identical in language, with the famous poor laws of Queen Elizabeth in England. The act of 1771, which was based upon the English poor laws, continued to be the general law of the state until the passing of the general poor law of 1836, which, in turn, was substantially a re-enactment of the same law, as no change of any consequence was made in the text. Inasmuch as there has been no general revision of the laws of Pennsylvania relating to the poor since 1836, we are confronted now with a system of poor relief that really dates back to the Elizabethan poor law of 1601.

But, the fact that we have witnessed no basic changes in our system of poor relief since the days of Queen Elizabeth did not help us to maintain the comparative simplicity of this earlier system. As the needs grew, remedial measures had to be adopted, regardless of the fundamental law. The tendency in our poor relief administration, having been away from

1. Journal editor's note: "Governor Pinchot's address . . . , from which the following excerpts are taken, is an effective plea for modern, enlightened care of aged dependents. Other states where old age pension legislation is needed may not have had as long a history of neglect as Pennsylvania, but even a decade is too long and the poorhouse system is generally a reproach to American standards. It is of more than ordinary significance that the great industrial state of Pennsylvania has pioneered in the adoption of old age pension legislation."

uniformity, each locality sought to relieve and remedy its own conditions through such legislation as it deemed best for its own welfare. As a result, we now frequently find the same parts or units of the state under local laws which show considerable differences. Thus, in twenty-eight counties poor relief is administered by a separate board of Old Age Assistance in Pennsylvania directors of the poor; in sixteen counties, the county commissioners also act as directors of the poor; in seventeen other counties, poor relief is administered on the township unit system by directors of the poor or overseers in every township, while in six other counties, a mixed system combining features of all the above, prevails.

Warnings against this endless and jumbling tendency of local legislation of poor laws have been sounded in Pennsylvania again and again. Indeed, our system of poor relief administration has been attacked by every commission that was delegated to study the problem. As early as 1833, a commission appointed to revise the laws of the state urged "that townships should be assimilated to counties, in respect to the mode of government, for the sake of regularity in the system," and, while, they contended, they did not "consider themselves at liberty" to dispense with the separate office of the overseer of the poor, they declared themselves as "not satisfied that any necessity exists for its continuance." In 1889, a commission appointed by Governor James A. Beaver, indicated this extravagant policy in the following words: "Up to the time of the adoption of the present state constitution, 1873, seventy-eight special poor-law districts were created by the legislature, and about three hundred and twenty-one acts of assembly passed relating to them." The commission went on to state: "The statute books from the foundation of the government are strewn with special acts. The late Chief Justice Woodward remarked in a case before the Supreme Court that it was difficult, if not impossible, for any lawyer to state the condition of the law relative to local matters in any district with accuracy. When the fact is mentioned that there are in the neighborhood of eight hundred acts of assembly upon the statute books which relate, directly or indirectly, to the poor laws, this difficulty will become apparent." This number, it is now estimated, is more nearly 3,000 than 800.

None of these difficulties having been remedied, the state dependents commission, twenty-five years later, in its report of 1915, continued this assault upon our system of poor laws by asking for its correction through repeal and amendment of existing statutes, and by the constructive enactment of new and comprehensive legislation.

The old age pension commission, in its report of 1919, after studies of the almshouses in the state, also reached similar conclusions and pointed out that: "In many county poorhouses the worthy, but unfortunate aged wage-earners are compelled, after a life of valuable service, to live and even eat at the same table with the insane, feeble-minded and epileptics, blind and deaf, sufferers from chronic diseases, persons with criminal records and prostitutes." And if all these were not sufficient, the commissioner of public welfare, in his first biennial report in 1922, in speaking of alms-houses, also stated that these institutions "were found to so over-lap in function with other counties, as well as state activities, that it is impossible to consider them as an agency by themselves . . . The needs of the several communities have grown so greatly in the lack of care of the epileptic, of the mental defective, of the insane and of the inebriate, and no other place being found available for these varied groups, the almshouse has gradually evolved into a common meeting place for these unfortunates, thereby directly diverting its use from its proper function. The consequence of this has been that the county homes have been so over-crowded and such an expense to the counties that for lack of proper funds for their support they have degenerated in many instances into a disgraceful condition in the smaller communities . . . The general mingling of the various groups of dependents in these homes at the present time makes the proper care of any single group almost impossible and pitiable is the condition of all." It would seem that the foregoing unanimous condemnation of our anti-quated poor relief system would alone warrant a reevaluation of our methods of care of our worthy aged. Dependency in old age to-day is obviously different from that of three centuries ago, and must be met by methods more suitable to the twentieth century. The modern problem of dependency in old age is not necessarily that of individual maladjustment, not the result of any lack of industry, or the inclination to be thrifty, but is due largely to our vast industrial expansion which, increasingly, finds less and less room for the decrepit aged worker or farmer. With the advan-tages of mechanical experiences decreasing continuously, as machines are steadily replacing human skill, and frequently finding themselves without friends and relatives able to help, the declining days of the aged man and woman are indeed, bleak and despairing. For, even more pitiful than poverty and suffering in youth, is that of old age when "hope no longer springs eternal in the human breast." To the man and woman past seventy years of age, the morrow can, by no stretch of imagination, be made to seem brighter than yesterday.

I considered it a pleasure and privilege, as Governor of this common-wealth, therefore, to sign the old age assistance act, not only because our present system of poor-relief is antiquated and inadequate; not merely because an old age pension system is a much more economical method than the present inefficient and costly poor-house system, but also, because

I am convinced that the man and woman who have helped, by their brain and brawn, to give to this commonwealth the prosperity we are all enjoying, and who have reared families who continue their honest and productive labor, have contributed sufficiently to our commonwealth as to be entitled to a somewhat more serene and happier life in their declining days than the heart-rending wretchedness we are according them to-day in our almshouses. May I, in conclusion, repeat what I have said upon signing the bill: "It has given me profound pleasure to sign this bill. Today we are righting the neglects of yesterday. As governor of this commonwealth, I am proud that ours is the first industrial state to adopt the law. Other states will soon see the wisdom of our procedure and enact similar legislation to make happier the lot of the aged within their borders. The highest duty of humanity is to care for those who have served the glory of the state and the nation as well, and as loyally as they knew how."

Politicians or the People?

The need for transparency in politics seems obvious to us now, yet in the early twentieth century, open elections and direct primaries in which all voters could participate were not the norm. In this article, published after his first gubernatorial term had ended, Pinchot alleges that some Pennsylvania pols hoped to control who could vote in party primaries so that they could shut out those whose votes could not be easily swayed.. The most recently enfranchised voters—women—were the intended victims of this scheme.

Originally published in *The Woman Citizen* 11 (November 1926): 23, 41.

————————————

————————————

One hundred and fifty years ago our ancestors laid down their lives for the principle that taxation without representation was tyranny and could not be tolerated by a free people. They won that fight and with it the right to vote and choose their own representatives.

Today that principle is under attack. A handful of politicians have set on foot a movement designed to rob the people of this country of their fundamental right to govern themselves. If the politicians have their way, they and not the people will really govern.

For that is precisely what the attack on the direct primary amounts to. It constitutes a raid on the rights of the American people, and especially of the women.

The convention system of choosing representatives is now being acclaimed by politicians who hate democracy, as the panacea for all our political ills and woes. The politicians are trusting to the traditional short memory of the American public to win their case and re-establish the convention system.

The abuses of that system are far too fresh in the minds of the public to require repetition here. We all remember the old political conventions where corruption and coercion walked hand in hand.

The direct primary was designed to put an end to the abuses that characterized the convention method of choosing party representatives. In theory, it was sound. In practice it has proven sound despite the abuses introduced by politicians who now seek an easier way of dominating party machinery through the convention system.

The direct primary curbed the power of the boss, the heeler, and their allies. The best proof that the direct primary has been a real step forward is to be found in the pleas that the worst elements in politics are bringing to bear in favor of the return of the convention.

Politicians everywhere are seizing on the revelations of corruption, misuses of power, and huge expenditures that characterized the recent primaries in Pennsylvania and Illinois as a club to beat the direct primary. But they are the very men directly responsible for the graft, vote stealing, and vote buying that characterized these elections. Yet they have the temerity to ask the American people to vest in the right to name all party representatives.

I am for the direct primary horse, foot, and dragoons. I believe it is the most effective method yet devised of giving the American people the opportunity to select the men and women who run their government. I intend to stand up and be counted in the fight that will have to be made by the friends of the direct primary and I shall do everything I can to resist the insidious efforts of our politicians to return them to supreme power via the convention system.

Even if I did not believe in the direct primary as I do, the character of the opposition to it would make me stop, look and listen before I cast my lot with the men who are fostering this movement.

Here in Pennsylvania, we find the worst elements in public life decrying the direct primary and painting a rosy picture of the convention plan. Gang politician after gang politician is going up and down this state telling people what a terrible thing the direct primary is. None of them mentions that the convention system was worse than the primary at its very worst.

One of the leading shouters for the convention plan is David A. Reed, the junior United States Senator from Pennsylvania. During the recent primary, he took up the cause of Senator [George W.] Pepper, and denounced Congressman [William Scott] Vare's candidacy. Pepper was beaten and Reed promptly denounced Pennsylvania voters as "dunderheads." He is now seeking to escape the consequences of his own folly by having the convention system re-installed before he has to submit his case to the "dunderheads" two years from now.

At the same time he is proclaiming his advocacy of Bill Vare's right to a Senate seat in the event that the latter is elected. It is interesting to note in this connection that Bill Vare would have considerable weight and power in any political convention that might be held—particularly any designed to select the Republican candidate for United States Senator.

I may fairly discuss the direct primary, because four years ago I won the nomination for governor in spite of the gang, just because of the direct primary. Without it I would not have been able to get even a decent start, and the State of Pennsylvania would have remained in the power of the political gangsters who had plunged the state thirty-one million dollars in debt.

More recently, I was a candidate for United States Senator. My opponents, Vare and Pepper, had spent in their behalf sums approximating $800,000 and $2,000,000 respectively. Vare had behind him every ward leader and gangster in Philadelphia. Pepper had behind him the gangsters of Pittsburgh, the financial magnates of the state and the press of Pennsylvania, with very few exceptions. We passed through a campaign that for sheer bitterness outstripped any held in recent years.

I lost, for one reason, because I refused to use the methods employed by my opponents. But I came out of the fight with my belief in the fundamental soundness of the direct primary stronger than ever.

What we need to do is strengthen, not repeal, the direct primary. Laws should be passed which guarantee the poor man a fair chance in a political contest. That can be done by limiting the expenditures of the candidates to a few pennies for each vote cast in the previous primary. Fiscal responsibility should be lodged in a financial agent designated by each candidate and failure of the financial agent to make full returns of his expenditures and obey the law should automatically result in the forfeiture of the nomination won by his principal.

Speaking for Pennsylvania, I feel that we need a general revision of election laws to make it harder for the gangsters of Philadelphia and Pittsburgh to steal votes. Laws restricting assistance to voters, requiring the opening of ballot boxes which are alleged to contain fraud or error, and prohibiting the chain system of voting will go a long way toward making our elections clean and honest.

I called a special session of the Legislature last winter for the express purpose of enacting such legislation. That session was dominated by politicians now clamoring for the convention system. It turned down every bill but one designed to guarantee an honest vote and an honest count and emasculated that one.

Strangely enough the very man who gave the orders to kill the election bills was the first victim of the old laws in the recent election. He claimed that his candidate for governor had been robbed of the nomination by the operation of vote thieves in Pittsburgh. He made an effort to have ballot boxes opened but encountered a stone wall. Today, I have no doubt he would have been a firm and ardent supporter of the very laws that he helped to defeat last winter.

The Women especially should oppose the abolition of the direct primary with all the vigor and influence they can command. They know what to expect of the gang under the convention system. They know how these politicians fought against the enfranchisement of women and the means they have employed to discourage women from voting now that the Nineteenth Amendment is a law.

The direct primary is the best guarantee that we have of the political rights of honest voters, women included.

Inaugural Address

Having won yet another surprising victory as governor, Pinchot used what would be his last inaugural address to challenge the then power elite of Pennsylvania. Among those forces who hoped to dominate public discourse and control the levers of government were the utilities corporations, and he lays into them in this opening speech, as he would for the next four years. He was their *bête noire,* as they were his. Pinchot relished the opportunity to undermine their clout.

Address delivered in Harrisburg, January 20, 1931.

———————————
———————————

Two forces are struggling for control of the governments of Pennsylvania and the United States. One fights in the open and has done so since the birth of this Republic. It represents the theory of government set forth in the Declaration of Independence and established upon this continent by the sacrifices of our forefathers. Its central principle is the right of a free people to govern themselves. It recognizes the duty and responsibility of the government to protect the people.

The other force operates under cover. It is directed by hidden forces for the advantage of a few as against the interests of the many. Its motives and methods are disclosed only when attacks upon it drive them into the open. Its central purpose is to control the government and so prevent it from protecting the people against manifold extortions, which take unjustly from the breadwinners many hundreds if not thousands of millions of dollars each year.

What is at stake in this conflict is the continuance of that government by the people which triumphed over government by the few when American declared and achieved her freedom.

In the great future that opens before us our people either remain masters of their own destiny, or they will once more become subjects of that type of government whose destruction was the object of the French Revolution in Europe, and the American Revolution on this continent.

In this momentous struggle every citizen eventually must take his stand with one side or the other.

It has become politically fashionable to doubt and flaunt the capacity of the people to govern themselves. It has become the custom to exalt and advocate the government by little groups of self-selected powerful men as against that government by the people in which our fathers so passionately believed.

The cynics who cast that doubt are everlastingly wrong. Government by the people is the American way, the right way. With all my heart and soul I believe in it. With all the power that I have, I shall defend it. The preservation of the Constitution, the prosperity of Pennsylvania, and welfare of the plain people depend absolutely on the perpetuation of the American form of government. . . .

Here in Pennsylvania a carefully planned, elaborately financed, and powerfully directed attack on the rule of the people under law has made substantial progress. It aims to substitute government by the public utilities for government by the people. It is not confined to Pennsylvania. Not a single state in the union is free from a similar attempt. . . .

I deny the right of this invisible government to exist in free America. I challenge the men who are working for it to come into the open, and to acknowledge in plain words what they are attempting to achieve by secret action.

The captains of the undercover army engaged in this raid on our form of government, like the captains of the armies that fought against Washington, have their mercenaries. The Hessians of those days have their counterparts in the controlled and corrupt political machines of today. . . . Back of the public utilities in their attack on our American form of government is the whole fabric of political corruption; the underworld, the protected racketeer, and criminals of high and low degree.

As the Hessians of the Revolution once held Philadelphia, so their successors hold it today. In their time our forefathers drove them out. So in our day must we.

For the second time in the history of Pennsylvania, a man has been elected twice to the high office of Governor. I approach my second term with firm reliance upon the Almighty with the clear purpose to do the right as God gives me to see the right, with a deep and humble sense of my responsibility, and with heartfelt gratitude to my fellow citizens.

I take office free of any promise that is not a public promise, from any obligation that would hamper my full liberty to serve the Commonwealth soberly, in honor, and in truth.

My allegiance is first of all to the plain people—the men, the women, and the children—whose servant I am, whose mandate I hold, whose interests I represent.

Eight years ago the task before the new Administration was to relieve the state from the huge burden of debt into which many years of maladministration had plunged it, to substitute honest, economical, and efficient government for waste and corruption, and to establish new political standards for the Commonwealth.

The task today is to defeat the attack of the public utilities. Government by utility magnates must not be substituted for government by the people. We have no more compelling duty than to destroy the corruption upon which the power of the utilities depends.

Clean elections was a principal issue in the recent campaign. The new administration will leave nothing undone to carry through the will of the voters that election crookedness shall cease to disgrace our State.

Other matters also require attention. Farm relief also exists in Pennsylvania and demands the most serious consideration. The farmer and his family need relief from excessive taxation and they need roads that will take them to their schools, churches, and markets throughout the year. The two objects can be secured at once. . . .

Prosperity is a general blessing. Substantially, we all go up and down together. Prosperous business, like prosperous farming, is necessary for the people who neither do business nor farm.

During my first term nothing was left undone to promote and defend honest business. Partly as a result, business grew better and work more plenty during those four years. I shall labor most earnestly for the return of the good times which marked my first Administration.

I recognize the obligation upon every man in public office to exert his full power to promote the prosperity of honest business, and to prevent and defeat attacks upon it. This is especially true when, as now, millions are seeking a chance to work.

Prosperous business provides employment. Just at the moment opportunity to work is our critical need. . . . As with so many other evils, the best way to deal with unemployment is by prevention. A concrete plan for that purpose prepared by the Committee on Unemployment will be laid promptly before the General Assembly.

. . . It is my intention to keep the voters of Pennsylvania fully informed as to the progress of the public business, and as to the way in which their orders are being opposed or carried out. They have a right to know.

It should be easy for the people to see their Governor. Therefore, the sign, "Governor's Office—Walk Right In," which was displayed in my first term on certain days will appear again, and the door will be open to all who choose to come.

. . . The platform upon which I was nominated in the Republican primary was the platform upon which I was elected in the fall. It was the only platform advanced by the Republican Party in the general election. It was adopted, and upon it I was chosen, by the electorate of the whole Commonwealth. It will be the sailing chart of this Administration.

I repeat that platform now as my pledge to the people of Pennsylvania:

I will use the full power of my office:

To break the stranglehold of the electric, gas, water, trolley, bus, and other public utilities on the cost of living and the margin of happiness.

To free the government of Pennsylvania from combined machine and public utility control.

To abolish the Public Service Commission. It is the catspaw of the corporations, unfaithful to the people, worse than useless.

To replace it with a Fair Rate Board elected (like our courts) by the people.

To have the Fair Rate Board elected by districts, so that every part of the state will be represented.

To review and reduce, through the Fair Rate Board, every unjust rate now charged by any electric, gas, water, trolley, bus, or other public utility under its authority. . . .

To lift the present unjust burden of taxes from the farmer, the home owner, and the business man by equalizing taxation throughout the state.

To give the country people good roads from home to market, church, and school—summer and winter.

To give every child an equal chance for an education, and security in office for competent teachers.

To abolish the coal and iron police, and replace it with officers selected and commanded by the Commonwealth, and paid by it at company expense.

To prevent the unfair use of labor injunctions.

To secure old age pensions for the helpless poor.

To get work for the unemployed, and advance the planned and orderly development of Pennsylvania. . . .

To see that the State assists disabled and neglected ex-service men, who need opportunity most.

To stop stream pollution, and to empower cities, boroughs, and townships to protect their own water.

To lift taxes from small inheritances.

To secure clean elections in Pennsylvania.

To maintain and enforce the law.

I will do my level best to give the children, the workers, the farmers, the fare payers, and the tax payers, a Roosevelt Square Deal. . . .

The Case for Federal Relief

The ravages of the Depression raised critical questions about how Pennsylvania, one of the most industrialized states in the Union, would support its growing number of unemployed women and men. The Republican Party, led by President Herbert Hoover, advocated voluntary relief programs. Pinchot disagreed, arguing instead for a robust federal relief plan that would support the most destitute and rebuild their capacity to contribute to the commonwealth. Well before Franklin Roosevelt's election in 1932, Pinchot was working out some of the arguments and policies that would emerge in the New Deal.

Originally published in *Survey Graphic* 67 (January 1932): 347–49, 389–90.

———————————

———————————

Is this nation, as a nation, to reach out a hand to help those of its people who through no fault of their own are in desperation and distress? Shall federal aid be granted in this great national crisis? It is not a question of ability to help. We are the richest nation on earth. If federal aid is needed, it can be granted. Congress has only to say the word. Shall the answer be yes or no?

My answer is yes. To my mind it is the only possible answer. Prolonged study and profound conviction support my belief that federal aid is our clear duty and our best hope of prompt and permanent recovery. Two solid years of bad times have taught us that we can no longer consider our condition as an unfortunate accident which will automatically right itself if left alone. Gentle bedside language can do nothing for us.

Our methods so far have been restricted substantially to local relief. Those in high places have continually insisted that a national emergency be met with local aid alone. They have left it all, with the exception of a bit of benevolent advertising, to the states and communities themselves. To requests and plans for federal aid they have cried "dole, dole." Why aid given by the nation should be a dole, and precisely the same aid given by a state or a city should not be a dole, I have never been able to understand.

Of course none of us wants the dole. None of us is in favor of establishing any system which will give the unemployed money or even food when work can be given instead. But that choice is not before us. Industry and business are not giving men the chance to work. Nor are they feeding the unemployed. We must feed them if they are to live. We must feed them if they are to retain any confidence in the government under which they live.

Crying "dole" has not helped the unemployed, but it has served a very definite purpose, that of restricting relief to local sources. Then what about local relief? In what direction has it headed us?

A nation-wide Community Chest campaign was backed to the hilt by the most persuasive and efficient forces that charitable leaders could muster. We can all rejoice that in many cases the quotas were subscribed. The quality of neighborliness, the virtue of sympathy, have not died out. We never feared they had. But if the full quotas aimed at were everywhere collected would they be sufficient to cover the needs of the winter? They would not. Responsible social workers tell me the quotas were fixed on the basis of what the chest managers believed that the communities could be made to subscribe. They were often small in proportion to the real needs. The people who think they can wash their hands, know that the chest drives are over, and go away on trips to Florida should think again.

Where does the bulk of local relief come from? Who carries the load? It comes from and is carried by those who pay taxes to the municipal and county and sometimes state governments. The Russell Sage Foundation, reporting for eighty-one cities, found that in past years private funds supplied only 28 percent of the relief. Tax funds supplied the other 72 percent. In some cities over 90 percent came from tax funds.

How are these taxes raised? The answer is that municipalities raise their funds mainly through real estate and other property taxes. Local relief of this kind means an increase in property taxes. This increase in property taxes and the sort of enforced charity by which industry takes a day's pay out of every twenty or so in the month from workers, even from scrubwomen in offices, to help swell relief funds—that is how the program of local relief works out. Yet it is substantially true that every cent a man of small means contributes to relief either directly or indirectly through increased taxes is taken out of consumption. His buying power is immediately slowed down by exactly that much. And the slowing down of buying power means the slowing down of the wheels of industry.

Here, then, is the heart of the local-relief plan. By cutting down consuming power, it can only serve to further our economic maladjustment and to sink us deeper in the hole.

Now in considering what plan we are to advance in addition to, or as a total or partial substitute for local relief, it might be well for us to investigate the flaws in our economic structure which brought our present troubles upon us. There ought to be very little doubt that the largest single cause was production beyond the power of the people to consume. Through the years called prosperous, no stone was left unturned which would help perfect or increase our national productive power. Technological improvements, financial devices such as mergers, high-pressure sales campaigns, instalment buying and other credit schemes, all tended to the same end. All helped to raise production to new and dangerous heights, and to leave normal consuming power farther and farther behind.

Instead of sharing the increased profits from production, industry shunted the wealth back to itself. Wage-earners were encouraged, persuaded, cajoled to spend their money buying goods. If they couldn't pay for them now, they should buy on the instalment plan. They should borrow money, if necessary. But they should buy. No real American, they were told, could be without his radio and his automobile.

And what happened to the money spent in buying? Did a reasonable part of it go back, in increased wages, to the working-man's pocket so that the circle of producing and consuming could go on? It did not. It went in staggering disproportion to dividends and capital. It went back to industry so that production might be increased, even at the expense of consuming power.

This is no wild guess. This is fact with figures to support it. Julius Klein, assistant secretary of commerce, tells us that in the decade ending in 1929, real wages increased only 13 percent while the returns to all industry increased 72 percent. Where did the 72 percent come from but out of the spent wages of the millions and millions of working-men? Dr. Klein tells us the dividends in industrial and rail stocks increased by 285 percent, twenty-two times as fast as wages. Is it any wonder that the crash of depression came? Increased production served only to turn the national wealth into two tremendously unequal channels. By far the bulk of that wealth went back in a torrent to capital and production. A tiny stream returned to purchasing power through wages.

Was over-production and the disregard of consuming power entirely accidental? I think not. To me it is inconceivable that the great experts in business and economics who have taken over the banking, industrial and political control of the country can have been blind to what was going on. As early as 1921 the Federated American Engineering Societies reported that many of our large industries were overdeveloped: Clothing 45 percent, printing 50 percent, shoes 50 percent, coal 50 percent. Yet throughout the whole decade the Department of Commerce used every power of persuasion to bring industry to the highest point of mass production.

If the driver for super-production had been coupled with a drive for an increased return to labor and consumers the result might have been very different. If it had been combined with an arrangement for providing men discharged because of labor-saving machinery and mergers with a dismissal wage it might have been helpful. It was coupled with nothing of the sort.

What it was coupled with was a campaign on the part of the Treasury Department to reduce taxation on great wealth. That campaign was not only successful but over-successful. Not only was the excess-profits tax repealed but the income tax on the higher brackets was reduced.

Meanwhile what was happening to consuming power? What about maintaining the buying ability of those millions of wage-earners who would have to use the extra goods turned out by glorified production? Take bituminous coal. In 1923 the people paid $900,000 for a Coal Commission to direct stabilization of that industry, already in bad shape. Its report and its recommendations were killed in cold blood while the administration looked calmly on. Take agriculture. For years the farm organizations have battled in vain for the stabilization measures which were so badly needed. Take the stock market. Some years ago when speculation was getting out of hand and the Senate had begun to study the situation, the then president concisely announced that the amount of brokers' loans was not too high. Never before had a president undertaken to support the stock market.

In all this record, not a plan was made—let alone carried out—for stabilizing purchasing power. Not a prop was put beneath consuming ability while producing ability was being reared to such dizzy heights. Our national leaders, those same leaders who have been insisting on local relief, lent willing hands in the development of a prosperity so one-sided that it could not stand.

Before going further let us see what sort of an economic structure these men have been building—these men who have consistently opposed the idea of federal relief. By the overstimulation of production, there has been developed in this country the most astounding concentration of wealth in the hands of a few men that the world has ever known. Here is the basic evil which has brought on the depression, and which we must guard against in planning relief for the future. Here is the evil which is protected and fostered by local-relief plans.

In 1926 the Federal Trade Commission made a report to the Senate on National Wealth and Income. They had studied the county court records of over forty thousand estates. The records came from twelve states and stretched over a twelve-year period. The counties studied had been chosen to represent not only every section of the country from coast to coast but also every sort of district from the farms to the congested cities. They found that in this sampling one percent of the people owned about 60 percent of the wealth, that sixty dollars out of every hundred were owned by one person out of every hundred. They found that 40 percent of the wealth, forty dollars out of every hundred, was left for the other 99 percent of the people. In other words, one person out of every hundred was considerably richer than the other ninety-nine put together. They found further that 13 percent of the people owned more than 90 percent of the wealth. And at the other end, 77 percent of the people owned only 5 percent of the wealth. Three quarters of the people could have added up all their fortunes and it would come to a bare twentieth of the total.

In 1929 the National Bureau of Economic Research made a careful study of all the incomes in this country for 1926. They found that four and a half thousand people received that year an average of almost $240,000 apiece. And at the bottom of the heap, forty-four million people had incomes of about one thousand dollars each, or less than one half of one percent of the separate incomes of those at the top.

Most recent figures are yet more amazing. In 1929 the per capita income in this country was $700 for every man, woman and child. But according to the Treasury Department's preliminary estimate, over five hundred persons had in that year incomes of over a million dollars apiece. Their total income was $1,185,000,000. They received, these five hundred odd, the average shares of 1,692,000 people.

The facts of concentration alone are impressive enough. But even more so are the indications of how tremendously that concentration increased in the years during which it received governmental encouragement. The figures for these years tell all too vividly the story of a nation building toward disaster by unbalancing its economic equilibrium. On March 20, 1931 the National Industrial Conference Board published in its bulletin figures representing the total income of the nation for several years back. In 1920 we made over seventy-four billion dollars. In 1928 we made eighty-one billion dollars. In eight years we had increased our income by a little less than one tenth.

But the Treasury Department's latest annual statistics of income reveal some particularly interesting things to compare with that one tenth. In 1920 there were 3649 people who had incomes of over $100,000. In 1928 that number had jumped to 15,977. It had doubled and then doubled again and was still going up. In 1920 those people made a total of over 727 million dollars. But in 1928, those who had the hundred-thousand-dollar incomes and up received about four and a half billion dollars—more than six times as much money. And all this, remember, while the incomes of all our people increased one lone tenth of its previous figure.

Then how about the men who receive a million a year? In 1920 there were thirty-three of them and they got 77 million dollars. In 1928 there were 511 of them, fifteen times as many, and they got over a billion dollars, or fourteen times as much. The national income had meanwhile increased by one tenth. Finally look at our fellow-citizens who get a paltry five million a year. In 1920 there were four of them and they collected not quite thirty million dollars. But by 1928 they had added twenty-two new members to their exclusive circle, and the twenty-six of them were forced to get along with an income of a little over 250 million dollars among them.

In other words, in the eight-year period between 1920 and 1928, while the total national income increased less than 10 percent, the number of men with incomes of over a million dollars increased over 1400 percent, or one hundred and forty times as fast. And the amount of money these men made in one year increased 1300 percent, or one hundred and thirty times as fast as the total amount of money made by everybody in the whole of the United States. They certainly got their share!

The same astounding concentration of wealth and power is seen in the industrial world. A study of corporate wealth and of the influence of large corporations was published this year in The American Economic Review. The conclusions reached are eye-openers. In 1927, there were over 300,000 industrial corporations in this country. Two hundred of the 300,000, less than seven hundredths of one percent, controlled 45 percent of the total wealth of all these corporations. The same two hundred received over 40 percent of all corporate income, and controlled over 35 percent of all business wealth. Furthermore, about 20 percent of the wealth of this entire nation was in the hands of those two hundred corporations.

Truly the growth of these two hundred giant corporations has been almost beyond belief. In the ten years up to 1929 their assets grew from under 44 billion to 78 billion dollars, an increase of 78 percent. The author of the study, Prof. Gardiner C. Means,[1] asserts that if their indicated rate of growth continues in the future they will own within twenty years virtually half of our national wealth. Professor Means then emphasizes an extremely important fact. He says that in 1927, less than two thousand men were directors of these two hundred corporations. Since many of them were inactive, the ultimate control of more than one third of industry was actually in the hands of a few hundred men. And according to present indications it will still be only a few hundred men who by 1950 will control half of the wealth of this entire nation.

It is this almost unbelievable concentration of wealth which has killed the consuming power of the average millions and has brought our misfortunes upon us. It is this same incredible concentration which is the chief

1. Gardiner Means, a New Deal economist, was coauthor of *The Modern Corporation and Private Property* (1932), a seminal text arguing that economic power in the United States was controlled by a mere 200 corporations. Pinchot shared Means's critique of this consolidation of power, fiscal and political.

obstacle in our path to permanent prosperity. . . . For if we examine statements and actions of the proponents of local relief, we find that they weave
together into a surprisingly harmonious pattern. That pattern does not
spell relief for the unemployed. What it spells is persistent shielding of
concentrated wealth—not relief for the needy but release for the millionaire.

The local-relief advocates are prolific in denials of any excessive distress. Yet I know that there are almost a million men unemployed in the
State of Pennsylvania alone. If my state were typical of the rest of the
nation there would be not far from ten million unemployed in the country.

Next we have statements to the effect that wage-earners are not so
badly off because prices have been dropping along with wages. That
argument is answered by the government's figures. Commissioner of
Labor Statistics [Ethelbert] Stewart of the U. S. Department of Labor
announced on October 1, 1931 that from June 1929 to June 1931 the cost of
living went down less than 12 percent. In the same period, he stated, the
total wage decrease was about 40 percent. Wages actually paid dropped
more than three times as far as prices.

The local-relief advocates have also laid unwarranted emphasis on
federal public works. Their construction program, they say, has greatly
relieved distress and they point out that the number of men employed in
the federal construction program last month [December 1931] was fifty
thousand. We have had the past summer half that number employed on
state highways alone in Pennsylvania. And fifty thousand is no large percentage of the millions unemployed after two years of depression. Is it any
wonder that President William Green of the American Federation of Labor
calls this "only a drop in the bucket" toward relieving unemployment?

Finally, there are the plans now under way to make up the federal
deficit the depression has caused.

Treasury proposals to increase the income taxes recommend that the
exemptions be lowered and the base of the tax be spread. In other words,
much or most of the increase is to come from the little fellows. Certain
leaders, among them Senator [David A.] Reed, advocate a sales tax. A
sales tax is simply another way of putting the burden on small business.
They do far and away the largest part of the nation's buying and a sales
tax would fall mainly on them. Does a sales tax reach the hoarded millions
of the over-rich? Does it take money from the coffers of the large manufacturing corporations? It does not. It is another way of seeing to it that
concentrated wealth shall remain concentrated.

There is only one conclusion to be drawn from all this: the safeguarding of money in the hands of an incredibly small number of incredibly
rich men. The force behind the stubborn opposition to federal relief is fear

lest the taxation to provide that relief be levied on concentrated wealth—
fear lest . . . the policy of shielding the big fortunes at the expense of the
little ones, should at long last be tossed into the discard.

In the name of those who are overburdened now, I demand that the
tax rates on the upper-bracket incomes be increased. In their name I
demand that the graduation of the inheritance tax be steepened. And in
their name I demand that the exemptions and the lower-bracket tax rates
be left untouched. To meddle with them is to trifle with disaster and to
invite the depression to stay. When I ask that the top rates of the income
and estate taxes be raised enough to pay for federal relief for the unemployed, I am speaking as a man directly affected. I pay an income tax in
high brackets myself. In time a goodly share of my estate will go to the
government.

I believe in levying taxes according to ability to pay. Our government
recognizes that principle in its dealings with foreign nations. Why should
it not do so at home? The burden of an income tax or an inheritance tax
cannot be shifted. It lies where it falls. The burden of a heavily graduated
tax falls on the man who is best able to bear it—who will feel the loss the
least. I am strong for it. I am strong for its use to help defeat that shame-
ful situation by which millions suffer from want in the richest country in
the world.

You may ask how federal-relief funds can be used. In two ways. First,
by supplementing the efforts of the states, cities and other municipal organizations for feeding and otherwise helping people who cannot get work.
Second, to give work. There is scarcely any limit to the number of men who
could be employed by the federal government in great public works of
many kinds in every part of the country. Flood control on the Mississippi
and other rivers, the development of inland waterways, reforestation and
fire prevention, the use of rivers for water supply, irrigation and power, the
checking of erosion, the construction of airports and the lighting of air-
ways, the drainage of swamp land, the building of highways—all these and
many others can be undertaken and will pay for themselves over and over
again in the recreated efficiency of national life. . . .

The picture is now complete. Local relief means making the poor man
pay. Local relief serves to weaken further our national consuming power
and block any hope of permanent recovery. Local relief is part of a vicious
policy to shield concentrated wealth—a policy which brought on the
depression and has kept it with us for two long years. Local relief means
release for the rich, not relief for the poor.

Federal relief is demanded by every principle of justice, of humanity
and of sound economics. Federal relief can be raised from the wealthy so

that the purchasing power of the millions of average citizens will not suffer. Federal relief can be spent in such a way that unemployment and distress will be defeated and the entire nation started well along the path to a permanent and balanced prosperity.

Best of all, it should be remembered that plans for a very considerable part of these developments are already in existence, and that work upon many of them could be undertaken with comparatively little delay.

This is no local crisis, no state crisis. It is nation-wide. I cannot believe that a national government will stand by while its citizens freeze and starve, without lifting a hand to help. I do not see how it can refuse to grant that relief which it is in honor, in duty and in its own interest bound to supply.

Lifting the Farmers Out of the Mud

Perhaps the most famous of Pinchot's relief programs was his ambitious effort to build new roads or repair the existing network across Pennsylvania. In part this was to create jobs that would put money in the pockets of those without an income; in part it was to increase the capacity of the state's many farmers to get their goods to market. Pinchot never forgot that he gained office with the support of this often marginalized constituency.

Source: Box 947, Gifford Pinchot Papers, Library of Congress; a revised version was subsequently published in the *New Republic*, October 19, 1932, 256–58.

––––––––––––––

––––––––––––––

Road building in America has passed into a new stage. Arterial highways, which heretofore have been our chief concern, are to yield their position of first importance, and secondary roads, farm-to-market roads, are to replace them as a major engineering undertaking of the nation.

Here in America in a decade and a half we ran our road bill to a billion and a half dollars a year. We thought we had settled into our stride. We thought we knew what we wanted in roads and how to get it. We concluded we must have an unbroken slab of pavement that would endure to the end of time. Such was our standard and we would live up to it.

But there was a certain exasperating ant in the molasses. These roads were back-breakingly expensive. In Pennsylvania they cost us $50,000 to $70,000 a mile. We spent as much as $85,000,000 a year to build them. Even where resources shamed Croesus there was a physical limit to the mileage that could be built on this basis. And while we got certain arterial highways people in the country stayed in the mud.

Several states decided the time was ripe to get roads to areas where traffic did not call for a boulevard that cost $60,000 a mile. Foremost were Pennsylvania, Virginia and North Carolina. Pennsylvania decided to develop the possibilities of so modest a sum as $6,000 a mile, or even less.

In the spring of 1931, 80,000 miles of Pennsylvania roads were the responsibility of the townships against 13,425 miles in charge of the state. Township roads have great local importance. They offer short connections between state highways, give outlets to villages and communities, provide the farmer with roads to market and to school and church, make the doctor available at all times of year, bring trade to wholesale and retail merchants, facilitate the transit of manufactured articles, relieve congestion on the main highways, give access to the great outdoor playgrounds of the state and allow hunters and fishermen to reach their objectives.

Part of the hard luck of the farmer everywhere comes from his difficulty in getting his product from his factory, which is his farm, to his market. Cheap and continuous transportation is even more important to the producer of milk than to the manufacturer of sheet because milk is quickly perishable. For all these reasons it was imperative that something be done for those who live on the back roads.

Today Pennsylvania is building all-weather highways that cost six thousand dollars a mile or less. Assumption of responsibility for local roads is no less a new venture in state government than the huge experiment in low-cost roads. Road builders of the nation are watching what promises to be the beginning of a new era in road building.

And that new era came through a mandate of the people. It was necessary that the legislature transfer rural roads to state jurisdiction. I suggested the proposed transfer and made it a plank in my platform when I ran for Governor in 1930. For many years I have traveled into every section of the state. I knew how hard it was to get back to the people living on the farms, and how much more trying it must be for them to wrestle all the time with the problem of miserable roads.

Rural roads are under the care of supervisors who, obviously, are not professional road builders. Sufficient money cannot be raised to improve all the highways a township needs. The state, I argued, should take over twenty thousand miles and transform them into dustless, mudless, hard-surfaced thoroughfares good every day of the year—and maintain the entire mileage.

My political opponents said this proposal made them laugh. They declared so gigantic an improvement program was impossible. Unwound on the map of the nation, the ribbon of proposed new road would reach from New York to Seattle, back to Philadelphia, across to San Francisco, slope down from the Lincoln Highway to Norfolk, cut by the Santa Fe Trail to Los Angeles, through the South to New Orleans, and double back all the way to Mexico City. Pennsylvania was already collecting more money for roads than any other state. Here was a proposal that it take over the burden always regarded as that of the local community. The thing was too ridiculous for consideration.

But the people approved the proposal and elected me. They gave me a legislature that without a dissenting vote transferred 20,000 miles of dirt road from the counties and townships to the state system. In the history of Pennsylvania or any other state it will be hard to find a legislative proposal more heartily supported, although it thrust on the state a huge expense that had previously fallen elsewhere.

Legislators from rural sections might have been expected to support it, for even though maintenance was ineffective, the roads taken over by the state were costing them $10,000,000 a year. But representatives of metropolitan sections supported the measure with equal enthusiasm. Senators and assemblymen agreed that good roads to farms would be a profitable investment.

Authorities had been in agreement for years as to durably paved main roads. Pennsylvania spent hundreds of millions to build them. They constituted its arterial system—the roads carrying heavy traffic between centers of population. But now all the main roads are nearly all improved. And clinging to the notion that only high-cost pavement should be built, the state frequently put down fifty-thousand-dollar-a-mile roads where they were not needed. In use for years, travel on them was so light that the pavement lacked the customary stripe made by oil dropped by traffic. The money spent on every twenty miles of such pavement would have brought a satisfactory surface to one or two hundred miles of purely rural roads. . . .

We were ready to go to work before the twenty thousand miles of township roads were turned over to us on August 15, 1931. In fact we began the first section on July 23, at Smith's Grove, in York County. The highway serves a very old Quaker community and connects Lewisberry, on an improved road to Rossville, five miles away. More than one hundred years old, it was often so muddy it could be traveled only on horseback. At each end is a Quaker meeting house, that at Rossville carrying the date 1769. The ancient Quakers convened for worship one Sunday at one end of the road and the next Sunday at the other. Smith's Grove was halfway between, and was a wide, straight stretch of dirt on which young Quakers are said to have tested the speed of their horses.

At Smith's Grove we broke ground on our huge statewide task of reconstruction. Barns and fences thereabouts had been freshly painted. Wherever we build these roads fences are likely immediately to be renewed, and farms cleaned up and new activities, including the coming to life of abandoned farms, inaugurated. Evidence of the public interest in the program was shown when five thousand people came to the ceremony.

We promised to complete as much as possible of our 20,000 miles in four years and maintain every foot of it. This means the expenditure of more than $120,000,000. The sum seems stupendous. But it is quite within the means of so rich a state as Pennsylvania. Here the gasoline tax totals $33,000,000 a year and the automobile license $31,000,000 more. My predecessor spent much more than that on limited mileages of high-cost roads. He spent so liberally, in fact, that the road treasury was quite empty when I took office.

In August we decided that we could build 1,700 miles of road before the ground froze in November. That meant a modest $10,000,000 to get the work started in every county. It was 8½ percent of the program, and that percentage of each county's roads was selected for improvement. Immediately we were buying and renting machinery wherever we could.

The magnitude of the task is evident when it is known that we spent $1,500,000 for purchase of equipment, and as much more for rentals, though we go light on machines and do as much work as possible with man power. Six hundred carloads of culvert pipe came rolling in while 2,500 tank cars of asphalt and 150,000 carloads of coarse aggregate were delivered to us.

The program provided employment for the needy. We distributed the work, giving men with families the preference. Construction was by the state direct, rather than through contract. The number of workers on our rolls increased rapidly. The November frosts failed to materialize, so we added another 666 miles of road to the program. By December we had 28,000 people working on the roads. By January 30,000. The unusual mildness enabled us to keep going all winter.

And we kept going all summer, too—and are still going. We shall keep going through the coming winter, so far as weather will permit. In late September our highway department had 40,000 men at work—twice as many as any other state. Since August 15, 1931, the department has finished 3,950 miles of the rural roads. And we are proud of the accomplishment. So, too, are the thousands of men and women who live along those roads.

If I may pause to brag a bit, I point to the fact that here in Pennsylvania we have over 34,000 miles of highway under care of the state. The huge state of Texas has only 20,000 miles of state highway and our wealthy neighbor, New York, [has] less than that mileage. No other state has ever approached our program. We challenge them all to do as we have done, to come along with Pennsylvania in a real, concerted effort to lift the farmer out of the mud.

Liquor Control in the United States:
The State Store Plan

A lifelong teetotaler and a staunch dry—meaning that he did not drink and was a public advocate for prohibition—Governor Pinchot had to come to terms with President Roosevelt's and Congress's decision to roll back Prohibition. The legislative fix that he promoted and that the state legislature enacted remains contentious: the state-store plan has made Pennsylvania the largest purchaser of alcohol in the United States, but the fact that Pennsylvanians still can only buy liquor through this system has grated on them since the establishment of the stores. (One consequence, presumably, has been a related boost in sales in the adjoining states of New York, New Jersey, Maryland, West Virginia, and Ohio.)

Source: Box 948, Gifford Pinchot Papers, Library of Congress; a revised version was later published in *The Rotarian* 44, no. 1 (January 1934): 12–13, 59–60.

—————————

—————————

Pennsylvania's liquor control legislation is based on five cardinal points. They are:

1. The saloon must not be allowed to come back
2. Liquor must be kept entirely out of politics
3. Judges must not be forced into liquor-politics
4. Liquor must not be sold without restraint
5. Bootlegging must be made unprofitable

Sincere drys and sincere wets and political leaders of all parties agree substantially on these principles. At a series of conferences, bills designed to carry out these principles were drafted and introduced as soon as the special session of the Legislature convened on November 13 [1933].

All Pennsylvania prohibition legislation was based on the Eighteenth Amendment to the federal constitution and, when the Eighteenth Amendment went into discard, existing control legislation died. Therefore we had only from November 13 to December 5 to enact new control legislation. As a result of the haste with which the bills were amended and finally passed, there are undoubtedly some imperfections.

Nevertheless, I believe we have sane and effective legislation which will have the approval of a vast majority of the people of Pennsylvania.

The cornerstone of the Pennsylvania plan is the McClure bill. . . . It establishes a state monopoly of the sale of liquor through state stores under the management of a State Liquor Control Board.

Through the state stores, liquor will be sold to private individuals for consumption off the premises, and to hotels, clubs, restaurants, railroad dining cars, and steamships which have licenses to sell liquor by the drink.

The Control Board also licenses those establishments which desire to sell liquor on the premises.

Sale over the bar is prohibited, except in the case of clubs; and sale on Sunday is also forbidden.

A hotel to receive a license must be of good reputation, must furnish sleeping accommodations and meals, must have at least ten permanent bed rooms for guests in cities, and six elsewhere, must have a public dining room operated by the same management, accommodating at least forty persons at one time, and a kitchen apart from the dining room in which food is prepared for the public.

A restaurant, to qualify, must have an area within the building of not less than 500 square feet, must be equipped with tables and chairs accommodating at least fifty persons at one time; and have a kitchen apart from the dining room in which at least three persons are regularly employed in the preparation of meals or incidental work.

A club can qualify for a license only if it is operated not for profit, has been in existence and operation for at least six months if incorporated, and ten years if unincorporated, before it applies for a license.

Annual license fees for hotels and restaurants run from $150 for municipalities having a population of less than 1,500, to $600 in municipalities having a population of 150,000 or more.

All license fees go to the municipalities in which the places are located. The hours for the sale of liquor for consumption on the premises are from 7:00 a.m. to 2:00 a.m., sales except Sundays and election days.

Politics will be kept out of the liquor business by the establishment of a civil service system for employees of the Liquor Control Board.

The personnel of the stores will be selected through competitive examinations held by the Department of Public Instruction. Examination papers of the applicants will bear no identification, and the successful candidates will be ranked strictly according to grade. Appointments will be made in the order of their standing. The candidate receiving the highest mark in the examination will be appointed first; the second, second; and so on. There is no political sponsorship at any time involved in the appointment of employees or in the taking of the examinations.

Private profit is to be eliminated as far as possible from the liquor traffic. The state system eliminates wholesalers and distributors entirely.

Careful analysis of costs indicates that the state stores will be able to sell liquor at a price much lower than prevailing depression bootlegging prices.

One of the first duties of the Control Board will be to make bootlegging unprofitable. And, of course, this is based on the sound theory that when crime does not pay it ceases to exist.

Under the Pennsylvania Plan a new source of revenue for social needs will be provided. No exact estimate of revenue can be made at this time. But millions of dollars will be made available from taxes to help meet the cost of unemployment relief; to make old age assistance payments; and to relieve school districts in which schools are in danger of being closed.

Thus millions of dollars that would go into the pockets of whisky dealers—and possibly into the pockets of politicians—will be diverted to the needs of society.

The money for these social needs, of course, will come from the profits of the operation of the liquor stores; from a floor tax of two dollars per proof gallon of all alcoholic spirits in storage in Pennsylvania; and a manufacturing tax of one dollar per proof gallon tax on distilled spirits.

This manufacturing tax will be refunded to Pennsylvania whisky manufacturers on exports to the extent that manufacturers show proof to the Board of Finance and Revenue that the tax places Pennsylvania whisky at a disadvantage in the state to which it is exported.

Another of the basically important principles under the control plan is that there will be no artificial stimulation of demand for liquor. Whisky will be sold by civil service employees with exactly the same amount of salesmanship as is displayed by an automatic postage stamp vending machine. The mistake that wrecked South Carolina's pre-prohibition dispensary system twenty five years ago—the payment of employees according to the amount of sales—will not be repeated. Store employees will be paid a salary without regard to the amount of liquor they handle.

If sales were in the hands of private retailers and wholesalers there would be sharp competition for business. People would be urged to buy this brand and that brand. Under our plan, anyone can purchase any brand or kind of liquor. If the article wanted is not in stock, the state stores must obtain it.

The state stores will be open from 9 a.m. to 9 p.m., except on Sundays, election days, and legal holidays. There is no limit on the quantity that may be purchased.

The law forbids the importation of liquor into the state except by the state stores and by importers licensed by the Board who may only resell to the stores or to persons outside the state.

Sacramental wine dealers may also import liquor for religious use. Permits will be issued to sacramental wine dealers on the recommendation of regular religious authorities.

In the last analysis, only experience will prove whether or not this liquor control plan will be thoroughly satisfactory. I believe it is the best yet devised.

While, to some extent, our plan is patterned on Canadian experience, it is too early to say whether it will work out as well as the Canadian system, but it is not likely to work out less well.

To many it may seem strange to read a dry Governor's ideas on the distribution of liquor. And so a word of explanation is necessary.

I am not only A dry, but I am dry.

But I accept the decision of the American people. That does not mean I have weakened or surrendered my allegiance to the dry cause. What I have done is what I hold every good American must do under the circumstances. I have accepted the decision of the majority.

This decision against my own view does not lead me to believe that the great majority of the people of the United States are for repeal because they want to guzzle whisky and wallow in the gutter. We are not a nation of drunkards. We were not before prohibition; we are not under prohibition; and we are not going to be after prohibition.

At the moment, very large numbers of American citizens do not believe, as I do, that prohibition at its worst was infinitely better than booze at its best. They have the same right to their opinion that I have to mine.

Roughly there are three opinions on this question of prohibition. The sincere drys are convinced that prohibition is morally and economically right.

Sincere wets believe that prohibition is morally and economically wrong.

And then there are those who have a selfish personal interest in the return of liquor. Whether their interest is a personal thirst, a personal money profit, or a personal political profit, it is not necessary to inquire.

The well-meaning, sincere wets, plus the group of selfishly interested, joined to overwhelm the sincere drys in the battle of the ballot.

The sincere wets and the selfish wets were together then but they will grow farther and farther apart as time goes on.

In Pennsylvania after the election, sincere drys and sincere wets got together and kept the liquor traffic out of the hands of the selfish wets. That can be done throughout the United States.

The Pennsylvania control legislation is an honest effort of sincere drys and sincere wets working together to prevent every preventable evil of the liquor traffic.

The drys realize that it was not their business to attempt to nullify the decision of the American people which, incidentally, could not be done, but to work with all men and women of good will to keep down the evils of liquor.

A large majority of the sincere wets recognized the great responsibility that fell on them with repeal and demanded a proper control of the liquor traffic.

So our Pennsylvania legislation is the result of honest effort to hold back by the dam of efficient control the flood of trouble which will fall upon our people if liquor were permitted once more to become the tool of unscrupulous politicians and the meal ticket for innumerable promiscuous dispensers of booze.

The Pennsylvania State Forests

Out of office, Pinchot struggled to remain in the limelight. Forests and forestry again offered him a public forum. In the 1940s, as his health failed, his mind remained alert, and this short article reflects Pinchot's continued insistence that Pennsylvania's forests, which he had done so much to protect, were essential to the state's continued prosperity. Destructive harvesting, even during wartime, was no substitute for conservative, sustainable management.

Source: Gifford Pinchot press release, August 1942; reprinted in *Science* 96, no. 2487 (August 28, 1942): 198–99.

―――――――――

―――――――――

In a letter to Harrisburg, I said that I had recently seen portions of the state forests of Pennsylvania butchered by lumbermen, and urged that it be stopped.

Harrisburg refused to stop it, and quoted in defense two men without professional training or practical experience in forestry. One of them set up our war needs in excuse. That excuse is worthless.

If the war needed every last tree in Pennsylvania, we should give it, of course. But the war does not need it.

The chief forester of the United States Forest Service says this: "I am convinced that in winning the war it is wholly unnecessary, and in addition the worst possible public and industrial policy, to destroy or depreciate the future productivity of our forests. We can cut all the timber we need to meet every conceivable war requirement and still cut in such a way that the productivity of the forest will be increased rather than impaired."

The productivity of our state forest is being impaired. Within the last two years the most destructive cutting of them ever perpetuated has been and is still going on.

This cutting, which Harrisburg defends, is not limited to trees selected and marked, as good forestry requires, but all trees above certain sizes have been sold and cut, without discrimination.

Trees too young for cutting, trees needed for seed, or to maintain the forest cover, help control floods, prevent erosion or otherwise necessary, have been cut regardless.

The second Harrisburg witness without professional training or practical experience alleged that this is good forestry. I say it is not forestry at all, but tree butchery. For the safety and welfare of Pennsylvania, it ought to be stopped. Will you help stop it?

PART FOUR

WATER, ENERGY, AND POWER

Gifford Pinchot believed in the public control, if not outright owner-ship, of natural resources and the energy that they produced. This was as true of forests and timber as it was of the power that water could generate. "Today, with electricity to give [water power] reach and scope, it is one of the most essential sources of the good life among men," he declared in *Breaking New Ground*. And it is, "unless atomic power shall move into first place, more dangerously subject to the evils of monopoly than any other. Here, if anywhere, public control is essential."

This had been a fundamental truth for Pinchot since early in his career. As a Progressive Era reformer, he was convinced that the key to bettering the lives of all Americans lay in an engaged and well-informed citizenry committed to efficiency and equity. Sustainable democracy required dem-ocratic ownership of the resources necessary for social progress. This conviction formed the basis of his job-ending decision as the nation's chief forester to challenge the Taft administration's commitment to open up Alaskan coalfields to exploitation. He gave the president no option but to fire him for insubordination, an act that then triggered a massive debate in and out of Congress, scuttling Taft's reelection ambitions.

Pinchot carried on this argument through his new work as head of the National Conservation Association, a public-affairs and lobbying opera-tion that provided him with a platform from which to fight for his beliefs. He was not opposed to the mining of coal in Alaska *if* the mining opera-tions were managed under regulations ensuring that the public directly benefitted from the coal's extraction. Neither was he unalterably opposed to the construction of hydroelectric dams in the Mississippi River water-shed, or to the use of this energy source in the production of fertilizer, but he was dead set against allowing capitalists such as Henry Ford to secure unfettered control of public waterways like the Mississippi and the power—electrical and political—that such domination would provide. While governor of Pennsylvania he was eager to bring power to the many rural counties not yet on the grid—communities that, not coincidentally, were a critical component of his voting bloc—but only if that electricity and its essential infrastructure remained in the public hands.

For Pinchot, the evils associated with power monopolies, what he called their "menace," were many, and he spent a considerable amount of his time and money detailing their deleterious impact on local, state, and federal governments, their corrupting influence on a once-free press, and their insidious effect on education at all levels. By contrast, public utilities (which he dubbed Giant Power), by their very nature, would produce incalculable social benefits: "the most substantial aid is raising the stan-dard of living . . . eliminating the drudgery of life, and . . . winning the age-long struggle against poverty." All in all, this beneficent initiative offered "the prospect of a thrilling episode of nation building."

Yet these benefits would never be realized, Pinchot warned, absent strong regulatory oversight insuring their equitable distribution. And for all the strengths of state government, which he had amplified during his two terms as Pennsylvania's chief executive, he argued time and again that the nation-state must be the locus of such control: "My firm conviction is that the questions which the utilities have put before the people cannot be settled by individual states acting alone; that the problem has become in many aspects essentially national; and that it can be solved only under the leadership of the Nation, supplementing the actions and powers of the individual states." This top-down leadership strategy was particularly critical, given the concentration of the utilities' political power and the great wealth that they deployed through lobbying to secure favorable legislation. Capitol Hill was the one place where it was possible to "meet them on something like equal terms. Unless we meet them where their strength is, we have in fact surrendered to them. And if we surrender in this field, there is less than little hope for victory in the more complicated matter of establishing an industrial order which can function without periodic depressions."

Stabilizing the flow of water, like that of electric power, also required a long and tough struggle, which Pinchot synthesized in his last published article. It appeared shortly before he died. It traces this test of wills over thirty years: from 1905, when the Forest Service was created and began to manage the watersheds that were located within the national forests, and to the 1930 and 1935 Federal Power Acts, which established an independent commission to "regulate the interstate transmission and sale of electric energy." That such regulation would be necessary well into the future, Pinchot had no doubt, for at its base this was an enduring and "always difficult contest between private greed and the public good."

What Shall We Do with the Coal in Alaska?

Although he was a forester by training, Pinchot's conservationism was broadly defined. What worked in the woods would also work in the mines, on the grasslands, and with rivers. He made this case in an extended essay about the Alaskan coalfields, an article written shortly after President Taft had fired Pinchot for challenging the administration's efforts to lease some of these rich veins in the distant territory. As part of his public campaign to keep this issue before the voters, Pinchot traveled to Alaska, visited the affected areas, talked with miners and the media, and published his findings in this article for the *Saturday Evening Post*. If President Taft thought that in forcing Pinchot out of the executive branch he was rid of him, this piece suggested otherwise.

Source: Box 943, Gifford Pinchot Papers, Library of Congress; subsequently published in *Saturday Evening Post*, August 26, 1911, 3–5.

———————————
———————————

What shall we do with the coal in Alaska? Use it, of course.

How much coal is there in Alaska ready to use? Alaska is two-and-a-half times as big as Texas. So far as we know now, about two square miles in every hundred contain coal—that is to say, coal can be found over about twelve thousand square miles. Not all of this coal, however, is high enough in grade or accessible or otherwise valuable enough to be worth mining under present conditions. Only about ten percent of it—of twelve hundred square miles—would pay for development and of this less than nine hundred and fifty square miles contain high-grade coal. In other words, the coal seams of Alaska are as extensive as Maryland; the useable part is as large as Rhode Island; while the valuable, high-grade coals cover less than a county.

Nevertheless, there is more good coal in Alaska than ever was in Pennsylvania. Most of the best of it, so far as our knowledge goes, is contained in two great fields of high-grade coal. The Matanuska field lies about one hundred and eighty miles by rail from the coast and the port of Seward on Resurrection Bay. It contains about six hundred million tons. The Bering River field is smaller, but nearer the coast and more accessible to the great markets which border the Pacific. It contains about thirty percent of the known high-grade coal in Alaska, or not less than four thousand million tons. Here are or were the well-known Cunningham claims, which have recently been declared fraudulent and invalid by the Interior Department.

These claims alone have enough coal to supply Washington, Oregon, California, and Alaska for nearly twenty years at the rate they are using it now. It is the Bering River field that is tributary to Controller Bay.

The quality of Alaska coal is as remarkable as its quantity. About half of the Bering River field is high grade bituminous coal comparable to the Pocahontas and New River coals of West Virginia; and about half is anthracite but little inferior to the best anthracite in Pennsylvania. It lies within twenty-five miles of tidewater. There is urgent need and strong demand for it in Alaska and beyond, and yet none of it has turned a wheel or smelted a pound of iron.

There must be a strong reason why these prodigious stores of fuel in seams measuring, some of them, twenty to fifty feet or more of solid coal—easy to reach, easy to mine, and easy to sell—should have remained locked up until now. The wonder grows when we consider that Washington, Oregon, and California are without any considerable supply of high-grade coal of their own, and that good steam-coal sells in San Francisco for more than three times what it brings in New York. The Government recently paid twenty-eight dollars a ton in Alaska for coal it could have bought in Newport News for less than three. Yet not half a dozen coal mines have been opened in Alaska and the combined product of all of them is altogether insignificant.

Here is a situation that well deserves to be called amazing and intolerable. Let it be kept clearly in mind that the non-use of Alaska serves no good purpose whatsoever. The less coal burned in the long Alaska winters, the greater drain upon the forests for fuel. The present industries of the territory are hampered and restrained by the high cost of fuel, transportation suffers, and the establishment of new industries is discouraged and deferred. If coal were as cheap as Nature has made it abundant underground the new growth for which Alaska has waited would now be well begun.

What power has checked the development of Alaska coal? From first to last, the delay lies mainly at the door of the obstructionists in Congress, who kept bad laws on the statute books, and in part also at the door of the men who tried to seize what they had no right to get—the syndicates of claimants, and their friends and backers, who preferred to take their chance of illegal gains under the old conditions rather than see the coal opened on terms that would benefit all.

The Bering River field was discovered in 1896, the Matanuska coal field about two years later. At that time and for years afterward, Alaska was little known in comparison to today. The possibility of a railroad to the Bering field lay in the future . . . and the prompt development of the mines was impossible. Nevertheless, the Bering River field was in time thickly covered with coal mining locations and the process of getting title from the Government was begun.

Unfortunately for Alaska, very many of these claims was fraudulent in character. The law under which they were located was a difficult one to work under, but nonetheless it must be obeyed. Since there were believed to be many infractions of the law, investigations by the Government became necessary, and that involved delay. Thus the well-founded suspicion of law breaking by the claimants retarded development at the start. Meanwhile coal-land frauds in the United States called the attention of President Roosevelt and his advisers to the reasons why the nation ought not to part with its coal. After careful study, the President, in 1906, withdrew from entry the coal still in the public lands both in the Alaska and the United States. In his message of December 3, 1906, he said:

> It is not wise of the nation to alienate its remaining coal lands. I have temporarily withdrawn from settlement all the lands which the Geological Survey has indicated in all probability as containing coal-mining coal. The question, however, can only be properly settled by legislation, which in my judgment should provide for the withdrawal of these lands from sale or from entry, save in certain special circumstances. The ownership would remain with the United States, which should not, however, attempt to work them, but permit them to be worked by private individuals under a royalty system with the Government keeping such control as to permit it to see that no excessive price was charged to consumers. . . . The withdrawal of these coal lands would constitute a policy analogous to that which has been followed in withdrawing the forest lands from ordinary settlement. The coal, like the forests, should be treated as the property of the public, and its disposal should be under conditions which would inure to the benefit of the public as a whole.

It has been charged that this withdrawal was a barrier to the development of the coal-lands in Alaska. Nothing could be farther from the fact. Practically the whole of the Bering River coal-field was covered with locations before the withdrawal was made, and every valid location was excepted from the withdrawal and could be freely developed and patented; and the coal could be put on market. It was not the withdrawal, but a defective and unworkable law and the lack of valid entries that locked up the coal.

President Roosevelt did not rest with a single effort to get the laws amended and to open the coalfields to legitimate development. Just two weeks after the message quoted above, he sent a special message to Congress in which he urged again the recommendations already made, and added that the result of the adopting laws would be "not only to stop the land frauds but to prevent delays in patenting valid land claims and to conserve the indispensable fuel resources of the nation."

In one more special and two more regular messages the subject was pressed again and again upon the attention of Congress and the whole power of the Administration was applied to get the law amended as private enterprise and public welfare both required. In 1907, among others, a model coal-leasing law was drawn up by Judge [George] Woodruff, then an Assistant Attorney-General under Mr. Garfield, and introduced by Senator [Knute] Nelson [of Minnesota]. In the same year another excellent bill was drawn and offered by Senator Robert La Follette [of Wisconsin] after consultation with President Roosevelt, and it has been introduced in every succeeding Congress. In House and Senate alike, it was impossible to get favorable action.

In 1909 and 1910 came the conflict between the Forest Service and the Interior Department over the Conservation policy and the Cunningham claims. While it was in progress Congress waited for the recommendation of the Investigating Committee, part of whose purpose, it was declared, was to prepare a plan for the wise development of Alaska. The investigation taught the public much that it never suspected about Alaska, and its conclusion opened wide the way for constructive legislation genuinely in the interest of the people.

Once more the friends of privilege stood in the road. Bills were reported from the Public Lands Committee of the House and Senate, each yielding to the demand for a leasing system where yielding was necessary, but each containing "jokers" so carefully devised in favor of special interests, and so plainly hostile to the public welfare when uncovered, that neither bill could pass. . . .

It is due, then, to the inactivity of Congress as a whole and the bad activity of certain elements in Congress that the problem of how to handle the Alaska coal is still unsettled, although the lines along which the settlement should come have long been known.

. . . At the time when, in message after message, the enactment of a law to lease Alaska coal was being urged upon Congress, when bill after bill was being introduced to provide for the development of the coal without injustice to the consumer, few men in Congress looked upon leasing as a practicable method of handling Alaska coal. Now substantially all are agreed that the leasing system is necessary and right, and that the title to the coal must be held in the public hands. The country knows that private ownership in the coal lands of Alaska means monopoly—and can mean nothing else.

Is it possible to draw a Government lease that will safeguard the public interests and at the same time be attractive enough for investors to secure prompt opening of the mines? It is done commonly and with entire success in Australia and other countries, and assuredly it can be done in ours, where the leasing of privately owned coal mines is well known. In the mining of the precious metals, also, it is a growing practice in our country, despite the hazardous nature of the undertaking. Coal-leasing, on the other hand, is comparatively free from the element of risk.

The man who puts his capital into the ground to promote the general welfare by supplying coal is entitled to fair treatment. Under a Government lease, the coal mine operator is not given the mine in perpetuity; but he must have it long enough to get the capital invested out again—a length of time we estimate at thirty or forty years. He must have coal land enough to maintain a profitable output during the whole term of his contract with the Government, and so may need in certain cases as much as five thousand acres under his lease. The royalty on a ton of coal must be set low enough and the price he may charge must be set high enough to insure a profit commensurate with the risk he faces; and the regulations under which he operates must be simple, practical from the point of view of the man who does the work and wholly free from unnecessary restrictions and needless red tape. . . .

The safety of the men who actually mine the coal must be provided for. If, for a single year, accidents on any railroad should become as great and horrible as the mining fatalities the newspapers constantly relate, the passenger trains on that road would pass empty day after day from the beginning to the end of their run. Yet the losses we hear about are smaller than those that never reach our ear. There is no reason why multitudes of men should die by suffocation year after year in the coal mines of the United States. There must be no repetition of these horrors in Alaska; and so the lease holders must guarantee, under the inspection of the Bureau of Mines, all possible safety to the men who do the work. To provide for the health and safety of the miners is a public duty and must be made a public charge.

Finally, and most important of all, the rights of the people of the United States—that vast, undying owner to whom the coal belongs—must be considered. The coal must be taken out clean in mining, for what remains is wanted and eventually the people will need all the coal. At the end of a reasonable time the lease must terminate, so that it may be renewed on such conditions as the public welfare in the future may require. The people must receive a reasonable but not large return for the use of their property. And there must be complete publicity of all business under the lease.

One of the principal reasons the great corporations have been able to control our politics as well as our business is that the public has no legal right to be informed of their affairs. Any company that mines the people's coal upon the people's lands may be fairly required to keep the people fully informed of what it does. The day is well-nigh over when the businessman who supplies a necessity of life, like coal or oil, can be considered to have no public function. How such a man conducts his business is of immediate interest and intimate concern to all the people who use what he supplies. So, under a coal-land lease in Alaska, the people may fairly require that what is being done upon their property by their agent, for that is what the lease really is, shall be laid fully before them.

. . . The opening of the coal-fields under Government regulation is but a start in the great work in Alaska which the Congress of the United States has yet to do. Alaska is the storehouse of the nation. Most of its timberlands are already fairly protected against destruction, while remaining open to use, for they have been included in national forests; but the fisheries, the copper, the gold, the power, the land, are other resources whose value to this country it is impossible to compute.

No comprehensive plan for the development of Alaska's resources ought to be adopted—and I believe that none can be put into effect— which fails to provide for equality of opportunity in the use of them under Government supervision and control. If conditions are such in Alaska that development without monopoly is impossible, then let us, the people of the United States, become our own monopolists and hold the monopolies in our own hands. As a nation, we can afford to assume the risks of development without taking from the consumer the huge profit of the promoter who succeeds, or saddling the public with the huge losses which are often shifted upon it by the promoter who fails. If conditions make for monopoly in Alaska let it be a monopoly by which the people are the owner, not the toll-payers—the beneficiaries, not the victims.

Testimony on the Hetch Hetchy Dam to the House Committee on Public Lands

Pinchot's testimony concerning the possible construction of a dam in the Hetch Hetchy Valley in Yosemite National Park offered a direct challenge to John Muir and other preservationists who argued that no dam should be built inside a protected national park. For Pinchot, utility—that is, the provision of publicly owned water and hydropower for an earthquake-shattered San Francisco—took precedence over Muir's no less powerful aesthetic claims made in an attempt to halt the remote valley's inundation. Pinchot, a longtime supporter of the dam, was no longer the nation's chief forester when he spoke to the Committee on Public Lands on June 25, 1913, yet his arguments still carried weight. The committee would vote in favor of the dam, and later that year Congress would pass legislation clearing the way for the construction of the O'Shaughnessy Dam. The vote was 43–25 (with 29 abstentions).

Source: *Hetch Hetchy Dam Site: Hearing Before the Committee on Public Lands, HR 6281*, 25–34. 63rd Cong. 1 (1913).

———————————
———————————

The CHAIRMAN [Rep. Scott Ferris, D-OK]: In deference to Mr. [Gifford] Pinchot's wishes, as he desires to leave the city, he will be permitted to address the committee at this time if there is no objection.

Mr. PINCHOT: Mr. Chairman and gentlemen of the committee, my testimony will be very short. I presume that you very seldom have the opportunity of passing upon any measure before the Committee on the Public Lands which has been so thoroughly thrashed out as this one. This question has been up now, I should say, more than 10 years, and the reasons for and against the proposition have not only been discussed over and over again, but a great deal of the objections which could be composed have been composed, until finally there remains simply the one question of the objection of the Spring Valley Water Co. I understand that the much more important objection of the Tuolumne irrigation districts has been overcome. There is, I understand, objection on the part of other irrigators, but that does not go to the question of using the water, but merely to the distribution of the water. So we come now face to face with the perfectly clean question of what is the best use to which this water that flows out of the Sierras can be put. As we all know, there is no use of water that is higher than the domestic use. Then, if there is, as the engineers tell us, no other source of supply that is anything like so reasonably available as this one; if this is the best, and, within reasonable limits of cost, the only means of supplying San Francisco with water, we come straight to the question of whether the advantage of leaving this valley in a state of nature is greater than the advantage of using it for the benefit of the city of San Francisco.

Now, the fundamental principle of the whole conservation policy is that of use, to take every part of the land and its resources and put it to that use in which it will best serve the most people, and I think there can be no question at all but that in this case we have an instance in which all weighty considerations demand the passage of the bill. There are, of course, a very large number of incidental changes that will arise after the passage of the bill. The construction of roads, trails, and telephone systems which will follow the passage of this bill will be a very important help in the park and forest reserves. The national forest telephone system and the roads and trails to which this bill will lead will form an important additional help in fighting fire in the forest reserves. As has already been set forth by the two Secretaries, the presence of these additional means of communication will mean that the national forest and the national park will be visited by very large numbers of people who cannot visit them now. I think that the men who assert that it is better to leave a piece of natural scenery in its natural condition have rather the better of the argument, and I believe if we had nothing else to consider than the delight of the few men and women who would yearly go into the Hetch Hetchy Valley, then it should be left in its natural condition. But the considerations on the other side of the question to my mind are simply overwhelming, and so much so that I have never been able to see that there was any reasonable argument against the use of this water supply by the city of San Francisco. . . .

Mr. JOHN RAKER[1] [D-CA]: Taking the scenic beauty of the park as it now stands, and the fact that the valley is sometimes swamped along in June and July, is it not a fact that if a beautiful dam is put there, as is contemplated, and as the picture is given by the engineers, with the roads contemplated around the reservoir and with other trails, it will be more beautiful than it is now, and give more opportunity for the use of the park?

1. Rep. Raker is noteworthy for having introduced the legislation to clear the way for the dam and for filing the bill that would establish the National Park Service.

Mr. PINCHOT: Whether it will be more beautiful, I doubt, but the use of the park will be enormously increased. I think there is no doubt about that.

Mr. RAKER: In other words, to put it a different way, there will be more beauty accessible than there is now?

Mr. PINCHOT: Much more beauty will be accessible than now.

Mr. RAKER: And by putting in roads and trails the Government, as well as the citizens of the Government, will get more pleasure out of it than at the present time?

Mr. PINCHOT: You might say from the standpoint of enjoyment of beauty and the greatest good to the greatest number, they will be conserved by the passage of this bill, and there will be a great deal more use of the beauty of the park than there is now.

Mr. RAKER: Have you seen Mr. John Muir's criticism of the bill? You know him?

Mr. PINCHOT: Yes, sir; I know him very well. He is an old and a very good friend of mine. I have never been able to agree with him in his attitude toward the Sierras for the reason that my point of view has never appealed to him at all. When I became Forester and denied the right to exclude sheep and cows from the Sierras, Mr. Muir thought I had made a great mistake, because I allowed the use by an acquired right of a large number of people to interfere with what would have been the utmost beauty of the forest. In this case I think he has unduly given way to beauty as against use.

Mr. RAKER: Would that be practically the same as to the position of the Sierras [sic] Club?

Mr. PINCHOT: I am told that there is a very considerable difference of opinion in the club on this subject.[2]

---

2. When Raker pressed Pinchot about the possibility of salvage logging large swaths of the area around the Hetch Hetchy Valley, Pinchot refused to go along, tempering a wholesale application of his utilitarian principles: "I do not believe that a national park should be used as a source of timber supply. . . . A place like a national park should be protected against that. I think we can have a little timber fall down and die for the sake of having the place look like no human foot has ever been in it," noting that Yosemite National Park "is one of the great wonders of the world, and I would leave it just as it is so far as possible."

Mr. RAKER: Among themselves?

Mr. PINCHOT: Yes, sir.

Mr. RAKER: You think then, as a matter of fact, that the provisions of this bill carried out would relieve the situation; in other words, that there is no valid objection which they could make?

Mr. PINCHOT: That is my judgment. . . .

Muscle Shoals

Through his position as the driving force behind the National Conservation Association, Pinchot kept in close touch with the principal challenges facing the movement. Most crucial, he believed, was the inimical relationship between the federal government and big business; corporations routinely tried to privatize what Pinchot argued must remain public. So when he learned that Henry Ford was offering to buy the publicly owned dams at Muscle Shoals, Pinchot's antennae went up. What follows is a detailed critique of Ford's (ultimately unsuccessful) offer; the particulars are less important than the larger claim that public resources should remain in the public's hands.

Source: Statement released by the National Conservation Association, August 27, 1921; cited in the *New York Times*, August 28, 1921, 2, and later excerpted in *American Fertilizer* 55 (September 10, 1921): 78, 82, 84.

_____

_____

The recent offer of Henry Ford to take over government property at Muscle Shoals, on the Tennessee River, is so important that I take the liberty of pointing out certain essential facts.

The first part of the Ford offer is to lease the Wilson Dam and dam number 3 for 100 years, with indefinite renewals, provided the government will complete them and install machinery to produce 850,000 horsepower. Mr. Ford offers to pay six percent on the $28,000,000 he estimates will be necessary to complete this work, or 3.4 percent on $48,000,000, Mr. Ford's own estimate of the whole government investment in dams, locks, and power houses.

Even if we add all other payments (the so-called amortization payments for the repair, maintenance, and operations of the dams, locks, and power houses) the total would be equivalent to interest at the rate of 3.6 percent. Mr. Ford also offers to give 300 horsepower to the government to operate the locks.

Please note that for the waterpower itself Mr. Ford would pay nothing and that he would be free from all taxes on the property. Other leases of waterpower from the government not only pay the total cost of building their own dams and powerhouses and pay taxes on them, but they also pay for the waterpower in addition. The Ford offer is like offering a man 3.6 percent on the cost of factory for rent, and then asking him to throw in a coal mine to supply fuel for the engines for nothing.

There is no allowance for depreciation, and the government would beyond question have to pay the cost of injury to the dams or locks from floods or other causes. Moreover there is nothing in the offer to indicate that the government, in order to protect its own property, would not have to bear the cost of replacing enormously expensive machinery when it had been worn out in Mr. Ford's service.

The second part of Mr. Ford's offer is to buy Nitrate Plant No. 1, which cost the government in round figures $13,000,000; Nitrate Plant #2, which cost the government in round figures $70,000,000, and other property, which brings the total to $88,000,000, and [for Ford] to pay $5,000,000 for it all. The property for which this offer is made includes steam machinery to produce 160,000 horsepower, which alone is worth far more than Mr. Ford's offer for the whole. In addition, the government is to buy from the Alabama Power Company the land upon which certain of the foregoing structures were built, and to turn that over to Mr. Ford also.

In return for the lease, the purchased property, and for the waterpower without charge, Mr. Ford offers in addition to the payments mentioned above, to do three principal things:

First, to maintain Nitrate Plant No. 2 ready to be operated . . . in time of war for the production of explosives, and in the event of war to turn it over for that purpose.

Second, to operate Nitrate Plant No. 2 to approximate present capacity in the production of nitrogen and other fertilizer compounds, and in this business limit his net profit from the manufacture and sale of fertilizer . . . to 8 percent.

Third, the offer as written suggests producing, but contains no direct proposal to produce, fertilizer for the benefit of American farmers. That could, of course, be corrected in the final contract, for I have no doubt that Mr. Ford desires to make fertilizer at a total net profit of 8 percent. Nitrate Plant No. 2, however, is not adapted to making fertilizer, but only cyanamid, one of several materials used in the production of fertilizer, and not one of the best at that.

The fact is that the Ford offer is not mainly a fertilizer proposition. It is seven parts waterpower to one part fertilizer, even if the fertilizer part should work out. For even if Nitrate Plant No. 2 would be permanently employed in the manufacture of fertilizer, it would consume but 100,000 horsepower out of the 850,000 installation. This is the heart of the whole matter.

As a waterpower proposition, the Ford offer is in every important point is directly contrary to the Roosevelt water power policy, which after 15 years of struggle was finally enacted into law last year.

The water policy provides that all water power leases shall be limited to fifty years. The Ford offer asks for 100 years with indefinite renewal.

The Roosevelt policy provides for return of the government works at the end of fifty years. The Ford offer provides for indefinite private possession of the government works.

The Roosevelt policy provides regulation of the price to the power consumer. The Ford offer, so far as the United States is concerned, provides no check on what the power consumer must pay.

The Roosevelt policy provides that public waterpower taken for profit shall make a return to the public. The Ford offer asks for many hundred thousand horsepower for nothing.

The amount of power Mr. Ford could develop, under his proposal, is greater by half than all that is now being developed at Niagara Falls. If Mr. Ford were to pay for it at the rates charged by the government to other companies that build their own works, as Mr. Ford would not, it could cost him about 150 thousand dollars a year.

Beyond question Nitrate Plant No. 2 ought to be maintained in condition for making explosives in case of war. Most certainly it ought to be used for making fertilizer for American farmers. The wisdom of developing waterpower on the Tennessee and its tributaries is beyond question. But all things can be done in fairness to the public.

I do not believe that Mr. Ford's offer should be summarily rejected. I do believe that it should be changed:

First, to make it fit the Roosevelt waterpower conservation policy, now the law of the land;

Second, to make it for the property of the people, something approaching what that property is really worth, and

Third, to make it clear what it offers the farmers without a doubt.

It is said that certain Wall Street magnates who hate Mr. Ford are anxious that his offer should be rejected. What these men think about Mr. Ford and his offer surely is no reason for giving him public property of enormous value for a consideration wholly inadequate and on terms utterly unfair to the public.

I should be glad to see Mr. Ford to make money, and plenty of money, out of taking over the property of the people as he proposed to do, but not such perpetual and gigantic profits as his proposal would assure. It is fair to consider the public also, and to remember that all the annual payments Mr. Ford offers to make would amount to only one-third of the yearly taxation necessary to meet the interest charge . . . on the government's net investment in the property he proposed to take over, and that he would get the waterpower for nothing.

Giant Power

Because he believed that the utilities and resources that sustained modern life ought to be owned by the people and not private capital, as governor, Pinchot became a forceful promoter of what he called Giant Power. It would unlock the state's potential, elevating the conditions of those laboring in the mines, on the farm, and inside factories and mills. This engine of change, under the watchful eye of state regulation, would make the Commonwealth a brighter and richer place.

Originally published in *The Survey* 25 (March 1, 1924): 561–62.

———————

———————

As in the story books of our childhood a giant—Giant Power this time—is about to do wondrous things for the human race. From the power field perhaps more than from any other quarter we can expect in the near future the most substantial aid in raising the standard of living, in eliminating the physical drudgery of life, and in winning the age-long struggle against poverty. For weeks and months after our entry into the Great War the effectiveness which we ultimately developed was held in check by what someone has called the distance disease—the battle-front was three thousand miles away instead of at the far end of a telephone wire. Principally because our utilities—even the largest and most far reaching of them—have grown up out of small and isolated beginnings we have been slow to recognize that distance is a rapidly disappearing factor in public utility development. In high tension transmission of electric current distance is as unimportant and state lines as meaningless as in the pumping of oil from the Oklahoma fields to the Atlantic seaboard. Giant Power now seeks a new form of cooperation among these vast enterprises in which the distance factor will be accorded only the importance which modern science and engineering gives it.

Giant Power is a term coined to suggest the realization of far-reaching social objectives through a vaulting engineering technique. We conceive Giant Power as a social force unshackling our people for the Great Adventure. Giant Power is also the equivalent of the sum total of controlled and interconnected mechanical energy within an area the limits of which are fixed—not arbitrarily as by state lines or by the historical development of some public or private enterprise—but by technical considerations. In a way we have always had such pools of power—every independent power

plant with its distribution wires constituted such a system. But now that
the distance factor is all but removed, these interconnected areas spread
out wondrously—their radial power lines extending hundreds of miles in
every direction from common generating centers.

Giant Power means giving to every producer of current an opportunity
to add to a common stock and to every user an opportunity to draw therefrom. Giant Power means the practice on the broadest possible scale of every
possible economy, such as the pooling of standby facilities and the elimination of every waste, such as that due to a low power factor. But Giant
Power also means the education of the public to the point where it can
intelligently and fully cooperate with public and private enterprise in these
objectives. We approach the time when the load factor of a community may
be made to mean more than the interest rate or the cost of living index.

The Pennsylvania Legislature at the session held during the Spring of
1923 made an appropriation at my recommendation for a Giant Power
Survey which in the words of the Act is to study

> the water and fuel resources available for Pennsylvania and . . .
> the most practicable means for their full utilization for power
> development and other related uses; to recommend such policy
> with respect to the generation and distribution of electric energy
> as will secure for the industries, railroads, farms and homes of the
> Commonwealth an abundant and cheap supply of electric current
> for industrial, transportation, agricultural and domestic use; the
> practicability of the establishment of giant power plants for the
> generation of electricity by fuel power near coal mines; the saving
> and the utilization of the by-products of coal; the transmission
> and distribution of electric energy throughout the Common-
> wealth; the electrification of railroads; the generation of electrical
> energy by water-power; and the coordination of water power and
> fuel power development with the regulation of rivers by storage
> for water supply, transportation, public health, recreation and
> other beneficial uses.

Further on in the Act the Giant Power Survey Board which is to direct
the work is charged—"to keep in view the mutual interest of this Commonwealth and other States and to outline plans for the interchange of
electrical energy with all other states within the practicable transmission
distance."

As Pennsylvania with her huge fuel resources and intensive industrial
development appears to be the heart of the Giant Power System—at least

for the northeastern section of the country—it is well to have her attitude toward sister and neighbor states thus clearly stated. In planning our Giant Power Survey—an "outline survey" the Legislature wisely called it—we are utilizing a method which, curious enough, appears to be almost unique in such inquiries, i.e. *we are studying the social needs first*. When we consulted the lawyers, they said, "Find out what you want to do and we will show you how to do it under the Constitution of the United States and the Constitution of the State of Pennsylvania." A little later the engineers—not to be outdone—responded, "You tell us what you want to accomplish and we will show you how to do it."

Perhaps another point of departure from the usual is found in the fact that our first concern will be with the small user—particularly with the farmer. No system of electrical development would be technically sound if not built on estimates of the industrial power load. Just so, no system can be considered socially sound which ignores the more or less immediate requirements of upwards of 900,000 farm population, a million or more rural population not living on farms, and perhaps as many urban and semi-urban householders—now without current.

One of the most pronounced and untoward effects of the Industrial Revolution with its mechanical power was the massing of population in urban centers. If, under the Giant Power dispensation, mechanical energy can not only be made cheap but distributed broadly, authorities agree in predicting a spreading out of population—a veritable "back to the land" movement. Only at a few points in the United States has a sustained effort been made to develop a rural load. Even so these efforts have been in the more densely populated country districts or in territory contiguous to urban or semi-urban centers of population and therefore easily reached.

Just how far we can go in carrying power to the farmers of Pennsylvania will not be known until the survey is completed. We have roughly 200,000 farms and 100,000 miles of road. Hence, over the whole State our farms are one half mile apart. In many of the counties the average distance between farms will be much less. In Ontario [Canada], where the Government owns the power system, they estimate the cost of constructing overhead rural lines at $1,200 a mile. Recently they have discovered that they can lay cable underground in rural districts at about $800 the mile. Interest and amortization charges on such an investment will evidently not act as a bar especially where farms average three or more to the mile. Experience in Ontario indicates that farms supplied with current sell for $1,000 more than those without.

France has recently created a fund of 60 million francs to be used in aiding groups of farmers to pay for rural lines. Under this arrangement the

Government meets half the expense of such construction. In Ontario under recent legislation the Government pays one-half the "prime cost" which is interpreted to mean one-half the cost of lines along public highways or about one-third the whole cost of making rural connections. I cite these two cases to show that in other countries it has been considered so important to put power on the farms as to warrant government subventions.

In much the same way, cheap and plentiful power is almost sure to effect a wider distribution of our industrial effort. One of the impressive points about the "Hydro" system in Ontario is the fact that all the small towns from Niagara to Windsor (250 miles away) have access to power on relatively equal terms. Here industrial development is widely diffused and even small towns—towns "where the community mind has a fair chance to grow up and function"—are on somewhat the same footing as the larger centers.

Giant Power looks forward to making current at the places and under the conditions where it can be made cheapest and then transporting it, if need be, great distances to points of use. Competent authorities say that this is now fully feasible. There was a time when the cost of making "juice" (the vernacular for electric current) at the mine mouth was without special interest for the Bucks County farmer or even for householders in our larger cities. In each instance the controlling factor was the cost of making the current quite near home. Now however, every Pennsylvanian is interested in knowing the cost of producing power at the point where it can be produced at the lowest cost. This is because current made at any point within the Commonwealth can now be transmitted to any other point with a loss so small as to be negligible in the rate charged.

Not one pound of the 400 odd millions of tons of bituminous coal used in Pennsylvania each year for making power is processed so far as I have been able to discover, for the recovery of those constituent elements which add nothing to its thermal effectiveness. In any school book on chemistry will be found a long list of desirable commodities which can be manufactured from these by-products: tar for roadbuilding, ammonia for fertilizers, delicate perfumes, and a wide range of medicines. To the by-product industry is given the largest share of credit for the industrial success of Germany before the Great War. Perhaps if we can learn how so to combine our Giant Power stations with by-products recovery plants as to stop this waste we can effect an economy which will more than offset the few mills difference between the cost of current developed from the best water power and that generated from modern steam or carbo-electric steam plants.

But under this new power dispensation there will be effected numerous changes, the gains from which largely elude the dollars and cents method of measurement, such as the elimination of the smoke nuisance from our cities. Again, our next peak of prosperity will see railroad facilities strained to the breaking point. There is no quicker or probably cheaper way of increasing present steam rail facilities than through electrification, thus not only adding to the mobility of equipment but making unnecessary the hauling of locomotive fuel. Cheap and widely distributed power would mean the removal of the coal load from the railroads, thus making room for larger quantities of graded commodities.

Right here I cannot refrain from referring to the improvements in living conditions in the coal mining regions which may conceivably be effected by Giant Power. Through the building at the mines of Giant Power plants supplying hundreds of thousands of consumers the fuel demand will be stabilized, with all that means as affecting both miners' wages and income. In operations of this magnitude there is every incentive for the utilization of machinery and the elimination of back-breaking effort. With the probable reductions in price of electric current which Giant Power implies, it will be used in the homes of the miners as never before, first for light and then for washing, cooking, etc.

Giant Power developments can best be considered entirely apart from the broader question of public as contrasted with private ownership and operation. We have in Pennsylvania outstanding examples of effective public operation of utilities. But for the most part our public utilities have resulted from private initiative. This is especially true of the electric utilities. It may not prove a difficult task to coordinate these private enterprises under common policies. Their owners will doubtless welcome the opportunity to demonstrate that far-reaching social ends are as readily obtainable under regulated private enterprise as under direct public ownership and control. At any rate it is usually good judgment to build on what is until we discover a better way.

Some leadership on the part of the State government is required in any event. In the first place, many of the questions involved in any broad consideration of Giant Power developments are inextricably interwoven with the theory of regulation of public utilities under which we now operate. Further, where any matter arises which is likely to effect vitally two such outstanding industries as coal and transportation, it is only the part of wisdom for the State to keep itself advised. Again, more and more society acting through the State must take cognizance of waste, which, both as an element of present day cost and in its influence on the conservation of natural resources, has long since become a matter of deep public concern.

Altogether, then, Giant Power presents the prospect of a thrilling episode in nation building. It would appear to be an altogether hopeful task in social engineering to show how recent discoveries of science and developments in the art of power production may be applied so as to effect immeasurably for good the lives of all the people.

Prevention First

The massive floods of 1927 that ripped down the Mississippi River and its many tributaries led the U.S. Army Corps of Engineers to propose an increasing number of levees and flood-control systems. Pinchot thought otherwise. Here and in a series of other articles, he applies the lessons he had first learned in Europe about the important role that forested headwaters play in the minimizing of flood damage. He was not alone in believing that these particular floods were a direct result of bad science and poor planning.

Originally published in *The Survey* 13 (July 1, 1927): 267–69.

―――――――――――
―――――――――――

The Mississippi flood is a man-made disaster. I do not forget that without an excessive rainfall it could not have happened. But neither does a great forest fire, set by a casual match, happen without an excessive lack of rainfall. In both cases men are responsible.

A river is a great natural balance sheet. It is the result of innumerable natural forces and phenomena—the rain, the earth, gravity, erosion, and many another. Where the river flows and how it flows represents a vast and beautiful natural equilibrium established among them all. When men destroy that equilibrium, inevitably they pay the price.

We Americans have been busy ever since we landed in America arranging things so that the price to be paid would be heavy. We have cut and burned the forests and have not replaced them. We have destroyed the natural reservoirs of the swamps. We have everywhere helped the water to run off quickly. We have confined the beds of streams between levees, or, as at Pittsburgh, we have used them as dumping grounds until the restriction of the channel became one of the principal causes of serious floods. In a word, we have done practically everything we could to force the Mississippi to make us trouble, and nothing effective to prevent floods.

In dealing with this greatest natural calamity in the history of the United States, we must, if we are wise, give as much attention to what men have done to the Mississippi as to what the Mississippi has done to men. What is wrong, and what is the remedy?

I heard Dwight F. Davis, secretary of war, at the recent flood control meeting at Chicago, point out with clearness and cogency that we must not act too hastily with regard to the Mississippi—that what we need first of all is a plan. He assumed that the Corps of Engineers of the United

States Army would make that plan. We have been dealing with the Mississippi River for half a century, but, when a great emergency arises on that river, Secretary Davis tells the country it must prepare a plan. That would not be necessary if it had a plan now. The worst enemy of the Corps could not formulate a more destructive charge against its efficiency in the regulation of the Mississippi. Unless my dates are wrong, the Corps of Engineers of the United States Army has had charge of the river since 1879. I do not forget that the Mississippi River Commission is nominally in charge. But that commission is mainly composed of and entirely dominated by the Army engineers. From 1879 to 1927 is forty-eight years. Forty-eight years is practically half a century. At the end of that half century of control work by the Army engineers comes the worst and most costly flood that we know anything about. And more than that, the Corps of Engineers, after half a century of active and responsible dealing with the river, does not know what to do next—is without a plan for its control.

How is it that it has no plan?

It is a cardinal principle of the engineers that the Corps must never be wrong, no matter what the facts. The Army engineers long ago took the position that levees, and levees only, were needed to control the floods of the Father of Waters, and have stuck to that opinion in spite of one demonstration after another, by one flood after another, that they were wrong. In 1912, and, to go back no further, in 1922, the Mississippi furnished conclusive proof that the "levees only" theory was utterly untenable. But it took a disaster that cost a billion dollars and made three-quarters of a million people homeless to shake the conviction of the Army engineers that what they had once said was so must always be so in spite of hell and high water.

The Corps has been shaken, but not very much. Its present position is that spillways shall now be added to levees, and that to consider any method of river regulation in addition to these two is evidence of moral turpitude. A lot of the rest of us, however, believe not only in levees and spillways but in forests and storage reservoirs and every other practicable means of regulating the river. We believe in prevention first. We believe that with floods, just as with epidemics and forest fires, an ounce of prevention is better than a pound of cure. We think that to keep a savage bull shut up is far better than to be forced to capture and control him after he has got into the china shop.

There has been no lack of weighty opinion behind our position. The Inland Waterways Commission was appointed by President Roosevelt to consider this question. It was probably (in spite of the fact that I was a member of it) the ablest and best-equipped body that has ever considered river problems in America. In 1907 it made a report, the essence of which was that every river is a unit from its source to its mouth; that it must be handled with due regard to every use of the water and benefit to be derived from its control; and that every good or bad influence on stream flow from the source to the mouth—forests, swamp drainage, soil drainage, levees, and every other—must be combatted or made use of in the unending struggle of men to utilize the earth without upsetting the natural balance which alone makes it habitable to man.

The report of the Inland Waterways Commission was transmitted to Congress with a message from President Roosevelt in which he gave it the strongest and most complete support. And his opinion was not a fleeting one. In his autobiography, he wrote of the report as being "at the same time sane and simple," "excellent in every way," and said: "The plan deserves unqualified support. I regret that it has not yet been adopted by Congress, but I am confident that ultimately it will be accepted."

Congress took no action on the report of the Inland Waterways Commission, and Roosevelt himself is authority for the statement that it was the Army engineers who defeated his plan. Levees—and levees only—was their cry.

On March 3, 1909, Congress appointed the National Waterways Commission which again took into account not only levees but other factors which influence the flow of streams, and other means for their control.

President Taft, during whose term this commission reported, was the second president who approved that general idea. President Wilson also, in a letter to the late Senator Newlands—father of our National irrigation policy and one of the best-posted men on waterways that ever sat in either House of Congress—likewise gave his emphatic approval to the same general plan.

Thus every commission, outside of the Army engineers, which has dealt with the question of the Mississippi since the Civil War, and every president who to my knowledge has expressed himself upon it, is agreed that the wide view which utilizes all means and not the narrow view which utilizes only one or two, the broad grasp and not the local prejudice, the generous and comprehensive plan and not the restricted one, ought to control in dealing with our inland waterways. So did the recent and very important flood control conference in Chicago. The Army engineers alone at Washington have stood out against this attitude, but their opposition has been strong enough to stifle progress.

If the foregoing statement is accurate, then the narrow policy of the Army engineers in putting all their eggs into one basket—the "levees only" policy—helped to cause and has a direct responsibility for the damage done by the present flood. And if that is true, then it is not wise to allow their point of view to be the only point of view considered in further dealings with this gigantic problem.

If anyone should consider that what I have said about the Army engineers is unduly severe, I refer to the opposition of the Corps to the construction of the Eads jetties, and to its persistent effort to prove that the jetties had failed long after ships were actually using the deep waterway they had made. If the Army engineers had had their way, there would be no jetties today and New Orleans would not be one of the greatest ports in America. The Army engineers as individuals are honorable men of good intentions. Many of their most distinguished officers are and have been my highly valued personal friends.

But the Corps, like many another body, has a bad habit here and there. My contention is that the habit of the Corps never to abandon an opinion once expressed should not be allowed to misdirect our national plans.

No one point of view ought to control. I am a forester, but I know that forests alone will not solve this problem. I do not insist that what I think forests can do in helping to solve it—what they can do toward the prevention of erosion and the regulation of stream flow—shall be accepted because I think so.

I do believe, however, that the part forests can play, the part reservoirs can play, the part spillways and levees and drainage and dredging and revetment and the rest can play, ought all to be considered not by the Army engineers alone, who have already taken their position and will not abandon it, but by a commission in which every point of view shall be represented by the best brains available and to which no conclusion will be sacred just because it is old.

Especially I am convinced that the vast expense of this huge undertaking ought to be lifted from the shoulders of the taxpayers if that can be done. I believe it can. I believe that production of electricity by the storage reservoirs which are needed for flood control will help do it. We know it can be done at Boulder Canyon on the Colorado. Why not on the tributaries of the Mississippi?

The Federal Water Power Act already contains the principle that private power developments below a new dam are required to contribute to the cost of storage in proportion to benefits received. That alone would help. The whole question is worth looking into.

The Power Monopoly:
Its Make-Up and Its Menace

Convinced that monopoly offered a clear and present threat to democracy, and certain that the private monopolization of energy, and in this case electricity, constituted a perfect example of this threat, Pinchot spent much of the 1920s gathering the necessary data about who owned what. In speeches, radio talks, newspaper articles, and in a monograph he privately funded (and which is the source of this excerpt), he identified those corporations and individuals who dominated the nation's power generators and its expanding electrical grid. The news was grim: the monopolists' control of energy gave them seemingly undisputed power over government at all levels, an evil Pinchot eagerly combatted.

Privately published in Milford, Pennsylvania, 1928.

———————————

———————————

Is there a Nation-wide, organized, persistent movement to monopolize the electrical powers of the United States?

Is there an electric monopoly? And if there is a power monopoly, has it been organized and financed for economical production and efficient service, with fair rates to the public, and fair profits for the power corporations and their investors?

Or are we facing a power monopoly organized and financed to secure the profits of extortion by the arrogant abuse of unregulated, unrestrained privilege?

As a private citizen, as a Federal official, and as the Governor of a State, I have given much time and some money to a conscientious study of the electric question. For years I have been in almost constant communication and consultation with many serious students of electric power, who have been spurred on in their investigations by deep-seated and public-spirited apprehension over the vision of our country entering the great electric era of world competition under the handicap of excessive cost of electricity, the one great modern driving power turning the wheels of our domestic, commercial and industrial life. The sum total of these investigations and studies is the positive and well-supported conclusion that a Nation-wide, organized, persistent, increasing movement to monopolize the electric power of these United States actually does exist.

There is an electric power monopoly.

Moreover, there is an electric power monopoly organized and financed, not for fair and efficient public service, but for ruthless exploitation, uninterrupted and unrestrained by anything approaching effective Government intervention or control.

We need not be surprised that State and Federal authorities have stood in awe before this gigantic Nation-wide power monopoly, because beside it, as its creator, financial supporter, and master, stands the concentrated money power of the United States, which today is the dominating money power of the world.

This dominating money power has seized upon the electric power resources of our country with a full realization of the fact that before very many years it will be not "the hand that rocks the cradle," but the hand that turns the electric switch that will rule the land.

Therefore the electric power monopoly deserves the fullest public attention. The people ought to know what it is, and why it is, and how it affects them. All the facts about it ought to be publicly available, either through Governmental agencies or through private effort. The people must learn to judge intelligently of its advantages and of its evils. Everything about it should be investigated fearlessly and published fully, because we must learn to regulate and control it before it smothers and enslaves us.

This pamphlet is intended as a contribution to public knowledge of the electric power monopoly. It is also intended to point the way for the additional authentic information needed for adequate protective legislation.

The power monopoly study submitted in this publication covers 4,362 corporations. . . . This list of power corporations may or may not be entirely complete. But it has attained so near to absolute completeness that it is without doubt the most complete list ever compiled or published. It includes the big holding companies, the smaller holding companies, companies owned or controlled by the holding companies, and what few independent companies remain. Some minor companies of recent origin, and some companies so long ago absorbed or dissolved that no current records are available, may be missing from this list, but that the list is practically complete, and does give a full view and a true view of the electric power industry is proved by the fact that one division of the corporations here listed—that of the 41 big holding companies—alone accounts for 82 percent of the electric energy produced in the United States.

In order to make the list as complete as possible, the listed companies also include those subsidiary organizations of power companies which are not engaged in the electrical power business, but through which electric holding companies control coal, coke, gas, water, street railways, bus lines,

bridges, lumber, real estate, amusement parks, and other interests contributing to their monopoly.

The records of corporations in this report are given as nearly as possible as of June 30, 1927, with the nearest applicable and available financial
and statistical figures—for the most part as of December 31, 1926.

Constant changes, never-ceasing mergers or consolidations, in the
never-sleeping zeal to concentrate extortionate control in fewer and fewer
hands, have altered the status of a number of corporations since the com-
pilation of this record. These changes, however, merely emphasize the
monopolistic tendency toward concentration by bringing together two or
more companies treated separately in this report.

The United Gas Improvement Company and the Philadelphia Electric
Company, for instance, are here treated separately, although since June
30, 1927, these two corporations have been merged. In the same way, the
Consolidated Gas Company of New York and the Brooklyn Edison Company are treated separately, although plans for their consolidation were
this year approved by the Public Service Commission of New York.

The most striking fact uncovered by this study of 4,362 corporations
in the power industry is the thoroughness with which concentration has
been achieved. Under this concentration the power corporations fall into
four general groups:

Operating Companies

3,108   controlled by 41 big holding companies.
877   controlled by 125 smaller holding companies.
126   controlled by 31 investment companies allied with the
        power interests.
85   entirely independent companies.
_____

4,196   operating companies.
166   holding companies.
_____

4,362   corporations owned or controlled by the electrical power
        industry, not including the 31 investment companies
        mentioned above.

The outstanding importance of the 41 big holding companies, which
own or control 3,108 of the 4,196 operating companies, is recognized here
at a glance. Yet the dominating importance of the 41 is still further
increased when their kilowatt hours of production and population served
are considered.

The records show that the 41 big holding companies control a little more than 82 percent of all the electric power generated in the United States. The records further show that almost 83 percent of the country's population depends upon the 41 power giants for the electric energy they need.

Since the six major financial interests dominate both the 23 corporations listed under their names and also the 12 corporations under joint control, we have only to subtract the figures for the six unidentified corporations in order to get a fairly accurate measure of the six-sided power monopoly held by the General Electric-Insull-Morgan-Mellon-Byllesby-Doherty community of interest. If we subtract the figures for the six still unidentified power corporations, we find that the six-sided master of the 35 big power corporations holds an amazing supremacy and domination . . . the General Electric-Insull-Morgan-Mellon-Byllesby-Doherty six-sided power monopoly controls but little less than two-thirds of the entire country's electrical power, and has a little more than two-thirds of the country's population at its mercy for its electric energy and service.

A monopoly of power is in itself not necessarily harmful. The public utility business requires monopolistic authority. Two telephone companies, two gas companies, two electric companies in one town usually amount to an economic extravagance if not a financial impossibility. The harm and danger of the six-sided power monopoly is not due merely to its monopolistic nature nor even to its enormous size. Its menace is due much more to certain other factors which may be summarized as follows:

1. The monopoly has been created by financial inflation.
2. The financial inflation of the monopoly has been supported by extortion.
3. This inflation and extortion are made possible and perpetuated by the control of investments secured through the blacklisting of investment houses which may refuse to sell the monopoly's inflated securities to the public.
4. Having forced its inflated securities on American investors, the monopoly now dodges behind these investors for protection against the arm of the law in much the same fashion that meaner elements of lawlessness, like common highwaymen, frequently have used their victims as shields against the bullets of policemen.
5. The power monopoly, fully conscious of its financial, industrial, and legal powers, as well as its extra-legal powers for evil, is seeking now in the open and in the dark, by fair means and by foul, to seize or continue control over the powers of government or, failing in this, to intimidate lawful authority to do its will.

The financial inflation of the power monopoly may have had its inception in the early clumsy attempts to limit its earnings. Public service commissions, supported by court decisions, have fixed 7 percent as the fair, equitable return on public utility investments. This rate was undoubtedly fixed in view of the special advantages which are given by the public to public service corporations, although many or most successful business enterprises derive a much higher return on their investment without being charged with either unfairness or extortion.

Under that limit several hundred electric light and power companies, usually small ones, have failed and been sold under foreclosure proceedings. Yet these same bankrupt companies have often been taken over by the big holding companies in the power monopoly and thereafter have prospered. But how could this possibly happen under a law that applied equally to the little and to the big company?

To the power monopolists the answer was easy. Wherever they took over a company, bankrupt or prosperous, for the purpose of establishing or extending their monopoly, almost without exception they paid for the acquired company with their paper—their stock. The prices have run from 1¼ shares of new stock for each old share to as high as five shares for one. Where mergers and consolidations were pyramided on top of each other, which has been the common practice, the inflation, of course, also has been pyramided far beyond the original ratio, which itself was usually unconscionable to begin with.

. . . We have seen the electric monopoly pick out State Governments. We have seen it crack its whip over State Assemblies. We have seen it with stupid arrogance and conscienceless boldness corrupt elections, and attempt to buy a seat in the United States Senate. We have seen it attempt to compel the United States Senate to deliver that purchased seat. We have seen it override the will of the people by its control over Congress. We have felt the application of its social pressure, its financial pressure, its political control. We have indisputable proof that the power banks, the power politicians, and the power monopolists are striving for nothing less than a power dictatorship over the Nation in all its parts. A private state within the public state is bad enough. But a private super-state, overawing and dominating the state, is intolerable.

Do we care enough about the future of America to save it from such a private super-state of electric power giants?

The Long Struggle for Effective Federal Water Power Legislation

It is striking that the last article that Pinchot published before his death in 1946 was a retrospective analysis of the decades-long fight to secure legislative federal regulation of water power. This was not a trivial issue for Pinchot, for whom the authority to manage energy production was tied directly to the Forest Service's ability to steward all the resources on the National Forests. Securing the rights of the nation—and thus of the citizenry—to protect and conserve timber, grass, minerals, and streamflow was one of his bedrock principles during his long public career.

Originally published in *George Washington Law Review* 14, no. 9 (1945–46): 9–20.[1]

———————————

———————————

The first and simplest form of mechanical power to be harnessed by man was water power. Today, with electricity to give it reach and scope, it is one of the most essential sources of the good life among men. It is also, unless and until atomic energy shall move into first place, more dangerously subject to the evils of monopoly than any other. Here, if anywhere, public control is indispensable.

Under the powers granted or implied in the Constitution of the United States, the Federal Government has control over navigable streams and their tributaries. Yet for a hundred years after the Constitution was adopted, Congress left the regulation of water power entirely to the states.

Before the long-distance transmission of electricity had revolutionized the situation, water power was regarded almost altogether as a local question. Fall River, Lowell, Lawrence, Manchester, Niagara Falls, and other manufacturing centers owed their superiority to water power. But in all these developments, power could only be used close to the water which produced it. Steam power, which came to the front because it was not subject to this limitation, after the Civil War became the country's chief source of power and has so continued to this day.

Federal stream legislation at its beginning had to do chiefly with preventing or removing obstructions to navigation. That was the purpose of the Rivers and Harbors Act of 1884 which authorized the Secretary of

---

1. A fully referenced version can be located at http://heinonline.org/HOL/LandingPage?handle=hein.journals/gwlr14&div=10&id=&page=.

War to remove unauthorized obstructions, including dams, bridges, and causeways.

The Act of 1884 was followed by the Rivers and Harbors Act of September 19, 1890, which forbade "the creation of any obstructions, not affirmatively authorized by law, to the navigable capacity of any waters, in respect of which the United States has jurisdiction."

In 1891 Congress granted free rights of way through the public lands and reservations for canals, ditches, and reservoirs. In 1896 it extended these rights to "any citizen or association of citizens of the United States, for the purpose of generating, manufacturing, or distributing electric power."

In 1899 Congress assumed fuller control over navigable streams and forbade the building of any bridge, dam, dike, or causeway over any navigable water of the United States "until the consent of Congress to the building of such structures shall have been obtained and until the plans for the same have been submitted to and approved by the Chief of Engineers and by the Secretary of War."

The effect of these Acts, however, was to prevent rather than promote development. And they applied only to navigable streams. The Act of 1901, however, empowered the Secretary of the Interior to permit rights of way through the public lands and Forest Reservations "for electrical plants, poles, and lines for the generation and distribution of electric power." It also empowered the Secretary to regulate the use of such rights of way and to revoke any permit when he saw fit. That was highly important, for a revocable permit meant that the title to the land remained in the Government.

Under the Act of 1901 the Secretary of the Interior issued regulations which related to filing applications for permits. But the Secretary never issued any formal permits. The practice consisted merely in making an endorsement on the map of the project that was submitted.

Licenses issued by Congress under the Act of 1901 gave away enormously valuable power sites without a charge and without a time limit— forever and for nothing. The first sign of change came when Theodore Roosevelt in 1903 vetoed a Bill to make a present of the now famous Muscle Shoals power site to private interests and thereby kept the door open for TVA, which, thanks to Senator George W. Norris, came in due time.

Until 1905, when the first steps were taken to bring about effective regulation and control by the government of the right to erect and maintain power dams, the custom of Congress to give away these extremely valuable rights continued unbroken. Unless some other interest happened to be after the same power site, all that was necessary was to get a bill introduced in Congress and sit by and watch it pass as a matter of course.

This time-worn habit of Congress to give away the public property was, of course, wholly unnecessary and wholly without excuse. Its only possible justification, aside from the pressure of the power interests, lay in the ancient bureaucratic shibboleth, "We have always done it that way."

When responsibility for the National Forests was transferred to the Department of Agriculture and the Forest Service, by the Act of February 1, 1905, most of the undeveloped water power of the Nation was still in the hands of the government. Undoubtedly more than half of the grand total was on the Forest Reserves and the Public Domain.

Under the Transfer Act, as mutually interpreted by the Departments of Agriculture and Interior, all grants of rights or privileges within the Forest Reserves which did not affect the title to the land or cloud the fee were under the jurisdiction of Agriculture. All those which did remained under Interior. But still no charge was provided for and the men who profited by these privileges and rights of way were not required to pay for what they got. But that situation did not long continue.

After the Transfer Act, the Forest Service, in dealing with the vast undeveloped resources in water power which had come under its control, could have followed any one of three paths:

(1) It could continue the indefensible policy of Congress by giving away these immensely valuable powers forever and for nothing.
(2) It could follow the policy of the Interior Department, which had a limited power of control in the public interest, but made little use of it, and did not require the companies to pay for what they got.
(3) Or it could develop a water power policy of its own.

There was no question which course to adopt. We must make our own policy and above all keep the title to the power sites in the public hands. *The Use of the National Forests*, a manual of instructions, issued July 1, 1905, contained this definite statement of policy: "A reasonable charge may be made for any permit, right, or privilege, so long as such charge is not inconsistent with the purposes for which the Reserves were created."

The Report of the Forester for the fiscal year 1905–1906, after noting the collection for the first time of a fee for grazing on the Forest Reserves, set forth as an underlying principle that a reasonable charge should be made for all permits which involved "the withdrawal of the particular resource or land from use by the people in general."

Furthermore, it definitely determined the basis upon which charges for the use of water for power should be calculated, as follows:

(1) A charge per mile for the length of the ditches, conduits, pipelines, transmission lines, etc. This applies when no greater width is allowed than that actually necessary at any one point for the enjoyment of the privilege.
(2) A charge per acre for land actually granted for occupancy, as areas flooded by reservoirs, land for power houses, residences, hotels, fenced pastures, etc.
(3) A charge for the conservation of water supply and the use of advantageous locations and other privileges. The water itself is granted by the State, not by the United States.

Thus, in a permit for a project to develop electricity the charge would be based upon: First, the length of the conduits, transmission lines, etc.; second, the area occupied by the power houses, reservoirs, etc.; third, the conservation of the water supply and the advantageous location which makes it possible to obtain a fall to turn the water-wheel.

Here was the beginning of a federal water power policy. It was deeply resented and bitterly fought by the power interests and their followers in Congress, but in all essentials it is in force today both on lands owned by the government and on navigable streams.

The Forest Service held that the quantity of water used was a proper measure of its conservation by the Forest Reserves and that the horsepower developed at the wheel, since it resulted from the water conserved and the fall furnished, was a proper measure of the entire conservation supplied by the Service to the permittee.

The Service was wise, I think, in deciding to enforce the new charge gradually, and not all at once. In the Spring and Summer of 1905, a few permits were issued for electric development without compensation but terminable at the discretion of the Forester. What we were after was not only a fair return in due time, but also good will and cooperation.

Later in 1905, the charge began. John S. Eastwood, for example, in August of that year renewed his power permit on the Sierra Reserve in California (now the Sequoia National Forest) with a new annual charge of $100. The Shasta Power Company on the Lassen Forest, California, and the Nevada Power Mining and Milling Company agreed to pay similar sums. Thus, for the first time, the principle of a charge was established in actual operation.

But the question of the duration of the permit was far less simple than the question of the charge. Before the Transfer Act the Secretary of the Interior had asked the Secretary of Agriculture "to suggest the length of time which should properly be fixed for the rights of way granted." A permit for a period of 99 years had been issued with the consent and approval of the Service to the Edison Electric Company of Southern California in the San Bernardino, San Gabriel, and Sierra Forest Reserves.

As head of the Forest Service I had personally approved the 99 years. And I recommended to the Secretary of Agriculture that permits issued by the Service should run for an even century. In that I was thoroughly and completely wrong. The power people had convinced me too easily that they needed so much time to recover their investments. The Secretary's judgment was better than mine. He cut the time suggested in two and he was right. Fifty years was long enough, as much experience has since fully proved. Fifty years is the limit today.

Another forward step was taken when on March 14, 1908, President Theodore Roosevelt appointed the Inland Waterways Commission. In his letter to the members he said:

Works designed to control our waterways have thus far usually been undertaken for a single purpose, such as the improvement of navigation, the development of power, the irrigation of arid lands, the protection of lowlands from floods, or to supply water for domestic and manufacturing purposes. While the rights of the people to these and similar uses of water must be respected, the time has come for merging local projects and uses of the inland waters in a comprehensive plan designed for the benefit of the entire country. Such a plan should consider and include all the uses to which streams may be put, and should bring together and coordinate the points of view of all users of waters.

And, the President added, the plans of the Commission should be formulated "in the light of the widest knowledge of the country and its people, and from the most diverse points of view."

It is worth noting also that the President's letter contained the first official recognition of the newly formulated policy of Conservation:

It is not possible to properly frame so large a plan as this for the control of our rivers without taking account of the orderly development of other natural resources. Therefore, I ask that the Inland

Waterways Commission shall consider the relations of the streams to the use of all the great permanent natural resources and their conservation for the making and maintenance of prosperous homes.

The report of the Inland Waterways Commission was based on two fundamentally important principles for whose formulation Doctor W J McGee, the Secretary of the Commission and the scientific brains of the Conservation movement in its early days, was directly responsible. These were:

First, that every river system is a unit from its source to its mouth and should be treated as such.

Second, that plans for any use of our inland waterways should "take account of the purification of the waters, the development of power, the control of floods, the reclamation of lands by irrigation and drainage, and all other uses of the waters or benefits to be derived from their control."

The Tennessee Valley Authority is the direct descendant of these two principles.

The principles of government control of power on the National Forests, established by the Forest Service, were thoroughly approved by Theodore Roosevelt. On April 13, 1908, he gave public proof of his approval by vetoing a bill to turn over important power sites on the Rainy River, a boundary stream between the United States and Canada, without the safeguards the [Forest] Service had developed. In that veto he declared that a time limit should be set for the termination of the grant, that a charge should be paid to the Government for the privileges received, that power sites should not be held undeveloped for speculative or other reasons, and that already the evils of monopoly were becoming manifest.

The Rainy River veto created consternation among the water power grabbers, but there was nothing they could do about it. Nine months later, on January 15, 1909, just before he went out of office, in his veto of the James River Bill, Theodore Roosevelt reaffirmed the principles of the Rainy River veto, and announced that he would sign no power bill which did not contain a charge and a time limit.

The President asserted that "the great corporations are acting with foresight, singleness of purpose, and vigor to control the water powers of the country. They pay no attention to state boundaries, and are not interested in the Constitutional law affecting navigable streams, except as it affords what has been aptly called a 'twilight zone' where they may find a convenient refuge from any regulation." And he concluded, "I esteem it my duty to use every endeavor to prevent the growing power monopoly, the most threatening which has ever appeared, from being fastened upon the people of this nation."

In 1910 the Second General Dam Bill limited the life of power permits to fifty years, provided for a charge, and for the recovery of the privilege by the United States. But these provisions were vague and indefinite, and made little improvement over those contained in the First General Dam Bill of 1906.

In 1912, the power interests and their friends in Congress staged a daring raid. Without hearings and without warning, the House Committee on Interstate and Foreign Commerce reported an Omnibus Water Power Bill which would have authorized 17 private power projects, without a charge and without provision for government regulation. Large water power interests would have controlled more than half of the grants proposed. Before, however, this piracy could be put through the House, President Taft's Coosa River Veto, based on the ground that no provision was made for a charge, broke it up.

For the next eight years a bitter fight raged in Congress between the power interests, eager for plunder, and the supporters of the principles laid down by the Forest Service and by Theodore Roosevelt in his epoch-making vetoes. The Adamson Bill, the Ferriss Bill, the Shields Bill, and the Myers Bill, some good, some bad, were introduced, fought for, and failed of passage. The most dangerous of these was the Shields Bill, behind which all the power of the great special interests was concentrated. After a long and bitter conflict, in the end it also was defeated.

In this long, often confused, and always difficult contest between private greed and the public good, the National Conservation Association led the fight against the power magnates and for the people. Charles W. Eliot, President of Harvard University, was its first president and I had the honor to succeed him.

The National Conservation Association had little more than two members for each Senator and Representative in Congress. Yet because it was right and because it knew how, it was able to protect the public interest against one of the most formidable attacks ever made against it.

The men who bore the heat and burden of this crucial fight cannot all be mentioned here. But since their efforts resulted in the definite, if not permanent, defeat of the power grabbers, and in the definite and permanent establishment of the principle of Government control over water power development, both in navigable streams and on the National Forests, some of their leaders should be named. All of them were or had been members of the United States Forest Service.

First came George W. Woodruff, Federal Judge, Assistant United States Attorney General, and Attorney General of Pennsylvania; then Philip P. Wells, Counsel in the Department of the Interior; Overton W. Price, Associate Forester, and O. C. Merrill, Chief Engineer, of the Forest Service; Harry Slattery, afterward Administrator of Rural Electrification Authority; and Thomas R. Shipp, Secretary of the Conservation Association. To these men and many others, and to public-spirited members of the Senate and House, such as Congressman William Kent of California, the Nation owes a great debt.

Before their fight was won and a Federal Power Commission was finally established, President Wilson took a hand. In 1918, a Committee on Water Power was created at the President's suggestion, and an administration bill, drafted by the Secretaries of War, Interior and Agriculture, was introduced. Followed two more years of backing and filling, and of conflict between the House and the Senate, until on June 10, 1920, the bill became law.

With all its faults the Federal Water Power Act of 1920, marked a great advance. It established firmly the principle of federal regulation of water power projects, limited licenses to not more than fifty years, and provided for Government recapture of the power at the end of the franchise.

For the first time, the Act of 1920 established a national policy in the use and development of water power on public lands and navigable streams. But it provided, unfortunately, for the administration of the Act by a commission of three men, the Secretaries of War, Interior, and Agriculture, whose hands were already too full to give it the necessary attention. This serious fault was corrected in 1930 by the passage of an Act which provided for an independent Commission of five full-time members authorized to employ a staff of its own.

The Act of 1930 took a great step forward. But it was not enough. In 1935 Congress passed the Federal Power Act which authorized the Commission to regulate the interstate transmission and sale of electric energy. Under that Act the federal control of water power operates today.

Beginning with the first effective regulation of water power by the Forest Service in 1905, the long series of conflicts and changes had at last, thirty years later, brought about the enactment of a law, and the organization of a Federal Power Commission, competent to deal effectively with this vital question on just principles of sound public policy. To deal with it as sound public policy was understood ten years ago. The Tennessee Valley Authority has made it clear that we have not yet reached the end of the road.

PART FIVE

NATURAL ENGAGEMENTS

That Gifford Pinchot was buried with his favorite fishing rod might seem odd. But only if you did not know how much joy he took in standing hip-deep in any stream, anywhere; or the thrill he took while trying to reel in a powerful swordfish leaping out of the rough waters off California's Catalina Island; or the chastened recognition every time a big one got away—and they got away more often than not—that human mastery of the wild was illusory. Pinchot, in short, was an inveterate angler and, among his contemporaries, an almost legendary fisherman. Journalist George M. L. LaBranche, for one, placed him in a pantheon of peers who, "despite the urgent calls of business, have yet found time to become past-masters of the piscatorial art." Pinchot's high status, LaBranche confirmed, was sealed when the forester-politician "once said that for him there was no answer to the question: 'What would you rather do than go fishing?'" His response depended on a level of wealth that allowed him to pursue this sport at his leisure. But it also bespoke Pinchot's deep affinity for the outdoor life and the visceral and vital connections to the natural world made manifest every time he ventured forth, rod in hand.[1]

He came to this enthusiasm at an early age, recording in his childhood diaries encounters with field, wood, and river, and the wildlife that inhabited these varied landscapes. That the young Pinchot was drawn to water, and its biota, is a function of his budding interests and his wider family's concerted efforts to nurture them. His parents and grandparents, who owned homes in rural communities in Pennsylvania and Connecticut, were themselves avid anglers and eager teachers. They also were keen-eyed observers of their child and grandchild: that Gifford shared their pleasure in the great outdoors, and that he hustled out to nearby ponds, creeks, and marsh with bated breath (and baited hook), only encouraged them to reinforce his proclivities.

These interests—call them affinities—proved critical in the choice of Pinchot's subsequent career. Emboldened by his family's support, and even nudged by his parents, James and Mary Pinchot, to think seriously about becoming a forester, he did. His decision was not unusual: as historian John Reiger has noted, most of the men and women who took up the conservationist cause in the late nineteenth century had spent their formative years outdoors.[2] These hunters and anglers learned to love the natural world, learning too that its scenic beauties and wildlife needed protection and management. Forestry was one such tool, but not the only

---

1. George M. L. LaBranche, "Six Famous Fishermen," *Country Life*, May 1920, 114.
2. John Reiger, *American Sportsmen and the Origins of Conservation*, 3rd ed. (Corvallis: Oregon State University Press, 2001).

one, and it is important to recall that its managerial vocabulary was developed at the same time that preservationism—the protection of landscapes from use—gained support. This energetic cohort helped establish the national forests and national parks, and they developed similar land-management institutions at the state and local levels, transforming the cultural discussion of and engagement with nature.

For Pinchot, these heralded large-scale outcomes depended on any number of unnoticed, intimate moments that reminded him of the need to be mindful of his place in the landscape. This became a central theme in his writings about his love of fishing, essays that Pinchot began as journal entries or letters during his many fishing and hunting trips, some of which would make their way into magazines or were later collected in his book *Just Fishing Talk* (1936).[3] "To be out in the open where fish are; to watch them at their great business of living; to see them in the water or out of the water; to fish for them, and even hook them and have them get away—all of this is wonderfully worthwhile," he once wrote, and "wonderfully better worthwhile than merely to catch and keep the stiffening fading body of one of the most beautiful forms of life." Increasing the challenge was a critical part of the code. In Milford, whenever Pinchot and his brother Amos fished the Sawkill, which runs through the family's Grey Towers estate, they snapped off the barbed portion of their hooks; they did the same wherever they cast their flies. Other insights came from close observation. In Oregon, white pelicans taught Pinchot how to snag trout in Klamath Lake. In Florida, he learned that if he wanted to hook a gray snapper, he had better learn to think like the elusive fish, a lesson that to his chagrin he had to relearn time and again; nature was a patient, if unforgiving, instructor. It was also a tough taskmaster (as reflected in Pinchot's gripping account of trying to land a hard-fighting swordfish) and a sublime presence (witness his reverential account of a South Pacific sunset).

So when in 1929 David Fairchild, president of the Tropic Everglades Park Association—an organization advocating the creation of what would become Everglades National Park—reached out to Pinchot to secure his support of the project, the forester was happy to do so, noting that the area's unique terrain made it a perfect candidate for a national park designation. "It is a region so different that it hardly seems to belong to the United States," Pinchot wrote about his many excursions to the mangroves and wetlands of south Florida. "It is full of the most vivid and most inter-

3. Gifford Pinchot, *Just Fishing Talk* (Harrisburg: Telegraph Press, 1936).

esting life on land, in the air, and in the water. It is a land of strangeness, separate and apart from the common things we know so well."[4]

In so arguing, Pinchot also signaled that nature was a trope, an enduring form of storytelling that bound one generation to another, a connection framed around the land and the water that helped to sculpt its contours and that turned time, in Pinchot's words, into "an ever rolling stream."

4. Gifford Pinchot to David Fairchild, January 19, 1929, Herbert Hoover Papers, West Branch, Iowa. Pinchot's letter was among a number of others that Fairchild solicited to share with incoming president Hoover in support of the new park proposal. Ultimately, President Harry S. Truman would establish the park.

One Afternoon at Pelican Bay

Pinchot was the youngest member of the National Forest Commission, which, under the auspices of the National Academy of Sciences and at the behest of President Grover Cleveland, conducted an 1896 inspection trip of the western forests and grasslands to determine their suitability for the new forest reserve system. Among those joining Pinchot were Harvard arborist Charles S. Sargent, celebrated naturalist John Muir, Yale biologist William Brewer, and geologist Arnold Hague, among others. For his part, Pinchot spent countless days surveying forest cover—and striking out on his own to camp, hike, hunt, and fish. He had never been to many of the regions the commission was visiting, and he believed that if ever he was to manage such landscapes he had better know them. He also sought release in the great outdoors because the commissioners were a pretty contentious lot. Distinguished and of strong ego, each had decided opinions about how the forest reserves should be regulated. Sargent wanted the U.S. Army to patrol the forests; Muir urged their preservation; Pinchot pushed for a professional cadre of foresters who, under careful regulation, would allow logging, mining, and grazing on the reserves. One of these debates erupted on August 26 in Ashland, Oregon. Pinchot's pointed and laconic diary entry captures the mood: "in evening had talk with Sargent & [Arnold] Hague about forest policy. Sargent utterly wrong on all points, as usual." Given this, it is not surprising that in the company of Brewer and Muir, Pinchot took a wagon over to Klamath Lake, where "I had some fishing I hardly dare tell about."[1] But Pinchot did talk about it, as the essay below reveals.

Source: Gifford Pinchot, Letterbooks, January 1, 1897–December 17, 1897, Gifford Pinchot Papers, Library of Congress; this would appear in only slightly revised form as "Pelican Bay" in Pinchot's *Just Fishing Talk*.[2]

———————————

———————————

. . . Pelican Bay . . . opens into Klamath Lake, which is a great body of water growing into land. The streams that fall into it are wonderfully clear, yet they carry fine silt enough gradually to change the Lake into a marsh, which in the process of time will change again into terra firma.

At the upper end of the Klamath Lake there are already vast meadows, miles in extent; and enormous stretches of bullrush (tule, in the local

1. Pinchot, *Breaking New Ground*, 101.
2. John F. Reiger, *Gifford Pinchot with Rod and Reel* (Milford, Pa.: Grey Towers Press, 1994), offers the best analysis of Pinchot's sportsman's ethic.

phrase) show where the next meadows will appear. Some miles to the north are the great Klamath Marshes, which prophesy a gloomy future for all the water in the lake.

The lake itself, with an average depth of ten feet, is an incomparable breeding ground for trout. These Klamath trout are reported to reach a weight of fifteen, twenty, or even thirty pounds, and in their shape and color, and in the quality of their flesh, they are more like salmon than any other trout I ever saw.

Pelican Bay has many little arms, and at the head of one of them a great spring sends a strong gush of water, three or four feet in diameter, straight to the surface through the clear depths that surround it. When I first saw it, it was full of trout swaying about in the rushing current till I had to look more than once to make sure they were not living fish. In fact they were not live trout but strings of silver cadavers, huge fish consigned by the men who caught them to the cool water as to an ice chest. And more beautiful fish there could hardly be. It was a sight to startle any angler to the depths of his enthusiasm and it certainly stirred mine.

About the spring someone had built a shanty or two, and provided a chance to eat and a chance to fish . . . there were boats near the spring. . . . [And after] dinner I made sure of one of them. My friend Will Steele volunteered to do the pulling. He said he didn't want to fish. Then at the little shop where repairs of every kind were tentatively attempted, I had a dented ferrule of my much-travelled rod made straight. . . . It was a good rod, and it had cost me all of four dollars. It weighed 4 1/2 ounces, was built of lancewood, and was as limber as a politician's conscience. My confidence in it had been growing over the course of the summer, but I confess that I joined in the general attitude of scornful amusement with which the onlookers regarded the proposed attack of such a weapon on the giant trout of Pelican Bay.

. . . Steele and I followed the little arm down into Pelican Bay. The marvelously clear water showed us trout, few and small at first. Of course I had to try for them. But the sun was shining, and they merely ran away from my fly. There was nothing strange in that.

. . . Ducks in multitudes were making a deafening clamor. But ducks I had seen before. What I had never seen was flocks of stately white pelicans dozing on the glassy water, or spreading their huge wings and rising slowly far ahead of the boat, till they sailed motionless into the hazy distance. That was something to write home about.

In the air the pelicans looked enormous, like tent flies in a hurricane. I never imagined that a bird could look that big.

Not even their size, however, was half so exciting as their organized fishing. These flying table cloths were like the hornets in the story, and like the hornets, they got results. And this is how I saw them do it, and more than once:

Six or eight pelicans would form a line beginning in very shallow water and extending out at right angles to the shore. Every bird was headed in the same way, and every bird moved steadily along, keeping in perfect alignment with the others. It was like the drill of a squad out of a crack regiment.

What was it about? Fish. It was a fish drive, pure and simple. And if one pelican didn't get a fish that met that line . . . , another did.

I couldn't see the fish, but I could and did see pelican after pelican plunge his beak into the water and then lift it to high heaven. And if that didn't mean swallowing, what did it mean? The trout those pelicans must have destroyed would be enough to drive a fish commissioner to drink.

Pelicans must know a lot, and here was the proof of it.

But while I watched the pelicans, I gave my fly no holiday. I whipped the water earnestly and in many places, but nowhere could I get a rise. At last it was plain that I must choose between trolling or no trout. The trolling had it.

In my fly book was a little spoon. I put it on. For some time nothing happened. Then Bang! A vigorous strike. After that nothing happened some more. . . . But better luck was on the way. A second tug! I struck in answer. A fish like a fresh run salmon threw himself two or three feet in the air, shaking his head savagely. Again and again he broke, wasting his strength until there was little left of it. . . . The little rod was doing magnificently, for that trout weighed eight pounds! . . . This was the sort of fishing I had dreamed about.

. . . [After reeling in a second trout] a third trout was hooked. He didn't break and I saw only a flash of his tail as he went down after the strike. But I could feel this was serious.

From the beginning this trout's strategy was better than good. His first fierce rush came straight toward the boat, and I should certainly have lost him if Will Steele hadn't pulled like a Trojan to help me keep the fish from getting slack line. . . . After that first run, a few moments of inaction. The little rod was so far below the level of the fish that he first refused to tire himself against it. Then came the next fierce rush, but off to one side. . . . Rush followed rush, then more rushes until it seemed certain I must lose him. There was no end of rushes up his sleeve. It was no trouble for that tireless fish to take out line, but lots of trouble for me to get it back in.

Like the fighting in a championship battle, there was something doing every second. First the fish went after me, then I got back at him. But at the end of every round he seemed to be as strong as ever.

I wasn't—not by a jug full. My hands and arms were aching, and every minute seemed like a week. The fight went on interminably. And during the whole of this long-drawn eternity the fish resolutely refused to show himself. I began to wonder what on earth it was I had got a hold of.

But this was no time for speculation. We were near the mouth of the bay where it was over a mile wide. The wind came up, and it took little time to kick up such a sea as we were obliged to take bow on. My unseen fish seemed to know all about it, for no sooner did it happen than he made runs on one side and the other and almost forced us broadside of the swells. If he had, we would have had to swim for it.

. . . Meanwhile heavy clouds had covered up the sunset, and the night began to fall. Heavy sea, heavy fish, and heavy darkness. . . . Only just before black night came down did he show himself. Compared to what he had been doing, at that first sight he looked small. His performance would have done honor to a ten-foot shark. Or that's the way I felt about it.

As the eternities drifted by he gained line but I gained more, until at length I had him almost at the boat. Not yet, however, within gaffing distance. . . . This was the time for all good men to come to the help of the party of the second part, and Will Steele didn't fail. The wind fell a little, the seas grew less, and, finally, what between good luck and good management, the gaff struck home and brought that gallant gladiator in. . . . When we knew we had him for good and all, both of us broke into vociferous and discordant whoops in celebration of the victory . . . when that part of the celebration was over, a combination of match and watch showed us that the fight had lasted one hour and forty seven minutes. Whew! I dream of it still . . .

Swordfishing

Pinchot learned to fish as a boy and for the rest of his life, wherever he traveled, he made it a practice to put hook in water. The chance to test himself against the elements was a huge lure, as is obvious from reading this account of his epic struggle to land a swordfish off San Clemente Island, one of the Channel Islands in southern California.

Source: "Swordfish Fishing," Box 1060, Gifford Pinchot Papers, Library of Congress; originally written in 1910, it was published in *Colliers*, April 6, 1912, 16. It was revised as "Marlin at San Clemente" for publication in Gifford Pinchot, *Just Fishing Talk* (Harrisburg: Telegraph Press, 1936), 202–8.[1]

―――――――――
―――――――――

Mexican Joe was sitting in the middle of the skiff and I in the stern, both facing backward, as the launch towed us under the cliffs a hundred yards from the shore. It was late, still afternoon, with a glassy heave on the ocean as the great Pacific rollers come in around the end of San Clemente Island. The western horizon was hidden from us by high shouldering hills, whose brown slopes fell away to black rocks at the water level. North and east the haze hid from us the heights of Catalina Island and the mainland of California. The time, the place, and the weather were all just right.

We were trolling for swordfish. Fifty feet of tow-line separated us from the launch, fifty yards behind us my bait, a flying fish, gleamed now and then through the side of a swell. We were fishing and hunting at the same time, for in such calm weather the swordfish often swims at the surface, with the half of his crescent tail and sometimes the whole of his dorsal fin above the water. You may have all the excitement of stalking big game before you hook your fish. Only the day before we had hunted a pair of this wonderful fish for four hours, carefully dragging our hooks across their line of travel over and over again. Each time the great fishes saw the bait they rushed for it together, and each time an agonizing thrill of indescribable anticipation swept through us. Every fisherman will know what I mean. But that was all. It was the wrong time of day, and they would not bite.

The next morning at sunrise I had found and followed, hooked, and after more than two hours of a lively difference of opinion had landed a

―――――――――
1. See another account: Charles Frederick Holder, "Gifford Pinchot and the Swordfish," *Outlook* 49 (March 19, 1910): 618–23.

swordfish eight feet nine inches long. That fish broke water forty-eight times in the course of the fight, and in one of his rushes took two hundred yards of line straight into the depths of the San Clemente channel in spite of the best I could do. The strength and grace of outline, the beauty of coloring of the superb creature—the rose, the blue, the olive, and the pearl—I shall never forget; but I had taken it from a large launch. I wanted to try now what sort of weather we should make of a similar fight from an ordinary fourteen-foot flat-bottomed skiff. So on the evening of the same day we went at it again. Down the coast to the eastern end of the island we ran, and near the Hook sighted the fin and tail that forecast the best fishing, so far as my experience goes, the red gods have yet vouchsafed to mortals. But that particular specimen, wiser than he should have been at the time of the day, refused the bait, swam directly up to the skiff, looked at us, and departed. Fifteen minutes later I had a strike. Joe cast loose from the launch and seized the oars. I struck with all my might, but the huge fish, hooked, as we saw later, in the bony side of the jaw, paid no attention. Joe backed the water, I reeled rapidly, and we were within fifty feet of the swordfish before he discovered what was wrong. Then out of the deep he came. Then rush followed rush, leap followed leap. High out of the water sprang this splendid fish, then lunged with his lance along the surface, his big eye staring as he rose, till the impression of beauty and lithe power was enough to make a man's heart sing with him. It was a moment to be remembered for a lifetime.

Then, the first fury over, the great fish started away. As rapidly as a man could row he towed our skiff a mile straight down the coast. As soon as the swordfish showed himself after the strike, the launch was sent back to camp for Dr. Charles F. Holder, who knows more of big game fishing at sea than all the rest of us put together. But Dr. Holder had never happened to take a swordfish or to see one taken. Indeed, I doubt whether two dozen all told have been caught in the history of angling in the Catalina waters. So the launch disappeared in the failing light, and scarcely had it done so when the swordfish turned and towed us out to sea. The utmost efforts of Joe with the oars and myself with the rod barely sufficed to keep us within reasonable distance of the rushing fish. Darkness was falling fast, and by the time we were three miles out in the channel I confess to many a wish and many a look for the launch. Sunset was gone when it came. Joe, wisest of old sea dogs, had been lighting matches behind my back and holding them in his circling hands for the launch to see, and so it found us. The tide was running strong, the wind rising against it, and the sea picking up. I welcomed Dr. Holder's arrival with distinct satisfaction. Afterward Joe asked me whether I had been nervous.

I gave myself the benefit of the doubt, and told him "No, because the launch was with us after dark."

"Well," said Joe, "the skiff would have stood a great deal more sea than the launch. The only thing I was afraid of was that the machinery of the launch would break down and the current carry her on the rocks at the Hook. We could always get in with the skiff, if there did not come a fog."

Straight into the rising sea went the swordfish, and there was nothing to do but follow him. For a time the crescent moon shone thinly over the dim shape of the island, then moon and island disappeared together, while the great fish, with a strength I could neither break nor check, dragged the boat against wind and sea.

An hour went by, and then another, yet the swordfish apparently was as strong as ever. But this time the sea was so high, as Holder told us afterward, that at times he could not see us between the waves. It was almost pitch dark, too, so that more than once, in the effort to keep close by, he nearly ran us down.

At last the steady strain began to do its work. The boat was gaining on the fish. I could not see, but I could tell. My line was doubled back for a few feet from the hook, and at last I felt the doubled part slide over the guide at the top of my rod. But the end was not yet. Over and over again I brought the fish in with a steady pull, leaning backward against the rod until my body was horizontal and Joe, just behind me, could no longer use the oars. And as often as the doubled line came in, the fish saw the boat and made a new rush I could do nothing to control. Once he came between the blade of an oar and the boat, so that Joe struck him as he dipped. Yet we could not see him. More than once I was afraid the line would foul the launch as it crept up and we yelled at it with all our united strength to keep away. Another half-hour passed, and the fish was getting tired. So, I admit, was I. But I doubt whether the stimulus of self-respect and the dread of failure were as strong in the fish as they were in me. A realizing sense of what it would mean to lose that fish kept me up to the work: and Joe's masterful handling of the skiff weighed heavily in favor of the rod and the fisherman. So when this great fighter was brought alongside for perhaps the twentieth time, still swimming upright, Joe managed to see him and gaff him near the head. But he was still a long way from being landed. One hand still holding the rod, thumb on brake, with the other I managed to pass over the tail a slip-noose which Joe had made ready. At the very instant it was done the launch ran into us, struck the skiff a resounding blow on the quarter, and the gaff slipped out.

You may have seen a cowboy sliding across a corral on his feet, one end of his riata round his hips and the other round the neck of a struggling bronco. Such an attitude seemed to me appropriate under the circumstances, and as I threw the rope behind my back it was clear to me that if the swordfish got away he would have to take me with him. That fish was mine, for I had earned him.

But there was to be no such watery end to this particular fishing. It appears that the motive power of fishes resides principally in their tails, and the tail of this one was in my possession. The other end of him was speedily gaffed again, and then with a strong heave we slid the great and beautiful creature into the boat as a wave passed under us. There we lashed him, from the point of his sword to the roof of his tail, with all the rope we had, and the war was over. Two hours and thirty-five minutes; nine feet, three and a half inches; and one hundred and eighty-six pounds. To-day he hangs up on my wall, with his mate of the morning, for a remembrance of the best day's fishing I have seen.

There had been seven swordfish taken already at Catalina during that summer. My morning and evening fish made nine. But that was not all my luck, for between the two lost to themselves but saved to me a third swordfish saved itself by the most remarkable rush in my experience of big game fishes. This fish we saw on the surface at a distance, at about eleven in the morning. When the bait came within its line of sight there was a rush like an arrow, but the strike, as with the other swordfishes hooked that day, was steady and quiet. When I struck, the line was snatched from the reel with inconceivable rapidity. With very little pressure on the brake, the new twenty-four-thread line was actually broken against the water. This statement will be incredible (until explained) to any man who has not taken heavy fish with light tackle. Every man who has will remember occasions when the reel had lost 100 or 150 yards of line, and the angler was letting it go with only the pressure absolutely necessary to prevent overrunning, and all seemed well; when a sudden and suspicious slackness brought his heart into his throat, and after much hoping against hope the frazzled end of a broken line came gloomily in. That was because the fish had turned at an angle to his former course, the line was forced to follow side-ways through the water in a sort of curved hypotenuse, joining the two sides of the triangle along which the fish was swimming, and then the pressure of the water broke it. So with my third swordfish, which I shall always recall and honor for that great rush.

A good many men have asked me whether the gentler kinds of angling still hold their charm after such big sea fishing as I have been trying to describe. My answer is emphatically, yes. I have taken also tarpon, kingfish, yellowtail, the Eastern jewfish, and the Western black sea bass, the albacore, and many kinds of shark, but in spite of it all I can still watch a float in a pond with the same pleasure, if not with the same thrill, as when I was a boy. To catch half a dozen trout through a long, late afternoon gives me the same deep satisfaction it always has. From the days when I angled for minnows with a pin, the delights of the running brooks have held me with a gentle firmness from which I have not escaped and never shall. One kind of fishing may be better than another, yet all are good. For me there is no answer to the question: "What would you rather do than go a-fishing?"

South Seas Reflections

Between his two gubernatorial terms, Pinchot and his family went sailing to the South Pacific, a journey that led to the publication of a book based on his detailed journals—and from which these impressionistic responses are drawn. This was also a voyage of discovery, partly scientific but mostly personal. Pinchot fell in love with life on the bounding main and he tried to recapture its varied meanings in prose that was clear and evocative.

Source: Box 958, Gifford Pinchot Papers, Library of Congress; *To the South Seas* (Philadelphia: The John Winston Company, 1930), 194–95, 345–65.

Doubtless there was a time when wild creatures in many places had not yet learned to fear man the killer. Outside the arctic circles what other places than the Galapagos are left?

The fishing in the Galapagos is probably the best in all the Seven Seas. That of itself is a reason why the islands cannot be long protected by mere isolation, as they are today. And it is also a reason why steadily increasing numbers of people will visit them, just as the fishing in our own National Parks brings countless visitors.

Communities of men learn slowly enough—communities of animals far more slowly. Long before these birds and beasts, unprotected by the fear of man as others are, can learn to dread him and avoid him, there will be none of the larger ones and few of the smaller ones left alive to profit by the lesson of experience.

On the many islands the Great Tortoises, of which I have said little, have already been exterminated. Only a pitiful and vanishing remnant still survives. So with the Iguanas. So with the Penguins and Flightless Cormorants.

As the Galapagos become better known, as what may be found there and felt there brings more and more visitors to the islands, as methods of communication improve (and they surely will), as more and more boats touch at the islands, and more and more settlers come to live on them—one thing will surely happen if we let it happen, and that right quickly—the last natural stronghold of the fearless wild will be destroyed.

Here is a region unmatched on earth in the ease and intimacy with which strange and fascinating wild animals and birds and reptiles can be seen and studied. . . . And that on a basis of mutual interest, for here people are as interesting to the birds and beasts as the birds and the beasts are to the people.[1] Such a region seems worth saving.

There is just one thing to do, and that is to secure setting aside of several of the islands as wild life refuges, just as we have done so successfully in the Yellowstone National Park and elsewhere at home. Whether the United States should approach the authorities of Ecuador, whether the League of Nations offers the proper channel through which this project may be best undertaken, I need not discuss here. But somehow it ought to be done.

Not a single one of the islands best adapted to be wild-life refuges is now inhabited, nor is any use whatever being made of any one of them. The way is open to act, if we act soon.[2]

. . . We sailed at dawn, the hour when the land breeze has its greatest strength, and three hours later sighted Fatu Hiva, some twenty miles away. High and very steep, incomparably bold, serrated, precipitous, and unimaginably green—the appearance of the island was breathtaking.

The little bay to which we were bound, a mere wrinkle in the coast line on the map, is gorgeous to the point of unreality.

. . . Centuries ago, Spanish explorers sailed into a bay on the west side of Fatu Hiva, past the tremendous ridge that falls a thousand feet and breaks into enormous pinnacles at the water's edge. The Spaniards called it the Bay of Virgins, not for an earthly but for a heavenly reason . . . because [the] huge rounded pinnacles of volcanic rock about its shores looked to them like cloaked and hooded figures of the Virgin of Mary enshrined for worship. . . .

French colonial administration, like that of other nations, may leave some things to be desired. But one thing whose value is incontestable that French have done for the Marquesas: They have built trails. As we entered the Bay of Virgins and were recovering a little from the almost physical shock of its prodigious beauty, some of us noticed, high on a hill so steep that it amounted to a grass-covered precipice, the zigzag of a trail climbing almost vertically above us, where it seemed as if no trail could possibly climb . . . [after a three hours' climb] at last we came to where we could look down to the Valley of Oma, scarcely less superb than that of Hana Vave.

1. This sentence is inserted from Gifford Pinchot, "A Refuge for Lap-Dragons," *Saturday Evening Post*, March 8, 1930, 177.
2. Ibid.

Directly in front of us the lofty peak lay hidden in clouds. Beyond the village the great pinnacled cliff rose straight up from the sea, with a huge swell of the Pacific breaking at its foot. We had seen it from the water, and across the face of it swung Frigate Birds, Boobies, Tropic Birds, and the delicate white Fairy Terns—the most characteristic flying things of the high islands of Polynesia.

The sunset was nothing less than violent, as sunsets in the tropics often are. Hidden behind masses of dark cloud the sun glared, like a burning eye. Out of a narrow crevice, and above and beneath the cloud wrack drove great fanlike beams of light, blue upward and yellow downward, to the zenith and the ocean. We watched the sun, which sets at home in temperate quietness, go down with the semblance of a vast explosion.

When we turned our backs to the sunset for a moment and looked eastward, the illumination of the titanic rampart which towered above the Valley of Hana Vave was unforgettable. It was almost impossible to leave the contemplation of it long enough to watch our footing and keep from stumbling down one of the grassy slopes, so steep that there would have been no chance whatever for the most active man to stop himself, once started.

On the walk back, the setting sun shot its level rays against precipice and rampart and gloried them. It changed the brown fern velvet on the nearer ridges into the warmest russet until they glowed like polished carnelians. . . .

The sea, clear of all vapor, was misty and mysterious with the white reflections of the trade-wind clouds, which gave it a depth and distance no sharp horizon can ever show.

We pushed on as rapidly as possible, finding, as many other travelers have found, that miles passed over easily on starting were much harder for tired men to travel back. At length we sighted the Bay of Virgins. . . . At length we reached the coconuts. At length we passed the bridge, slipped through the darkened village, and could just see the outline of the skiff that was waiting to take us out beyond the surf.

A day of days—rather a day of years, of lives. Titanic wildness and sylvan peace, flown over by white birds.

Two's Company

Gifford and Cornelia Pinchot shared a love of politics and fishing. Indeed, on her first visit to the Pinchot estate in Milford, they headed over to Pinchot's favorite spot on the Sawkill to cast in its swift waters. It may have been at that moment he realized he was hooked for life. Their lifelong political engagement was balanced by their equal enthusiasm for rod and reel, a companionate relationship captured in the title to this essay.

Source: Box 1060, Gifford Pinchot Papers, Library of Congress; revised for publication in *Just Fishing Talk* (Harrisburg: Telegraph Press, 1936), 54–60.

———————————
———————————

It may be foolish to confess it, but I like to fish alone. Not, of course, if I can persuade Rubia [his wife, Cornelia Bryce Pinchot] to go along, and not always when I can't. For there are few things more delightful than to fish the right water with the right companion, whether on ocean, lake, or stream.

But for me there is a powerful charm in being solitary in the companionship of woods and waters or the sea. It may be the sign of a crabbed nature; it may be the mark of a soured disposition; it may be just natural cussedness, but at least I tell the truth about it. To know the woods especially, you must be alone in them, and you will never know them fully until you are alone in them at night.

Whether you approve or not, let it be admitted that I love to fish alone. Now fishing alone on foot, or even on horseback (which isn't as foolish as it sounds), is simple and practical from every point of view. But fishing from a boat is different. Moreover, pond fishing from a sturdy flat-bottomed skiff on a still day is one thing, while fishing from a light canoe in a breeze or wind is very much another.

A canoe is the most temperamental of all the craft that float. If it knows you and likes you, well. It will do anything for you, go anywhere with you, and ride out to a sea that looks like sudden death. It will refuse to upset under the most aggravated provocation, will let you climb in again out of deep water if for any reason that might seem desirable, and will open to you more waterways to happiness than all the yachts of all the millionaires.

There seem to be no limits to the sweetness of a really kind canoe. I have seen Rubia take sharks of over seven feet with a rod and reel from a canoe, and at the finish shoot them with one hand the while she managed the rod with the other. Meanwhile I knelt in the other end, like Patience on a monument, and kept my paddle in the water and my tongue between my teeth. But the canoe loved her, and sat up on the water like a church on a hill.

I have fought many a tarpon from a canoe, and landed not a few of them standing in it, rod in the left hand and tarpon in the right, up to 90 pounds in weight. The canoe liked me, and I never was thrown out till a movie camera came along and insisted on an upset. Whereupon the canoe yielded, and the overturn was duly photographed. You can see it, tarpon and all, in the picture.

The best harpooning I have ever known has been from a canoe. A porpoise at one end of the line and a canoe at the other will keep your mind off all your other troubles. But why multiply instances? A canoe that really likes you in spite of all your faults is close second to a perfect wife.

But there's nothing more sensitive than a canoe, and never let yourself forget it. Any evidence of ill temper on your part it will instantly recognize and resent. Never speak harshly to your canoe, lest the next minute find you swimming. Address it urbanely and with deliberation, and it will eat out of your hand. Rub it, as it were, gently between the ears, scratch it beneath the chin, keep your feet in the middle, and it will purr through the water like a kitten under a stove.

But the canoe with a hostile disposition, or even the canoe that feels a little strange—from all such deliver us. If you cannot sell it or give it away, then take your courage in both hands and use an axe. There is nothing in this world more prejudiced than a prejudiced canoe, and nothing holds a grudge longer. If it does not get you today, it will tomorrow. Therefore beware. As the ancient Romans used to say: *Cave canoem*.

At Beaver Run there is a 16-foot canoe that gladly calls me Master when Rubia is not by. It is docile and considerate to a fault, and lets me walk about in it, and refrains from dumping me out when I drive it full speed against a hidden snag, or when I pole or paddle standing on the gunwales for a better view. It is more patient that Griselda and kinder than the most sugary heroine in all the works of Louisa M. Alcott or Mrs. Aphra Behn, on whom be peace.

The praises of such a character who shall celebrate, who shall fittingly recite? The lion of Androcles was not more devoted, the daughter of what's his name more filial. It is, as the reader has doubtless remarked before this, a perfectly good canoe, and why make all this fuss about it?

Into this canvas-covered paragon, when the time and the mood woo me to be alone, I put a long spruce pole shod with iron, a paddle (more as a precaution than because I mean to use it), a five-foot casting rod, the fly rod Rubia picked out for me, a landing net adapted to the monster pickerel never get, and in a creel nearly all the plugs and spoons and fly-rod wigglers and other barbed atrocities I ever owned.

Into it I also put a coat, remembering that pickerel bite better toward evening, when it will be cool. I put it in the bow because it will be drier there, or else I put it in the stern because it will be drier there. Full well I know it will get wet enough in either place before I put it on.

Then stepping in with a show of careless ease, in case there would be anybody looking, I fasten to the thwart near either end some 18 inches of strong line tied to the neck of a little bag of gravel (shot would have been better). Then I am off.

When I have reached the spot where I propose to take the first pickerel, my pole goes deep down into the mud, and one of the little bags is given a twist about it. When it falls back into the canoe, I am at anchor, and there I stay, let the breezes blow how they will, till I have fished what water I can reach and choose to move again.

Just beyond where I am anchored to the bottom slopes deeply into the old channel, which here is all of 30 yards across. This is the place to try a wiggler. So the casting rod flips it as fast as I can manage, and I reel it in as soon as the backlash is straightened out. For I have the faculty to getting more backlashed in less casts with more kinds of guaranteed anti-backlash reels than any man who reads this sad confession. I am letter-perfect at it. Yet I do sometimes catch fish.

Once, just hereabout, I was casting with a wiggler ringstreaked and speckled, when there came a check, not as solid as when you hook a stump, but yielding and alive. The line began to cut through the water, but without the proverbial hiss. Speaking of which reminds me to say that I am skeptical of hisses. You will recall perhaps that when Ajax hurled the great rock in Homer's Iliad, it was reported to hiss through the air, that [Longinus] Podbipienta heaved another rock in [Henryk] Sienkiewicz's *With Fire and Sword*, that Iliad of the Poles, which also was made to hiss. Few self-respecting writers ever catch a fish on paper without a hissing of the line. Myself, I feel like hissing all these hisses out of the court. Even poetic license has license to hiss.

We have nearly all heard a line sigh, and occasionally when a big fish has made a sudden dash right near the boat your line or mine has hissed, but mighty seldom.

All of this time my pickerel has been surging against the rod. Now I have him almost within reach. As his smooth round back shows for a moment, I know him to be big. How big I'll never tell you. I'm all jazzed up about him. But the rod and the line are too much for any pickerel in weedless water, and he gains no single inch. Then into the net and into the canoe and onto the scales. His size is my secret.

I wonder is there anywhere a fresh-water fish whose protective coloration is more perfect than a pickerel's? If so, it must be a frequenter of very shallow water, like the flounder, or the countless little fishes that disappear against a sandy or a rocky bottom. When the sun is shining squarely on the water in the middle of the day, you may see a pickerel where he lies, but not always even then. As the shadows lengthen, how many times have you and I had a strike close alongside the boat, and have seen nothing more that the complete or partial disappearance of the bait, as the invisible jaws closed over it.

See that rotting stump of an old white pine. There ought to be a pickerel somewhere round it. I cast my wiggler so that it falls ten feet beyond, and drag it slowly past. Nothing? Then try the other side. Sometimes it takes a lot of teasing before you can make him strike. Or that's a likely opening among the lily pads. There ought to be a big one hiding there. Perhaps I get him, and then again perhaps I don't. And so when that place is fished out, up comes my pole, and the canoe takes me serenely onward to another spot.

Maybe there's something doing under that old log. Off goes the wiggler on its predatory mission, and bang it comes down on top of the log, and, what's worse, a hook goes into a seam the weather opened. And I've got to go and lift it out. And if there were 40 pickerel under the log I'll get not even a smell of them until next time.

And so with this and that, before the fish stop biting I have perhaps six or eight pickerel, perhaps but two. But few or many, I have had was "T.R." (Theodore Roosevelt, Sr.) used to call "a corking time." I always have to quit.

A canoe and one is company, and no amount of pickerel can make it a crowd. There is nothing better than such solitary fishing, except of course when Rubia comes along. One evening when she did, we took— between us—16 pickerel, enough for my brother's household and my own.

Not one of them quite reached two pounds, and most of them were under one. We had more fun than if we had caught a hundred pounds of fish, twice over, and the whole world was filled with calm contentment as we paddled homeward in the twilight, bringing the captives of our rod and our reel along with us.

Another time, as I sat motionless and alone, with not a ripple in the surface and not a living thing in sight, came the sharp whistle of a buck across the water. I never saw him, but he brought back memories that made the ants crawl up and down my back. Suddenly the familiar pond grew strange, the wood about it full of questions. It was like old days in the wilderness again.

Another breathless evening as a blue jay cried his autumn challenge in the thicket, a winged seed from a milkweed pod floated with slow dignity over the listening pond, and came unhasting to its light rest upon the silent water. Scarcely had it done so when over the hillside resounded a hammer stroke of the greatest of woodpeckers, and in a moment at the Cock of the Woods flew wavily across and struck a new anvil on the other bank.

Then from the quiet distance three grebes came winging close to the darkening surface, lighted upon it without a sound, and on it drew smooth lengthening broad arrows as they went about their noiseless personal affairs. A little breeze breathed and ceased. To move seemed like a sacrilege.

Such things are best remembered when a man goes fishing. As these and many another incident of quiet evenings serenely moved and lingered in my musing memory, while the light faded into darkness and all the world was still, a smashing strike in the lily pads brought me with a jar back to the earth again. Swiftly the rod bent to my hand, then to the fish, and the last pickerel of the day came in out of the wet.

By that same time the pond had faded into unreality. Strangeness covered it as with a mantle. There was just light enough to puzzle the wayfarer on the long pull back, to shift the channel from where I knew it so well to be, and move all the snags away from their remembered lairs to new ambushes for the hurrying canoe, which still held fast to its angelic disposition, and kept me right-side-up and dry in spite of every trap. Right glad I was of that, and grateful, too, for it was 30 miles to supper from the landing, and the nights were getting noticeably cold.

Of such times and places are quietness and peace.

Time Like an Ever Rolling Stream

Rivers are as real as they are metaphorical, and for Pinchot the chance to reflect on the Sawkill, a beloved stream that tumbles through his family's property in Milford, Pennsylvania, led him to craft this epistle to his son and namesake, Gifford Bryce Pinchot. It also offers an imaginative reconstruction of the Pinchots' place in the land they called home.

Source: Box 1060, Gifford Pinchot Papers, Library of Congress; a revised version appeared in *Just Fishing Talk* (Harrisburg: Telegraph Press, 1936), 233–38.

Men may come and men may go, but the Sawkill brook flows on—feeding its trout, protecting its insect, molluscan, and crustacean life—a home and a hiding place for myriads of living creatures—a thing of beauty and a joy forever.

Along its banks giant Pines and Hemlocks have germinated and grown, flourished and died, decayed and vanished, uncounted generations of them, each leaving its contribution to the richness and glory of the place—in their branches generations of squirrels and birds have fed and quarreled and mated and carried on the business of the world.

Under the shade of little needles on great limbs deer and bear drank and listened as they drank. About their roots cubs, fawns, and baby otters romped and rested and romped again. In winter their cones and leaves strewed the snow after every breeze, and on sunny days melted little cavities for themselves, and froze there as the shadows fell across them.

Buffalo, elk, moose, wolves, and panthers left their tracks beside semi-human tracks of bears and coons, the webbed tracks of beaver, and triangular imprints of mink.

Great flocks of passenger pigeons hid the sun, and where they settled on branches of stout trees branches were broken off and crashed to earth, to the thunder of innumerable wings.

Kingfishers clattered up and down the gorge in high water and low, as through the years the weather and the water shaped the rocks and the floods ground out great potholes with their in-arching rims.

Century upon century of millenniums passed over the Sawkill and left it much as they found it. At times great Pines and Hemlocks fell across the stream, at times the rush of the torrent after great rains moved them away to new positions, to be moved again or to disintegrate where they lay by the slow action of the elements.

Now and again a sandbar changed its course, a pool was deepened by a fall of rock or shallowed by the cutting of a new channel. Great trout grew fat and lazy in the slow current of beaver ponds, and the full-fed water snakes sunned themselves where countless forebears had coiled in comfort before them.

When the redmen came, life on the brook changed, but only a little. For they were no slaughterers, but conservationists, blood and bone, and took no more than the natural increase. Each family had its hunting grounds in which no other family might hunt except for food while passing through, and the penalty for breaking that game law was sometimes death.

Now and again through the centuries a forest fire set by lightning swept one or the other bank, or maybe both, and changed the lives of the land and water dwellers for a few or many generations.

For uncounted ages the redmen hunted on the Sawkill, and still the greater and lesser tribes of wood and stream lived with them, not one destroyed, not one dangerously reduced in numbers by anything the Indians did. Then came the change.

White men appeared. With new weapons of destruction, new zeal for slaughter, new appetite for conquest, they made new demands on nature for the means to live a new kind of life. With their coming the axe began to modify the face of the earth, and the days of the wilderness were numbered.

The slow and inevitable march of the centuries over the Sawkill changed almost overnight to the rush of oncoming civilization. The old order, grown out of thousands of generations of adjustment, and the old balance, painfully won through the life and death of myriads of forms of life, suddenly found themselves powerless before a new and strange attack, against which they had no time to develop a method of resistance.

The Indians gave way before it, and disappeared. The buffalo, the elk, and the panther followed them. The primeval forests went down before the need for houses and ten thousand other needs for wood. The white man was reaping where he had not sown, and nature paid the price of the better living, the faster thinking, and the more stable existence of the heirs of all ages.

Hemlocks that overhung the riffles and pools of the Sawkill when Columbus discovered America were still vigorous trees when the first Pinchot [Constantine Pinchot] to set foot in Pennsylvania twitched his first trout out of the Sawkill, and found it good. With him came his son [Cyrille], a boy of nineteen, who the year before had been on his way to

join Napoleon's army as a recruit when the battle of Waterloo put an end
to his soldiering.

The son threw himself into the life of his new country with the vigor
that distinguished him. The tribes of Pine and Hemlock along many
streams paid him tribute, with years much land passed into his keeping,
and he prospered and grew strong, while the Sawkill hurried and tarried
on its never ending march to the sea.

His son, my father [James Pinchot], was born and grew up in the
little village which occupied the level plain between the Sawkill and the
Delaware, and in the days when artificial flies were yet unknown, became
so skillful an angler with more natural bait that few fly fisherman I have
known could match him.

I in my turn became a lover of the Sawkill and its sister little rivers,
and under my Father's eye I learned the uses of the worm. I took full many
a trout with it, and in due and early season graduated to the wet fly and
the dry.

But my best performance with any fly was far below the high crafts-
manship of my father's handling of a worm.

When my son [Gifford Bryce Pinchot] announced his participation in
the affairs of the world by the barbaric yawp of infancy, his Mother and I
destined him to be a fisherman. Anxiously we waited for the time when
he might take his first trout, and take an interest in taking it. At the age
of three, accordingly, we explained to him about fishing, which disserta-
tion he obviously failed to comprehend, and asked him if he wouldn't like
to catch a tiny speckled little trout.

Being, like other youngsters, ready to try anything once, he assented—
and the cortege moved in solemn procession to the stream. It was no light
matter. The son and heir was about to begin his career—catch his first fish.

So I hooked a trout, handed Giff the rod, and urged him to pull. He
pulled; the trout struggled on the bank; and the boy, casting an indifferent
eye on what should have engaged his whole I.Q. passed on with no interval whatever to matters of greater juvenile interest.

What a shock there was, my countrymen! Rubia and I were struck
with horror. I couldn't be consoled even by the fact that I had just taken
several trout on a leader made by myself out of a knotted succession of
single strands of Rubia's hair. Was it possible that the son of such parents
could fail to love to fish? We couldn't believe it, and, what was more, we
didn't intend to stand for it.

And we didn't have to. We let nature take its course, and, because we
did not press him, before he was ten Giff was casting a workmanlike fly.
From then to now on more than one occasion he has brought back more

trout than his instructor and progenitor. And he loves to fish about as much as I do.

"Dad," said the fifth generation of Pennsylvania Pinchots on a day when everything was right, "how about fishing this afternoon."

"I thought I would," said I.

"Hot dog!" replied this worthy son of a slang-infested father. "What rod you goin' to take?"

"Well, I thought I'd take the two-and-three-eighths-ounce Leonard. There's too much wind for the one-and-three-quarters."

"What fly you goin' to use?"

"A spider," said I.

"Hot dog!," said Giff again, out of limited objurgatory vocabulary of youth.

So father and son settled the preliminary details, and when four o'clock came off we went in the open car, up over the hill behind the house, out past the red Schocopee schoolhouse where Rubia and I cast our votes at every election, to the brook I have been fishing for more than fifty years.

There we put our rods together, first carefully anointing the ferrules by rubbing them on our noses, as good fishermen do. The we chose white and brown spiders, with long hackles and little hooks, out of my horn snuff box, with Napoleon's tomb carved on relief on the cover; made that the barbs had been broken off with a pair of sharpnosed plyers (we never fish for trout with barbed hooks any more); tied leaders to spiders with the Turtle knot; and oiled the hackles of our spiders with three parts albolene to one of kerosene. Then the war was on.

It was a good war, and swift. Before you could say Jack Robinson, Giff had a nine-inch native. Untouched by human hand, back into the stream he went, thanks to the debarbed hook, with nothing but a little healthful exercise to remember his adventure by. I always get great satisfaction out of that.

Then no more rises for a while, until, as the sun sank low, thick and fast they came at last—the little to swim away unhurt, and the less little to drop into the creel after they had been put to sleep with the back of a jack-knife. We had all we wanted long before it was time to quit. So we sat down on a log and held a session on the State of the Union.

"Dad, how long has this brook been here?" asked Giff, after long pondering.

So I told him, as best I could, and when we got home I tried to write it down. And that's what you have been reading.

ACKNOWLEDGMENTS

I have been hanging around Gifford Pinchot for so long—one of my first graduate school papers was about his impact on the twentieth-century conservation movement—that he deserves a shout out; I have learned a great deal reading his words about the prospects and politics of conservation that constitute this book, and I hope you will too. I am as deeply indebted to a host of colleagues and institutions for their engagement with this project, including Al Sample, former president of the Pinchot Institute for Conservation (and to whom this volume is happily dedicated), as well as the institute's engaged professionals; the remarkable folks at Grey Towers National Historic Site in Milford, Pennsylvania; Mike Wood of High Ridge Leadership; and many peers who work for the U.S. Forest Service that Pinchot founded. All of them have given me opportunities to test out my ideas about the significance of Pinchot's life in activism and have provided lots of constructive feedback. At Pomona College, the Environmental Analysis Program's administrative assistant Anne Tessier and my research assistant, Maia Welbel, provided crucial support. Librarians at Honnold/Mudd Libraries in Claremont swiftly responded to my many interlibrary loan requests, and this project benefitted as always from the kind attention of the great staff at the Forest History Society in Durham, North Carolina. I am also grateful to the many editors and archives that have given me permission to publish some of these documents. The book has benefitted as well from the smart guidance of two reviewers of the manuscript whose comments were spot on and from Kathryn Yahner at the Pennsylvania State University Press; she and her colleagues have been a joy to work with. With abashed thanks to my wife, Judi Lipsett—sorry, as always, about the mess.

Typeset by
COGHILL COMPOSITION COMPANY

Printed and bound by
SHERIDAN BOOKS

Composed in
BASKERVILLE 10 PRO

Printed on
NATURES NATURAL